SEA CHANGE

Other Books by
James C. Abegglen

Kaisha: The Japanese Corporation (with George Stalk, Jr.)

The Strategy of Japanese Business

Management and Worker: The Japanese Solution

Waarudo Bijinesu no Keiei Senryaku

The Japanese Factory: Aspects of Its Social Organization

Big Business Leaders in America (with W. Lloyd Warner)

SEA CHANGE

PACIFIC ASIA AS THE NEW WORLD INDUSTRIAL CENTER

James C. Abegglen

THE FREE PRESS
A Division of Macmillan, Inc.
NEW YORK
Maxwell Macmillan Canada
TORONTO
Maxwell Macmillan International
NEW YORK   OXFORD   SINGAPORE   SYDNEY

The Free Press
A Division of Macmillan, Inc.
866 Third Avenue, New York, N.Y. 10022

Maxwell Macmillan Canada, Inc.
1200 Eglinton Avenue East
Suite 200
Don Mills, Ontario M3C 3N1

Macmillan, Inc. is part of the Maxwell Communication Group of Companies.

Printed in the United States of America

printing number

1 2 3 4 5 6 7 8 9 10

Library of Congress Cataloging-in-Publication Data

Abegglen, James C.
    Sea change : Pacific Asia as the new world industrial center/
James C. Abegglen.
      p.   cm.
    Includes bibliographical references and index.
    ISBN 0–02–900155–2
    1. East Asia—Economic conditions.   2. Asia, Southeastern—
Economic conditions.   3. East Asia—Commerce.   4. Asia,
Southeastern—Commerce.   5. Competition, International.   I. Title.
HC460.5.A516   1994
338.095—dc20
                                          93–36426
                                          CIP

To Hiroko
with love

CONTENTS

●

Chapter 3 • Japan in Asia   57

Chapter 4 • Asia's New Economies: The China Factor   81

●

●

ACKNOWLEDGMENTS

The great economic growth taking place in East Asia is changing the very structure of world business and industry. The region is vast in area, population, and diversity. Its changes have occurred only relatively recently. To write about so great a region, one not well known yet to many in the West and one recently developing, has considerable hazards—risks of too broad treatment or too much detail, or being too topical and yet being overtaken by headline events. But this is a historic change in the economic and social map of the world, and description and analysis must be undertaken.

Any success of this book in deepening the understanding of the sea change in world industrial structure taking place in East Asia is owed to the considerable help of a large number of people. Robert Wallace of The Free Press was critical to the effort, not only in providing the initial stimulus to undertake the research and writing but in later patient support as the project proceeded. John Rolander, President, Gemini Consulting (Japan), and his colleagues in the Gemini Consulting organization provided unstinting and indispensable support that made it possible to carry out the work.

In the research on which most of this book is based, several associates played important roles. Brian Riordan was deeply involved in fieldwork

●

and analysis in Korea. A good deal of the material on coastal China and Asia's new economies is owed to Richard Sparks. Both Riordan and Sparks are Gemini Consulting (Japan) staff members.

Work in Vietnam, and a good deal of interviewing and data collection elsewhere as well, depended greatly on Tran The Huy of Asia Advisory Service K.K. Orlando Camargo, AAS staff consultant, was an important source of interview material and data analysis, with additional help from Hiroyuki Sasaki, also of AAS.

It is not possible to note here all of the government, business, and academic individuals across East Asia who made time to provide advice, information, and assistance in the course of preparing this book.

Special appreciation must be expressed, however, to Tasuku Takagaki, President, Bank of Tokyo, and Hisao Tahara, Director of Matsushita Electric Industrial Co., Ltd. in Japan. Special thanks are owed as well to Tran Duc Nguyen, First Secretary to the Vice Prime Minister, for hospitality and support in making our Vietnam fieldwork both effective and fascinating. In Indonesia, Kristanto Santosa, Partner of PQM Consultants, was a source of important assistance.

Jane Withey was of special help as a patient and also, when needed, impatient editor, in the best sense of critiquing substance as well as style. Her help was critical, as was that of Tomoko Saito, who carried out the tedious work of manuscript preparing with a rare combination of diligence, competence, and charm.

With all these obligations to friends and associates, and to informants named and unnamed, the greatest obligation is to my wife, Hiroko Sasaki, research aide, creative critic, and constant supporter. She makes it possible and worth doing.

James C. Abegglen
Tokyo and Kanaya

1

●

SEA CHANGE

A sea change is underway in the world economy, as the center of world industry moves from the North Atlantic to the Pacific. The long-held economic wealth and power of the Western economies is now being increasingly shared by East Asia's hundreds of millions. The map of world business and industry is being redrawn as East Asia's economies continue their extraordinary rates of growth.

Northeast Asia—Japan, Korea, and Taiwan—now provides one-third of world vehicle output. In autos, the prototypic twentieth-century industry, Japanese firms alone are estimated to hold nearly a 40 percent share of the entire world market. It is predicted that this will move to 45 percent, nearly half of world market share, within two or three years.[1] And these estimates do not include the fast-growing production of autos in Korea. It seems nearly certain that Northeast Asia will control half of the world auto market in a few years.

As autos have been central in twentieth-century industry, so electronics are fast taking over that role as the twenty-first century approaches. Here too East Asia—Japan, Korea, Taiwan, Hong Kong, and Singapore—holds world lead in production. Two-thirds of all consumer electronics products are produced in the area and nearly half of electronic components. In more sophisticated electronics, the region supplies about one-third of the world's computers. In 1990, Asia accounted for nearly half, about 45 percent, of world trade in electronic products.

East Asia's industrial strength is by no means limited to these two key sectors of autos and electronics. About one-quarter of world steel production is now in Northeast Asia. Textile production is centered in the area. Much helped by East Asian investment, Japanese machine tool makers dominate the world industry as 15 of the 25 largest machine tool makers in the world are Japanese companies. Shipbuilding moved to East Asia some years ago. The list of sectors in which East Asia holds major industrial power is long and growing. Computer games is the most recent addition.

POTENTIAL FOR CONTINUED SUCCESS

East Asia includes Japan, the newly industrializing economies (NIE) of Asia—Korea, Taiwan, Hong Kong, and Singapore—and the four large nations in the Association of Southeast Asian Nations (ASEAN: Thailand, Malaysia, Indonesia, and the Philippines). In the broadest sense, East Asia also includes all of China (see Table 1–1).[2]

China's coastal provinces, linked now economically and industrially to the rest of East Asia, have become an integral part of the area. When these coastal provinces are included, East Asia includes some 800 million people and the combined economies are nearly $4 trillion in size (see Table 1–2). This is not a great deal less than the combined economies of France, Germany, Italy, and the United Kingdom—most of the economy of western Europe. The region is already a major part of the world economy, with 15 percent or so of world population and a similar share of the world economy.

The growth of East Asia is the critical dimension in gauging the region's importance. To estimate the region's size in the near future, at the end of the century, assume that Japan grows at a 4 percent annual rate, down from its 1980s performance as the economy matures. Assume further that the rest of East Asia grows at an annual rate of 7 percent to the end of the 1990s, a bit less than its 7.6 percent annual rate over the past 20 years or so. Not unreasonable assumptions, it appears.

If East Asia performs in this fashion, that is, much as it has been for

•

Table 1–1   Population and Economic Size

	Population (millions)	GDP (US$ billion)	GDP per capita (US $)
Japan	124	$3,362	$26,930
Hong Kong	6	68	13,430
Singapore	3	40	14,210
Taiwan	20	179	8,788
Korea	43	283	6,330
Malaysia	18	47	2,520
Thailand	57	93	1,570
Philippines	63	45	730
Indonesia	181	116	610
China	1,150	370	370
TOTAL EAST ASIA	1,665	$4,603	$2,765

Source: Data from *World Development Indicators 1993,* board draft, Tables 1 and 3 (Washington, DC: The World Bank, April 21, 1993) and from C. H. Kwan, "Economic Interdependence in the Asia-Pacific Region—Towards a Yen Bloc," *Nomura Asia Focus* (Tokyo: Nomura Research Institute, April 1993).

nearly a generation, then the total East Asian economy would be about $6 trillion in 1990 prices and exchanges rates. That will make the area a bit larger by the turn of the century than the United States, Canada, and Mexico—the North American Free Trade Area (NAFTA) economies— are today. The growth over the period would be the equivalent of add- ing the 1990 economies of German and France to the area.

The size and growth of the region will be increased as Vietnam moves to full participation in the world economy, with its 60 million population and considerable potential for rapid economic growth. The economic size of the region will seem even greater than these figures suggest, owing to another factor as well. This kind of rapid growth means rapid productivity increases, which in turn should mean generally appreciating currencies, especially against the U.S. dollar, which in trade- weighted terms has lost one-third of its value since 1985. In dollar terms, then, East Asia is likely to be larger still than these projections suggest, by perhaps an additional 10 percent or so.

The growth of East Asia at high rates began in the late 1960s, a turn- ing point for much of the area. Japan, the main external driving force for the area's growth, was completing its era of double-digit growth and

●

Table 1–2   East Asia Now and in 2000

	1990–92		Year 2000	
	GDP ($ billion)	Population (million)	GDP ($ billion)	Population (million)
Japan	$3,500	125	$4,800	130
NIEs: Korea, Taiwan, Hong Kong, Singapore	600	70	1,000	80
ASEAN: Indonesia, Malaysia, Philippines, Thailand	300	315	600	370
Coastal China	150	300	300	330
TOTAL	$4,550	810	$6,700	910
Percent of World	20–22	15	23–25	15–16

Assumes: 4% Japan GDP growth, 7% rest of East Asia; 1991 prices and exchange rates. Vietnam and North Korea not included.
Note: 1991 United States, Canada, and Mexico, $6,400 billion; France, Germany, Italy, and United Kingdom, $4,800 billion.
Source: Data from *World Development Indicators 1993*, board draft, Table 1 (Washington, DC: The World Bank April 21, 1993); Asian Development Bank, *Asian Development Outlook 1993* (Hong Kong: Oxford University Press, 1993), p. 259; and Japan Center for Economic Research, *Takyokuka Jidai no Sekai Chizu: 2000-nen Sekai to Nihon* (Tokyo: 1992), p. 255.

becoming a major industrial power. In Indonesia and Korea, government changes in the mid-1960s led to strong economic growth policies. Singapore became an independent nation. World trade was growing rapidly in a generally positive economic environment. As Figure 1–1 indicates, East Asian growth took off and has continued at an extraordinarily high level, despite oil crises, sustained recessions in the developed world, and war in the region itself. Even in 1975, 1982, and 1991, when world economic growth went to zero, East Asia's economies continued to grow 6 to 7 percent annually. Note too that as the base has broadened, East Asian growth rates have not slowed. An assumption of continued growth rates that double these economies in real terms in a decade seems a reasonable one.

In fact, there appears to be a considerable, even surprising, degree of agreement among various observers on the continued rapid growth of East Asia. The prospects for the region as projected by a major Japanese research institute show growth in Japan in the 1990s at an average rate

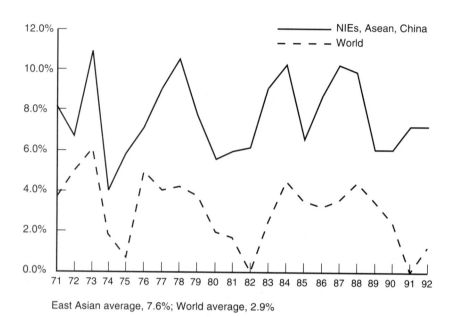

East Asian average, 7.6%; World average, 2.9%

Figure 1–1   **East Asian and World Economic Growth, 1971–1992 (percent per annum, real)**

Source: Reprinted from C. H. Kwan, Economic Interdependence in the Asia-Pacific Region: Towards a Yen Bloc (London: Routledge, in Press).

twice that of the United States and Germany and in the rest of East Asia, at triple the U.S. and German rates. In an OECD study of world economic futures, the authors posit four different scenarios of growth over the next 25 years. In the least favorable scenario, termed the Global Crisis scenario, the "dynamic Asian economies," as the authors term East Asia less Japan, grow at an annual rate of 6.0 percent in the 1990s. In the more positive scenarios the growth of these East Asian economies is seen as up to 7.3 percent per annum.[3]

A British observer offered an interesting way of viewing the prospects. "Let us assume that all these countries together can achieve a growth rate averaging 6 percent per annum (in total, not per capita). If the established industrial countries achieve a growth rate averaging only 2 percent, they will be overtaken by 'Asia' just after the year 2040, within the lifetime of the majority of people now living. Even if Western

●

growth rates buck up to 3 percent or Asian growth rates are slightly lower, the catch-up will come around 2060, still within some people's lifetimes."[4]

Even the World Bank, not given to rash enthusiasm, predicts a virtual end to East Asian poverty within the decade, in contrast to a continued or even increased incidence of poverty in much of the rest of the developing world. These are truly sea changes, for widespread poverty of peasant masses is surely a general view of East Asian societies. The World Bank expects a spectacular drop in Asian poverty levels in only fifteen years (see Table 1–3). National wealth and general prosperity are no longer exclusive to the nations of the West—all of East Asia is joining in.

KEYS TO GROWTH: INVESTMENT IN INFRASTRUCTURE

A corollary of this growth is a problem that exists throughout East Asia of requirements for the whole range of infrastructure facilities—road and air transport facilities, harbors, electrical power generating capacity, and telecommunications. The surging growth puts demands on the infrastructure that require massive investments even in highly developed Japan. These investments, across a broad range of products from steel and cement to radar and cellular phones, are necessary for growth as bottle-

Table 1–3   **Proportion of Population Below the Poverty Line (percent)**

	1985	2000
East Asia	13	4
South Asia	52	37
Latin America	22	25
Eastern Europe	7	6
All Developing Countries	31	24

Source: The World Bank, *World Development Report 1992* (New York: Oxford University Press, 1992), p. 30.

necks keep occurring and are themselves a force for growth, a main source of increased demand. Each government in the area has announced huge investment programs in the whole range of infrastructure needs, led by Taiwan's $300 billion six-year plan, for a grand total in East Asia of announced plans of just under $600 billion—not including Japan's ten-year, $3.5 trillion commitment. The changes in life-style and standard of living implicit in these huge budgets make up a good deal of the shift from poverty that the World Bank expects. At the same time, world companies that fail to capture a significant share of this massive demand will fail in the competition of the 1990s and after.

The growth of East Asia and the ambitious infrastructure investment programs on the planning boards will be drawing down the world's supply of new capital at the same time that the needs of eastern Europe and the republics of the former Soviet Union continue to be very great. Given competing demands for capital, made greater by the needs of the United States and Britain to rebuild their industrial bases, can East Asia in fact fund the kind of growth that is expected in the region?

KEYS TO GROWTH: SAVINGS

The issue is key to the future of the region. Clearly, most observers do not see a capital shortage as a major issue or their estimates of East Asian growth would be less sanguine. Capital supply will come first of all from very high levels of domestic savings throughout the area, savings rates that are a multiple of the savings rate of the United States and that have increased over this period at exceptional speed. Note that in both Korea and Indonesia the savings rate in the mid-1960s was less than 10 percent of GDP. Not surprising then that investment rates in the two countries were so low as to preclude real economic growth; the problem eased somewhat for Korea by substantial foreign aid flows from the United States especially. In the 1960s, however, savings rates throughout the region were at or below the level that is creating a major problem now for the United States of inadequate investment (see Table 1–4).

By the 1990s, savings rates throughout East Asia were at very high levels. Gross savings in most of these economies were at the level of one dollar for every three dollars produced. Indonesia, with a long period of stable and reasonably competent government, has moved from its disas-

●

Table 1–4 Savings and Investment as Percent of GDP, 1965 and 1992

	Gross Domestic Savings		Gross Domestic Investment	
	1965	1992	1965	1992
Japan	30	34	28	33
Singapore	10	46	22	40
Hong Kong	29	34	36	31
Taiwan	20	28	23	24
Korea	8	35	15	40
Malaysia	24	30	20	36
Thailand	19	34	20	36
Philippines	21	15	21	22
Indonesia	8	36	8	35
China	25	38	24	37
United States	21	15★	20	16★
World	23	23★	23	23★

★1990.

Source: Data from Yanagihara Toru, Ed., *Ajia Taiheiyo no Keizai to Chiiki Kyoryoku* (Tokyo: Ajia Keizai Kenkyujo, 1992), p. 7; Asian Development Bank, *Asia Development Outlook 1992* (Hong Kong: Oxford University Press, 1992, pp. 294–295; The World Bank, *World Development Report 1992* (New York: Oxford University Press, 1992), p. 235.

trously low savings rate of only 8 percent to the startling level of 36 percent—a level that can fund a good deal of growth. And so, less dramatically, for the rest of the area as well.

The major exception is the Philippines, whose savings rate was not high and has deteriorated to a lower level still, equal to U.S. levels, although aid programs, mostly from Japan, make a somewhat higher level of gross investment sustainable. The Philippines remains plagued by political instability, corruption, and governmental incompetence, with land reform still only a dream and ghastly disparities between a few of great wealth and a great many of extreme poverty. A cliché of pre–World War II days described Turkey as "the sick man of Europe." The Philippines is "the sick man of East Asia" and shows little sign of addressing the terrible problems that have prevented this one East Asian country from participating in the move to relative prosperity.

•

KEYS TO GROWTH: RECYCLING
JAPAN'S SURPLUSES

Except for the unhappy case of the Philippines, East Asia's high savings rates find their reflection in the trade surpluses of the more mature of the region's economies, Japan and Taiwan in particular. There has been a certain fashion in America to describe Japan as a production-focused economy, said critically because somehow Japanese consumers are seen as deprived as a result of this production emphasis. The United States is in the same fashion described favorably as a consumption society. This is true enough in a way. Japan's economy produces more than is consumed, and the difference is savings. American's economy consumes more than it produces, and the difference is the awful situation where the world's richest nation by many measures is maintaining its consumption level by drawing on the savings of the world, through world funding of U.S. deficits, to the disadvantage of those poorer nations badly in need of capital investment funds. The fact is that consumption is easy; production and savings are more difficult but absolutely essential if the world is to enjoy economic growth. These savings find one expression in balance-of-payments surpluses.

Assessing the importance to the world of Japan's balance-of-payments surpluses, Derek Healey notes the high level of East Asian savings and their impact: "Besides Japan, only Germany and Taiwan—and until recently although to a lesser extent the Republic of Korea—are generating balance of payments surpluses. Of these, the German surplus will undoubtedly be used, first, for the rehabilitation of the former East German Economy; second, for the restructuring of the East European countries . . . ; and third, for assistance to the Soviet Union in its reconstruction process. Thus only Japan and Taiwan are currently in a position to provide capital to assist the economic development process in the rest of the world."[5]

Healey might have added China to the list, given its recent surpluses and its growing foreign exchange position—although no doubt those surpluses can be absorbed domestically in support of China's growth. In any case, Japan is setting record surpluses, with foreign exchange reserves of $80 billion. Taiwan has even greater reserves, at some $90 billion, probably now the world's highest, leaving gold out of account. China's additional $45 billion or so means that East Asian exchange reserves rep-

•

resent a very substantial part of world totals, $200 billion among these three nations.

Recycling the Japanese surplus in particular has provided additional capital to the economies of East Asia in two forms: first, aid funds, and second, direct investment. Japan is the largest aid donor nation now in the world, with a special emphasis in its aid programs on East Asia. In 1990, bilateral aid amounts were similar for Japan and the United States, about half again as great as the German aid program. However, the six major recipients of Japanese aid were all Asian nations, with Indonesia as usual receiving the largest amount of Japanese aid funds, but China and the Philippines also major recipients. In contrast, one-third of U.S. aid goes to Israel and Egypt, with the Philippines the only East Asian nation among the top ten U.S. aid donees, the U.S. grant to the Philippines being less than half that of Japan's. German aid goes to a broader geographic range of nations, with some focus on the Near East and South Asia. The concentration of Japanese aid funds on East Asia is strikingly different than the aid patterns of the other major donor nations.

In addition to the concentration of aid in East Asia, "another characteristic of Japanese aid is the high percentage directed toward infrastructure. In 1989, for example, 32 percent of the spending went for things like roads, railroads, ports, telecommunications systems, and power plants. The United States, by contrast, provides relatively little money for physical infrastructure. It gives far more food aid than the other leading donors, and it also invests fairly heavily in "social infrastructure."[6] As noted earlier, the shortfall in physical infrastructure is precisely a main barrier to more rapid economic growth throughout developing East Asia, and much of Japanese aid is aimed precisely at helping to clear away those bottlenecks in transport, energy supply, and telecommunications that are both a major problem for these economies and a major opportunity for Japanese suppliers.

Taiwan and Korea are beginning to develop aid programs as they move to the Japanese position of savings accumulations and current account surpluses. However, programs from Taiwan are limited by political issues, as Taiwan's government does not have formal diplomatic relations with many of the countries in the area, and Korea's programs are constrained by sheer lack of funds as Korea struggles to reestablish a trade surplus again after several years of deficits. Both of these economies, however, join Japan in being major suppliers of direct investment to the economies of Southeast Asia.

•

KEYS TO GROWTH: FOREIGN
INVESTMENT AND AID

With this has gone as well a general inclination to encourage foreign
investment as supplying capital, technology, and skills badly needed in
these developing economies. The moves of Deng Xiaopeng in China to
use foreign investment as an instrument of economic growth have been
an unexpected and unusual Communist recognition of the positive effects of foreign investment, and have been as well a brilliant success along
the China coast, with steady increases in the openness of China to foreign investment.

The potential for investing abroad has been essential to the continued economic growth of the investing as well as the receiving nations.
The first wave of investment from Japan, and then in turn Taiwan and
Korea, had been to secure raw material sources—Japan's large investment in Sumatra to obtain aluminum, the Korean and Taiwanese ventures elsewhere in Indonesia for plywood and pulp. However, the investments have driven mutual growth in the next wave, from the
mid-1980s, in search of labor as Northeast Asia encounters labor shortages and increasing labor costs, in search of less expensive land, and to
balance the pressures of increasing exchange rates against the dollar that
make exports more difficult, from Japan and Taiwan in particular.

This is not a "hollowing out" of the Northeast Asian economies.
The industries that are moving into the Southeast and into coastal China
are the lower value-added industries that must move if the Northeast
Asian economies are to continue to increase their income levels. These
economies would be "hollowing out" in the U.S. sense only if critical
higher value-added products and components such as those for electronics manufacture were being sourced from offshore. This is not the case,
at least not yet, for Japan, Taiwan, or Korea.

The combination of development aid and direct investment provides
a measure of the total capital contributions made to the area. In 1990, the
flow into East and Southeast Asia from the United States was $3,856
billion in combined aid and investment, nearly all investment. The EC
nations together provided an almost identical amount of aid and investment to East Asia, a total in 1990 of $3,947 billion. The total Japanese
flow that year was $9,647 billion, or two-and-one-half times greater than
the flow from either the United States or western Europe.[7] It appears that
Southeast Asia is to Japan as Latin America is to the United States and

●

eastern Europe to western Europe. The Japanese appear to have the best of it.

Nor are Japanese flows diminishing. Aid in 1993 is up again by about 7 percent, with the Asian proportion of Japan's total aid declining as more Japanese aid flows to South Asia and the Middle East, but the amounts to East Asia are continuing to increase. Japanese direct investment to the world declined sharply in 1992 as the economy slowed, down nearly 20 percent from the year earlier. Direct investment into East Asia, however, increased. The large flows of capital continue.

The role of the United States in this process has been critical. "The spectacular Asian economic 'miracle' owed much to the United States. First of all, the latter continued to provide a military presence through its bases and fleet in the region . . . although it might be questioned (as it was in various parts of Asia) whether such a presence was really needed. . . . Secondly, the United States more directly helped the Asian countries' economic growth through purchasing large quantities of their goods. . . . It may be said without exaggeration that the accessibility of American markets to Asian goods was a principal cause of the expansion of Asian export trade in the 1980s which in turn fueled its growth."[8]

KEYS TO GROWTH: EXPORT PROMOTION

It has been remarked often, and accurately enough, that one of the reasons for the economic success of East Asia has been the emphasis on export promotion in managing these economies, rather than import substitution. Import substitution as a way of dealing with trade deficits and of supporting domestic growth was a standard part of the development strategy of many nations, including at an earlier period many of the East Asian developing economies. Led by the Taiwanese and Korean examples in particular, however, and those economies' great successes, the region as a whole has opened itself to trade to a considerable degree and has sought growth through export promotion rather than through protectionism and import substitution.

Trade has been a critical part of the performance of these economies. Exports were seen as the route to success, and this helped determine their openness to foreign investment, viewed as another support to trade growth. The performance has been spectacular, just as total growth has

•

been. East Asia now accounts for one-quarter of world trade. While Japan's export growth has slackened with growth driven by the internal demand of a maturing economy, nearly all the rest of the area has experienced double-digit export growth, and these rates are continuing. While world trade in 1991 grew only 3 percent, East Asia's major trading economies increased their exports by 13 percent and imports by 17 percent.

Eight of the ten economies of East Asia are now among the 25 largest traders in the world, and East Asia's quarter share of world trade is up from only 10 percent three decades ago. Japanese expectations are of continued rapid export growth for the area (see Table 1–5). In this growth, the U.S. market was a major factor, as noted, especially with the Asian NIEs. As recently as 1986, nearly two-fifths, 37 percent, of the exports of Taiwan, Korea, Hong Kong, and Singapore were to the U.S. market. Only 10 percent went to Japan. By 1991, dependence on the U.S. market by the NIEs had dropped by one-third to just under 25 percent, while Japan remained at 10 percent.

The ASEAN 4 present a quite different pattern, with Indonesia, Malaysia, and Thailand never so dependent on the U.S. market as the NIEs. The United States has taken about 20 percent of the exports of the ASEAN economies, with Japan at about 25 percent. As intra-Asian trade increases, dependence on both Japan and the United States has lessened slightly. The Philippines, no doubt for historical reasons, is in the NIE

Table 1–5　　　**A Greater China Economic Zone:** *A Second Japan?*

	Population (million)	Area (thousand km^2)	GNP 1991 ($ billion)	GNP per capita 1991 ($)
Japan	124	378	3,362	26,930
South China Economic Region	121	339	306	2,535
of which				
Guangdong	64	178	34	527
Fujian	31	124	10	326
Hong Kong	6	1	82	14,396
Taiwan	20	36	180	8,815
ASEAN 4	319	3,053	302	947

Source: Reprinted from Nak-keung Mak, "The Guangdong Economy: Another Small Asian Dragon," *Nomura Asia Perspectives* (Tokyo: Nomura Research Institute, December 1992), p. 29.

•

pattern of heavy, and in this case even increasing, U.S. dependence. Here again, as in so many ways, the Philippines seem the odd man out in East Asia.

China needs special mention. As Overseas Chinese investment flooded into South China, and as Guangdong and Fujian production and export of such light items as textiles, shoes, toys, and the like took over the place in the U.S. market held earlier by Taiwan and Hong Kong in particular, China's trade with the United States has moved into substantial surplus. The predictable political reactions in the United States are occurring with some risk of U.S. protectionist moves against Chinese exports to America. Isolation of China is unlikely to serve U.S. purposes overall and would certainly have a negative impact on East Asian economic development and U.S. relations in the area.

EAST ASIA INDEPENDENT FROM
WESTERN ECONOMIES

In economic terms East Asia has been the beneficiary of a curious period in U.S. history, during which U.S. consumption increased greatly as tax levels were slashed in the 1980s. Individuals, corporations, and governments in the United States all reduced savings to very low levels, and the national government became a massive dissaver. Import restrictions on textiles, steel, autos, and other products were drowned by the surge of import-satisfied consumption. This all occurred at precisely the time that it best served the interests of the economies of East Asia, as their production levels and quality of output moved to meet world standards.

This era is no doubt drawing to an end as dependence on the U.S. market diminishes and as the need of the United States to remedy its savings failures becomes more urgent. It is clear that the economic progress of East Asia is no longer dependent on the West but has become self-sustaining. East Asia is now a more important market for Japan than North America. Asian trade with Asia is nearing half of total trade and on current trends will be more than half by the end of the decade. There are clear implications in this for trade policy and for the issue of trading areas and trading blocks, to be discussed below.

In military and strategic terms too an era has ended with the collapse of the Soviet Union. Remnants of the cold war remain in East Asia—there is no peace treaty between Russia and Japan; the Korean peninsula

•

remains potentially explosive; the problems of Cambodia continue. Three major countries in East Asia are still led by Communist parties, even with China's "Socialist market economy" and Vietnam's *Doi Moi* reformation.

So it is not so easy in East Asia to speak of the end of the cold war. Still, there is not—nor has there been for some time, in the opinion of a great many—a serious military threat or issue in the region. There is interest in a continued U.S. military presence, but that interest seems driven by a desire to avoid taking regional responsibilities as much as by a felt need for U.S. troops in the area. And certainly, barring some catastrophic change in world conditions, the U.S. military will continue a steady reduction in Asian bases and troop deployments. Domestic U.S. conditions and attitudes will require and demand a steady military withdrawal from Asia. The question is whether the United States has the wit or will to devise for itself a different role in Asia than marketplace or policeman.

One conclusion must be that the growth of East Asia has moved past dependence on the United States or any other single factor and has now become truly self-sustaining. "Growth in Asian demand is now more than compensating for falls in demand in the U.S. and elsewhere. The impact on Asia from the global economy has become very small," according to Chi Hung Kwan, senior economist at the Nomura Research Institute.[9] As seen earlier, East Asian GDP growth, and export growth, has continued without significant pause despite a sustained downturn in what have been considered until recently the regions' main markets of North America and Europe. A key clue in a classic Sherlock Holmes story was that the dog did not bark. The key to understanding the new autonomy of East Asia is the recession of 1989 to 1992 that did not take place.

A neglected aspect of East Asian development is its heavily urban focus. To a considerable degree, it is misleading to speak at length, as here, about these economies as national. First, the notion of the nation-state is essentially a concept developed in the West. In a good deal of East Asia the nation-states' boundaries are more porous. Indonesia, Singapore, and Malaysia are examples of recently established nations where religious, ethnic, and subregional identities are likely to be a good deal stronger than national identities. Taiwan and Hong Kong are further examples. No doubt this aspect has made for the development of regional economies in much of the area—national boundaries are less important,

•

for example, than language and area identities to many of the Overseas Chinese, who play so important a part in these regional developments.

A second way in which the Western emphasis on nations can be misleading is the size and importance of Asia's cities. In evaluating Asian markets, Western businesspeople must learn to look at urban markets rather than national ones to understand their true scale and configuration. In developed and homogeneous Japan and Taiwan, the differences in per capita income from main city to country are not great. The income advantage of the average Tokyoite is only a little more than twice that of residents in Japan's poorest prefecture, Okinawa. In Taiwan, the income spread from high-income Taipei to the poorest region, Yunlin, is about 2.5 times. National averages in these economies can be a meaningful guide to the configuration of the market.

However, the income differences in sprawling and developing countries like those in Southeast Asia can be very great. The income difference between the Bangkok average and Sisaket in Thailand's remote northeast is nearly 14 times in per capita income. Similarly, from Shanghai in China to China's lowest-income province, Guizhou, the income spread is 8 times.[10] Yet these main cities are very large markets in their own right. Bangkok has a population of six million persons, nearly 15 percent of the entire nation—and no doubt this understates the real size of the Bangkok urban area. Manila, Taipei, Kuala Lumpur, and even Vietnam's Hanoi have 10 to 15 percent of the national population, with Seoul the highest, at 26 percent. The market is not a remote province, nor yet the national average. The market for most industrial products and most services is in these great cities. Hong Kong and Singapore, of course, are pure city-states, entirely urban. These are also young populations, with an average age under 20 years, half the average age of most Western populations.

URBAN CENTERS AS KEY ECONOMIC CENTERS

The economic growth of the great urban centers of East Asia powerfully supports the argument of Jane Jacobs that cities, not nations, are the relevant unit for understanding economic growth. "Nations are political and military entities, and so are blocs of nations. But it doesn't necessarily

•

follow from this that they are also the basic, salient entities of economic life or that they are particularly useful for probing the mysteries of economic structure, the reasons for the rise and decline of wealth."[11]

"It is important, if we are to understand the rise and decline of wealth, for us not to be fuzzy about an abstraction like 'expansion' but to be concrete and specific about how expansion occurs and of what it consists. The expansion that occurs from city import-replacing consists specifically of these five forms of growth: abruptly enlarged city markets for new and different imports consisting largely of rural goods and of innovations being produced in other cities; abruptly increased numbers and kinds of jobs in the import-replacing city; increased transplants of city work into non-urban locations as older enterprises are crowded out; uses for technology, particularly to increase rural production and productivity; and growth of city capital."[12]

The cities of Asia, notably the city-states of Singapore and Hong Kong, fit this pattern well. Note too the great shift of population in Japan from the countryside to the cities in the 1950s and 1960s, and in Korea in the 1960s and 1970s. Something like this is now happening to Bangkok and Jakarta. The process is not pretty and is especially harsh for those who hold nostalgic feelings for these cities as they once were. But the process is development, and the loss of charm is often quite simply the overcoming of poverty. What was seen as East Asia's problem—overcrowded cities as refuges from a desperately poor countryside—would in this view have in fact been a principle cause of East Asia's more recent successes.

An accurate assessment of the configuration of East Asia's move to industrial power involves therefore an appreciation of the special role, importance, and wealth of its cities. It involves as well an understanding of the position of Japan in the area. The stark fact is that the Japanese economy is a full three-quarters of the entire economy of East Asia (see Table 1–2). Even assuming slowed growth of the Japanese economy and continued rapid growth of the rest of East Asia, at the turn of the century Japan will still be 70 percent of the entire region in economic terms.

This mirrors the relationship of the United States to the Western Hemisphere. The U.S. economy accounts for some 75 to 80 percent of all the Western Hemisphere's economic activity. The rather large numbers of corporations in the United States and Europe who failed to develop positions in Japan are inclined to seek an alternative to Japan in East

Asia. There is no alternative. The position of Japan is one of economic dominance in the area, like it or not, and that position will not change significantly in this generation.

JAPAN'S ROLE IN EAST ASIA

The importance of the Japanese economy in the area is especially striking in terms of size of companies. Nearly 90 percent of the top 500 companies of East Asia are Japanese. The largest 34 are all Japanese, with Korea's Samsung in 35th place with sales of about $14 billion. Ninety of the top 100 companies are Japanese, 6 are Korean, with 1 each from Malaysia, Indonesia, and Taiwan.[13] This is due first of course to the massive size of the Japanese economy relative to others in the area, but also to the fact that in these recently developing economies many of the firms are rather new and still under family management. It can be assumed that the number of large East Asian companies, competitive in size to Japan's companies, will increase rather rapidly over the coming years. These companies, like Japan's, will be reaching out from the region to world markets, and growing proportionately.

The position of Japan's companies in East Asia is examined in some detail below. Asia is now by a good margin the most profitable area of investment for Japan's companies. It is, clearly, the area where the growth is. East Asia not only provides growth and profits but resources, labor supply, inexpensive land, and growing local markets. These factors are all reinforced by a steadily appreciating currency. Japanese companies' production abroad is still well under 10 percent of total output, compared with 20 to 25 percent for U.S. and German companies. However, continuing very large Japanese trade account surpluses, along with the forces at work that make investment attractive, mean a continuing increase in offshore production by Japan's *kaisha*.

Japan's business executives seem convinced of East Asia's advantages. When Japan's powerful association of business firms, Keidanren, asked a sample of top managers, "What priority does your company assign to markets of the future?," 62 percent placed a higher priority on Asian markets than on the U.S. market.[14] The most recent foreign investment data suggest that the largest proportion of Japanese direct investment is

•

still going into the United States. This no doubt will continue to shift toward East Asia, the more so as Asia continues to welcome Japanese investment and U.S. attitudes toward Japan become more critical.

As we have seen, East Asia is now Japan's largest export market and the fastest growing, with exports in late 1992 to Asia up 15 percent on the year. Jardine, Fleming Securities noted in late 1992, "In October, Asia replaced Europe as Japan's second biggest export market for transport machinery (cars, trucks and motorcycles.)"[15]

Japan's historic move to a leading position as an industrial power has made possible the development of East Asia, and that is still the single most important factor in East Asian development, while East Asia in turn is now supplying Japan with a new and important support for Japan's continued industrial growth. These patterns of investment, trade, and mutually reinforcing growth are clearly not zero-sum games, and there are no moves in East Asia toward protectionism or closing borders to foreign investment. A winning game for all is now being played in East Asia.

The question remains, is there to be a second Japan in East Asia within the next generation? Can some nation displace Japan as the region's economic power? If Japan falters economically, is there a successor economy to step into the lead?

No one of the East Asian nations seems to qualify. Korea lacks the infrastructure of education and scientific skills that Japan built over a century, and with a population of 40-odd million is too small to be a major power. In combination with the North this could change, but only after a long period of great difficulties, in the manner of the German reunification. Indonesia has the population and resources but has a very long way to go to build the economic base from which to move to leadership. It is a candidate, but only far into the future.

NEW REGIONAL ECONOMIC ZONES

One of the most striking phenomena in the current economic growth of East Asia is the rise of regional economic zones, combining the capital and technology of Hong Kong, Taiwan, Korea, and Japan with the coastal provinces of China, opened as markets and investment sites by the reforms led by Deng Xiaopeng. The most dynamic of these are the Hong

•

Kong–Guangdong combination and the Taiwan-Fujian combination. Both of these regional economic zones are Chinese—of different dialects and regions though—with growth in both being led by Overseas Chinese, both focused in light industry, and both providing access to the vast Chinese hinterland of labor supply and potential market.

It takes no great ingenuity, then, to suggest that these might become a single economic zone—or that indeed they are in process now of becoming such a zone. The flow of investment, trade, and people into Fujian from Taiwan is now mainly through Hong Kong, given the lack of direct connections between Taiwan and the mainland. Table 1–5 provides some basic data on the regional zone compared with Japan and with ASEAN. The similarities to Japan in population and area are striking, with GNP estimated at about one-tenth that of Japan in total and per capita.

"Some Taiwanese leaders are advocating the formation of a greater China economic zone that would encompass mainland China and Southeast Asia. This concept is seen as a means of competing with the world's three major economic zones (Europe, North American, Japan) and preventing the expansion of Japanese economic influence in Asia."[16] Clearly, there are political barriers to a formal structuring of this zone, but clearly too the market place and economics are driving these entities together, and the absorption of Hong Kong into China in a few years will mark a step toward actual integration. In any case the concept does not require a formal structure but instead a continuation of recent and current economic trends. Nomura Research states, "The greater China economic zone is already a reality, albeit an invisible one."[17]

Whatever configuration this and other regional economic groupings may take over the next years and decades, their existence and dynamism is characteristic of the sweeping changes that continue in East Asia. The economic growth of the area is now self-sustaining as East Asia for the first time in nearly three centuries moves again to a central position in world affairs. There has been a sea change, as the industrial center of the world has moved to the western Pacific. No country nor company will go unaffected as the region's success reorders the economic structure and marketplaces of the world.

2

•

ENSURING
COMPETITIVE SUCCESS

CORPORATE STRATEGIES IN EAST ASIA

By near-unanimous reckoning, the economies of East Asia are where growth will be over the next decade. And by near-unanimous judgment, the corporations of Europe and the United States are failing to make investments in production and marketing commensurate with the reality and potential of East Asia. One consequence is lost opportunity, as markets that Western companies might profit from are captured by Asian competitors.

The failure to take markets has not only the immediate consequence of loss of profits, however; it also has the strategically disastrous consequence of allowing competitors to take share, gain market volumes and production scale, and move to industry leadership by exploiting the high growth left to them without competition from Western firms. Asian competitors are, by default, provided a base from which to build global competitive position.

It should be no comfort that as yet few companies in East Asia, apart from the Japanese, are world competitors. Japanese companies too were unknown to the West as Japan's economic growth took off in the early 1960s. Sony hardly existed, Toyota's cars were a joke. Japan's fast growth

•

made these companies into world leaders—fast growth not captured by Western competitors.

Like much of East Asia now, as Japan's economy moved to high-velocity growth in the 1950s and 1960s, Japan was seen by the executives of most of the world's businesses as a small, remote, insignificant, and difficult market. Much as Indonesia and China might be seen today, the hazards were considered formidable and the returns hardly justified by the costs and risks. In addition to the disastrous neglect of the Japanese economy, a great many Western firms made what proved to be a competitively fatal mistake.

Invaluable technology that would have made entry into Japan possible was sold off for windfall income—and, after improvement by the Japanese company, was later used to batter Western vendors. Elaborate justifications for their entry and investment failures have been developed by Western companies—official and unofficial barriers are described as having prevented investment—but none acknowledge their competitive mistakes.

In fact, however, some of the great companies of the West, with an appreciation of the massive potential of the Japanese economy, used their technology and capital to build major positions in Japan that now provide solid platforms for aggressive strategic moves into the rest of East Asia. Texas Instruments and IBM in electronics; Hoechst and DuPont in chemicals; Nestlé and McDonald's in food; Ciba Geigy and Merck in pharmaceuticals—all with billions of dollars of sales in Japan and with fully integrated facilities, including research and product development—are examples. They are all too few, however, and as a result Western corporate competitive problems as well as national current account problems reflect the failure of most Western corporations to address the Japan challenge.

IS FAILURE IN JAPAN TO BE REPEATED IN THE REST OF EAST ASIA?

In industry after industry, East Asia is where the growth will be in the 1990s. If this growth is captured in significant part by Japanese firms in autos and consumer electronics, the advantages Japanese companies al-

•

ready have in these products will be greatly increased by the addition of scale from Asian growth. Moreover, much of East Asia's growth will be in rather basic industries—bulk chemicals, for example—where Japanese and Korean firms are now relatively weak, owing to lack of scale and world share. They can emerge as formidable new competitors by capturing East Asia's growth through the kind of aggressive production and market investment that these companies are now undertaking in China and Southeast Asia.

In a great many industries, therefore, those in which world market position is critical to strategic success, Western companies must move rapidly into the markets of East Asia and organize themselves to be effective in this complex group of economies. Western companies, of course, are active already throughout East Asia, and it is useful to examine their position and experiences. They are too few, however, and generally too small in scale to meet the competitive challenge of the area. Some are of real importance, and in any case they and their Japanese competitors illustrate many of the opportunities and issues of doing business in the area.

EAST ASIA AS A PRODUCTION PLATFORM

East Asia as a production platform is a first, and still for many products, appropriate and effective approach to the area. Perhaps the best-known examples of this approach, at the extremes of the technology continuum, are the fashion and other apparel companies that provide designs and specifications to Asian workshops and that ship, even airfreight, the products back to the Western marketplace, and the semiconductor companies that hire the assembly of products in East Asia for final finishing and marketing in the West.

This kind of contract production will no doubt continue so long as East Asia presents well-disciplined and reasonably well-educated labor, at low prices. As Taiwan and Korea have moved beyond this role, Hong Kong and Malaysia are now of interest, as will be Guangdong and Vietnam in the near future. The arrangement is attractive to the host country, providing employment and foreign exchange but little by way of capital

●

investment or yet of training or technology. Some of these contract labor arrangements lead to major investments—Texas Instruments has been in Penang for 20 years and employs 2,800 persons there.

However, these apparel production and electronic assembly operations are not generally an integral part of the economies in which they have contracted for labor supply. That is, the pattern is that only part of the total manufacturing or assembly process takes place in Asia, and the commitment to a given supplier or location is temporary. Moreover, the Asian production represents only a part, and usually a quite small part, of the Western company's total production.

Nike

A quite different pattern of utilization of East Asian costs and skills is appearing in two companies that warrant close examination—America's Nike and Japan's Mabuchi Motors. The two companies are very different, operating in quite different product areas, but have the common characteristic of depending on offshore, East Asian supply of their products to all their markets. (Mabuchi produces some very specialized motors, made-to-order, in its Japan facilities.) They are using different approaches to obtaining product—Nike through subcontract, Mabuchi by investing in facilities—but the basic logic of the two positions is similar.

"All but 1 percent of the 90 million shoes Nike makes each year are manufactured in Asia. If costs in a particular country or factory move too far out of line, productivity will have to rise to compensate, or Nike will take its business elsewhere. The firm uses about 40 factories; 20 have closed in the past five years or so and another 35 have opened.

"'We're always looking for new manufacturing sources,' says David Taylor, Nike's vice president for production. 'People ask why we don't produce more in Eastern Europe; but we've concluded that the most capable manufacturers are in Asia.' "[1]

It would appear that Nike is a helpful barometer of relative Asian labor costs and development stages. "Until recently, almost all Nike's shoes were made in South Korea and Taiwan, but as labor costs there have soared, the firm's contractors in these two countries have moved much of their production to cheaper sites in China, Indonesia and Thailand. Now, Vietnam looks like the next country on the list."[2]

Nike does not manufacture its products itself. At its U.S. headquarters, the company's designers and marketers come up with the products for the new season (and Nike introduces a hundred or more a year). The speed of design change is the assurance against copying, because the designs become obsolete fast and could in any case be reverse-engineered for production by companies not subcontracted by Nike. The designs are produced in multiple locations, a sort of "double sourcing" to reduce risk.

"Out of Nike's 7,800 employees, only 610 work at the contractors' sites in Asia. They are primarily involved in ensuring factories produce shoes of the right quality and meet their delivery schedules. Some 75,000 Asian contract workers are making Nike products, four-fifths of them producing shoes, the rest apparel."[3]

A little hard on the U.S. balance of payments perhaps, but arguably U.S. capital and labor should not be dedicated to so labor-intensive a sector as shoes in any case. This certainly represents a brilliant strategic approach to this kind of product. The U.S. company holds control at the front end of design and engineering, in the production process of quality and delivery, and keeps its control of the marketplace—the point of ultimate power in this kind of branded consumer goods business. Capital investment is minimized; response time is very fast. The key to competitive success becomes design and marketing, the high value-added ends of this business. And it might be noted too that Nike further reduces its financial exposure by having the major Japanese trading company, Nissho Iwai (a preferred shareholder), handle the financing of Nike's purchases from its Asian subcontractors.

Clearly this approach to Asia is not for everyone. It assumes that production capacity is in place or can be quickly adapted to the product's needs, and that no capital or technology need be supplied from abroad. It also assumes a rapid change in product design such that the subcontractors are not advantaged by setting up production for their own or a third party's account. That said, there is no place on earth where more effective arrangements of this kind can be made than in East Asia—good-quality labor capable of working to high product standards, hard-driving entrepreneurs to provide the production management, governments supportive of this kind of contract production, and fast reaction time in the system to provide competitive edge.

●

Mabuchi Motors

Japan's Mabuchi Motors, like Nike, is a fast-growing, highly profitable company with most of its production abroad and sited in East Asia. The products are very different. Mabuchi produces micromotors, used in audiovisual equipment, cameras and appliances, and increasingly in auto applications such as locks and windshield wipers. About two-thirds of Mabuchi's total sales are outside Japan. Founded in rural Japan right after the war by the Mabuchi brothers, the company has current sales of about $560 million, with an after-tax return on sales of 13.6 percent. The profits are those that go with the 50+ percent world market share that Mabuchi Motors has maintained, and in going public a few years ago its founders became very wealthy indeed.

"The company is among the most attractive in the electronics sector. High margins, good growth, commanding market share, aggressive reduction in manufacturing costs, and geared to economic reform in China—the stock is very attractive. Mabuchi still holds a 52 to 53 percent share of the world market for small motors, and to increase their competitiveness Mabuchi will shift more production to China and Malaysia, from Taiwan. At present, production in China accounts for 67 percent of the company's total production, Malaysia provides 7 percent, and Taiwan, 22 percent."[4]

The Mabuchi move to overseas production was made early in the company's history, to Hong Kong in 1964, with an investment in Taipei following in 1969—both while the yen was still 360 to the U.S. dollar. They got well ahead on the cost power curve, with facilities running in low exchange rate and labor cost areas as the yen and Japan's costs went sky-high. The jewels in the Mabuchi production crown now are the Guangdong operation, the largest in the province, with 12,000 employees in a subcontracting plant, and the Dalian company, which set a precedent in obtaining approvals from the Chinese government in three weeks, and the first approval for a 100 percent investment for Dalian in the bargain. Mabuchi's Dalian company is tenth in profitability of all Japanese companies' overseas affiliates, while its Hong Kong subsidiary is sixth in profit among Japanese companies in Hong Kong.[5]

Eastman Kodak is a major customer, buying millions of these tiny motors, and reports it has had no quality problems whatsoever—and this despite the fact that all the products are from offshore Japan locations, with only 1,000 of its 27,000 employees Japanese and only 70 of these stationed abroad. Mr. S. Gotoh, general manager, said to this issue, "It is vital that education levels be adequate. Employees need to be able to evaluate and judge for themselves whether this is a usable or unusable product and act on that decision. Standards are set by the home office and directed to all our operations. Vital to this is the dispatch of employees to oversee production at each location. Conversely we make every effort to bring technicians, trainees and managers here to Japan to receive training, the longest for about one year, with the average in either direction from three to six months."

Mabuchi growth prospects are improved by the rapid increase in the use of small motors in autos, from 20 units in 1980 to 35–40 units in 1990, and a total of 100 in sight. To help ensure market position, Mabuchi just opened a new $80 million "Technology Center" near Tokyo to focus on production technology and basic research.

Like Nike, Mabuchi controls design and engineering from corporate headquarters, supervises quality and production scheduling but with all production offshore, and controls marketing of the product. The differences derive from the nature of the product, in Mabuchi's case a product that requires that plant and equipment investment be made—an investment easily justified by the quite exceptional profits that Mabuchi enjoys.[6]

Uniden Corp.

A company that has pursued a similar approach in Asia to Mabuchi's is Uniden Corp., a maker of cordless and cellular telephones and radio equipment. An even younger company than Mabuchi, although achieving comparable total sales, Uniden was founded in 1966. Taking advantage of the citizen band radio boom, it focused on the U.S. market, with manufacturing in Taiwan, Hong Kong, and the Philippines—but now shifting to China.

Managing Director Y. Okazaki reviews the situation: "Because our products were manufactured for 100 percent sales abroad there was no reason to have a manufacturing facility in Japan. We had factories in Yamagata, Saitama, Kanagawa and Chiba and decided to close them all. Our earnings from the U.S. citizen's band boom allowed us to pay re-

•

cord high severance allowances to our Japan factory employees. Our production moved to Taiwan and Hong Kong. Because the Taiwan dollar was tied to the U.S. dollar we could deal directly in currencies that would not result in a loss as would have happened if we worked on a straight yen conversion basis.

"The second reason is that communications equipment are assembly dependent production, labor intensive. Gradually this type of labor became more difficult to attract throughout Japan. Taiwan at this time was the natural choice at one-third the cost. The third reason was the existence of a 6 to 6.5 percent duty on communications products exported from Japan. At that time both Taiwan and Hong Kong had special status as NICs under the General Systems of Preferences allowing them non-levied access to the U.S. market."

Hit hard by its diversification plays and speculation during Japan's "bubble" period of 1990–92, Uniden took write-offs and losses, but "This term Uniden's consolidated sales will grow by 16.3 percent, buoyed by strong orders from the U.S. U.S. sales are forecast to provide 72.5 percent of total sales this term. Thanks to the start in May 1992 of full operations at their China factory, consolidated recurring profit will probably grow by 42 percent. Due to increased personnel expenses and other expenses in Hong Kong, Uniden closed its Hong Kong factory last term and constructed a factory in China. At the China factory personnel expenses per head are ¥10,000 (U.S.$83) per month, about one-fifteenth of that in Hong Kong. Due to the start of full operations in the new China factory, the operating margin will improve by an estimated 2.8 percentage points."[7]

TARGETING EAST ASIAN SALES

Uniden is now looking to Asia not only for production but for markets as well, despite its continuing heavy dependence on the U.S. market. Again, Managing Director Okazaki says, "Regional movements such as NAFTA indicate that in the future it will not be realistic to see products manufactured in Asia being exported to the U.S. in the same numbers as before. Our approach is thus 'manufacturing in the market.' We have our sights on China for this very reason. Only 2 percent of the population have telephones and the land mass is inviting for CB expansion. We have up to now focused our efforts on the U.S. and Europe but Asia now shows the greatest new business expansion potential."

All three of these companies—Nike, Mabuchi, and Uniden—have based their production in East Asia and in the developing part of East Asia, taking full advantage of the very attractive labor supply. Nike's strategy is basically different, however. Nike is a gypsy—attracted by efficient, low-cost labor and ready and indeed forced to move on as labor cost and availability changes. Nike is in Asia but is not of Asia. Protected by its fast design changes from copying, Nike's product does not require the company to invest in Asia.

Indeed, it appears that on the sales side of the business Nike either ignores or fails in Asia. The company reports more than 93 percent of its sales in the United States and Europe. In other words, less than 7 percent of sales are to 90 percent of the world's population, and certainly one would conclude that less than 5 percent are to the 50 plus percent of the world population in East and South Asia. Curious, because a great many fashion firms—Chanel, Vuitton—realize one- to two-thirds of their worldwide sales in East Asia. This is a paradox in the Nike case—Asian production and virtually no Asian sales. Still, for companies in businesses with fast-moving design changes, but where unique capital investment is not required, the Nike strategy is a superb way to take advantage of East Asia's strengths.

The Mabuchi Motors and Uniden cases are basically different from the Nike case. These are not gypsy companies, for all their histories of having moved production facilities. Their manufacturing requires investment and full management, not only quality control and scheduling. Mabuchi especially, but Uniden increasingly, is looking to Asian markets for a good proportion of total sales. The lesson here is that East Asia's developing economies can justify dedicating the entire manufacturing capacity of a substantial company to its developing economies, offshore even from Japan. That lesson needs to be driven home to Western companies, which, as we shall see, are consistently failing to make the appropriate commitments to and investments in the economies of East Asia.

Each of these companies presents a rather special case, in their history, products, and approach to East Asia. In world trade competition, the vehicle industry and the electronics industry play the largest roles. The situation of these industries in East Asia warrants examination for lessons that might apply broadly to Western companies as they approach East Asia.

●

EAST ASIA'S AUTO MARKETS

The auto industry is of special interest, because vehicles and parts make up a major share of world trade and the industry's great size and diversity of inputs of material and parts impacts profoundly the entire economies in which autos are produced. Toyota, for example, claims that one in ten of all Japanese workers is involved in an activity related to automobiles, and the situation in Germany and elsewhere cannot be greatly different.

Japan's leading tire producer, Bridgestone, an interested third party to vehicle production, has based its production and marketing plans on world vehicle growth in output of only 10 percent from 1991 to 1995. However, Bridgestone projects 41 percent growth in the non-Japan East Asian markets. Given the low expected growth in North America, Europe, and Japan, that means in Bridgestone's view that East Asia will account for a full 70 percent of the growth of the world vehicle market over the next several years.[8]

Bridgestone is in an industry that is approaching the competitive endgame worldwide, with 60 percent of world share held by three companies—Bridgestone, Michelin, and Goodyear—and another seven or so companies dividing the balance of share. With East Asian growth at twice world levels, and with production not only in Japan but in Thailand, Indonesia, Taiwan, and the Philippines as well, Bridgestone appears well positioned to capture much of the Asian growth in competition with its European and U.S. main competitors.

In the industry itself, Honda plans on a doubling of the auto market in East Asia and Oceania over the decade of the 1990s, from about 2 million annual sales outside Japan to about 4 million. This will be as great, in Honda's view, as the total growth in the European market and considerably more than the total growth of the North American market. Some estimates of the market growth are even more optimistic as East Asia's economies continue to surge: the Thai market for autos, for example, increased by 70 percent in 1992 over 1991, to a total of about 350,000 passenger cars, and 25 percent growth is expected.

These growth estimates are for an industry that is scale-intensive not only in manufacturing but in sales as well. With lean production, sheer manufacturing scale is less critical than before, but the costs of establishing a distribution and sales system and a credible system of after-service require considerable investments justified only by substantial sales volumes. Moreover, the auto industry of the world is going through a

•

shakeout, with overcapacity in most producing centers and manufacturers in North America and Europe especially cutting back on facilities and dismissing large numbers of both factory and office personnel. Billions of dollars of losses have been reported by General Motors alone, and even Japan's makers, Toyota and Honda excepted, have been experiencing red ink, cutbacks, and efforts at rationalization.

The opportunity for this huge, troubled industry is in East Asia. It is a neutral and geographically isolated market, perfect for cutthroat price competition. No doubt, then, the world's makers are battling it out there. Well, not exactly. In the ASEAN markets, which are relatively open and are now probably some 700,000 vehicles in total size, Japan's auto companies have more than 90 percent market share. European and U.S. companies are virtually nonexistent in these fast-growing markets. Even in Hong Kong, surely an example of a truly open market, the Japanese share is over 80 percent, led by Toyota with over 25 percent of the total market. Mercedes and BMW lead the rest of the world with about three share points each.

Korea is for the Koreans. No open markets there, as Korea uses total market protection as a device to build its own, it hopes, world-competitive auto industry based on its growing domestic market of what is now about 750,000 cars per year. Taiwan is the one exception to the pattern of total domination by Japan. Its majority-owned company in Taiwan, Ford Lio Ho Motor Co., holds about 25 percent of Taiwan's 350,000-unit market.[9]

What was happened here? How could General Motors, the world's largest manufacturing company, totally miss the East Asian market? One might expect that almost by chance they would have some position somewhere in the area. Or Fiat, Italy's largest private company. Or Daimler Benz, Germany's leading industrial company. Only Ford of the great auto companies of the West has the elements of an East Asia position, with a major holding in Taiwan, a substantial interest in Japan's Mazda, and together with Mazda, a holding in Korea's number-three producer, Kia.

Where Are the Americans?

The auto industry is the exemplary case of the importance of having a major position in Japan—or rather, of the terrible costs of missing, or mismanaging, Japanese opportunities. The American auto companies

•

have made an effort. In the 1960s, Chrysler bought into Mitsubishi Motors in a dramatic defiance by the Mitsubishi management and Chrysler of the wishes of Japan's Ministry of International Trade and Industry. Chrysler never effectively incorporated Mitsubishi Motors into its world system, however, and as Chrysler got into deep trouble, it divested its holding rather than use the Japan company as a base for restructuring.

The real failure of the U.S. industry, however, is the total bankruptcy of the Asian strategy of General Motors. It was GM that early in the 1970s bought a major holding in Japan's Isuzu, originally a 34 percent interest. Isuzu had long been a leading truck and bus producer but was in deep trouble from its failures in the passenger car business. GM offered the alternative to takeover of Isuzu by Nissan, and was to bring to Isuzu the design, engineering, and sales skills that would make Isuzu as successful in autos as it continued to be in trucks. Even while taking its share position to a high of 44 percent at one point, GM never helped Isuzu in its problem areas, and indeed was felt by Isuzu to have made its problems worse on several occasions. In any case, Isuzu has finally dealt with continued losses in its auto business by getting out. It will try to help GM in GM's U.S. truck business, but Isuzu will sell Honda passenger cars through its Japan dealers.

The Isuzu situation—which could have been the basis for a strong position in East Asia, given effective management—has its counterpart in the failure of General Motors in Korea as well. GM had a full 20 years of 50 percent ownership of a Korean auto producer before abandoning the investment and selling out to its partner, Daewoo, in 1992. In both cases, GM proved unable to deal successfully with local partners or with the local market. (In Japan the black executive cars that are now Mercedes Benz's products were all Buicks and Cadillacs in the 1960s.) With either a Japanese or Korean base, GM might well have had the platform, for a major East Asian position. As it is, the periodic announcements by GM of plans to invest heavily in Indonesia (GM pulled out of that market too, in 1972) or in China simply lack credibility, given GM's Asian record of failure and its serious problems in North America and Europe.

The European auto companies too have established no manufacturing bases in Korea or Japan. The German companies have done very well in the Japanese auto market, Mercedes Benz, Volkswagen, and BMW each with annual import sales in Japan of over $1 billion. This does little for them in terms of market penetration in the rest of East Asia, however, and European firms in general seem not prepared to make the kind of

•

world-scale investment in East Asian manufacture that competition requires and that the market potential would justify.

Ford, as noted, has the elements for a major East Asian position. Ford
has worked hard to build a valuable relationship with Mazda, despite
holding only a 25 percent equity position. Mazda will come under severe
pressure, however, as the Japanese auto industry shakes out (the Isuzu
withdrawal from passenger cars was only one of a number of needed
changes in the industry structure). Nor has Ford yet made use of its Taiwan investment as a platform for other moves in East Asia. A move from
Taiwan into Fujian, for example, could be an effective point of entry
into the Chinese market, but to date only Mazda's venture into Hainan
involves Ford in China, and only indirectly.

The interesting auto play in China is Honda. Most of the world's
vehicle producers are venturing into China, and the Chinese government clearly sees some advantages in playing off each against the others.
The market remains small and fragmented, and slow to develop. The
Honda edge is unique. Bear in mind that China is a land not of motor
power but of leg power, just as Japan was at war's end and as much of
East Asia still is. It is likely (an exact count is not possible) that China has
something like 600 million bicycles in use. Every visitor to China must
have a sharp recollection of a great wave of bicycles moving through
every street at all hours. And what comes after bicycles? Not automobiles, but autobikes—motorcycles. So it was in Japan in the 1950s; so it
is now in Taipei and Djakarta. And so Honda, still the world's largest
motorcycle producer for all of its automobile success, stands squarely in
the path of the next major vehicle market in China.

Honda announced in the single year 1992 three joint ventures for
the manufacture in China of motorcycles, not by chance located in central, northern, and southern China. Each motorcycle venture will of
course have its work force and management, parts suppliers, and sales and
after-service network, all of which will be of enormous value when auto
production lines are added but which in the meantime should provide an
explosively growing business opportunity. GM, Ford, and Chrysler do
not make motorcycles, nor does Daimler, Fiat, or Renault. And BMW's
look too large.

So the East Asian auto market could be Japan's. Of the U.S. companies, only Ford is still in the running. The European companies seem to
have no interest in or capacity for the magnitudes of bets on Asia that are
required and justified by the market's size, growth, and ultimate impor-

●

tance. After all, half of humankind lives in East Asia, a good number of
candidates for auto purchase. The potential gain to the Japanese industry
from the capture of East Asia's growth is great—as is the loss to the
American and European makers.

EAST ASIAN DOMINANCE IN
ELECTRONICS PRODUCTION

The second of the key trading industries on which so much of national
economic position depends is electronics. Although the auto industry is
still dominated by the West, with Japan and Korea accounting for about
one-third of world production, the electronics industry presents a more
complex pattern. As shown in Table 2–1, the industry can be divided
into three broad categories—consumer electronics, industrial electronics,
and electronic components. If these are summed, the full impact of the
importance of East Asia can be seen in that East Asia—in fact, Northeast
Asia—has now a larger position in electronics production than does the
United States or western Europe. East Asia dominates world production
of consumer electronics and is, by a considerable margin, the leader in
production of electronic components. It is only in industrial electronics—telecommunications equipment, computers, test and measuring instruments, and office equipment—that East Asia's production is less than
that of North American and western Europe.

Table 2–1   Electronics Industry Output, 1992 ($ million)

	United States	Europe	Northeast Asia (Japan and the NIEs) Total
Consumer electronics	9,183	14,310	42,623
Industrial electronics	158,426	133,423	111,167
Electronic components	64,144	30,300	88,738
Total	231,753	178,033	242,528

NIEs includes Korea, Taiwan, Hong Kong, and Singapore.
Figures for Europe and NIEs are estimates and are calculated at 1991 exchange rates.
Source: Reprinted from Electronics Industries Association of Japan, "Facts and Figures in the Jap-
anese Electronics Industry" (Tokyo 1993), p. 109.

•

That the consumer electronics industry has come to totally dominate the world market as the U.S. industry has lost position is well known and an often-told story. The remaining major competitors for the Japanese companies in consumer electronic products are European—Philips of the Netherlands, with a marginal position in Japan but a major position in Taiwan and substantial investments in China, and France's Thompson, now owner of the former RCA facilities and holding a substantial investment in Singapore's Batam Island development, but with no position in the critical Japanese industry.

What makes consumer electronics of special interest with respect to strategies for East Asia is first, the very large market that East Asia now offers for consumer goods in general, with consumer electronics one measure of market size, and second, the investment strategies being pursued by Japanese electronic firms in East Asia and their impact on the area's growth potential.

Japanese exports to East Asia provide one estimate of the size of the market. Production of the simpler consumer electronic products—radios, cassette players, stereo headphones, and the like—has already been shifted out of Japan, with Hong Kong, Korea, and Taiwan, in that order, the world's largest producers of radio cassette products. These are for both local and world markets and are produced in good part by Japanese firms investing in the area.

For more sophisticated consumer products like color television and video tape recorders, Asia is now the major market for exports from Japan (see Appendix Table 1). Equally important, the area is now the largest market for electronic components from Japan; in Southeast Asia a good proportion are no doubt used in the assembly in plants of products for local marketing and export to world markets. Sharp Corporation, for example, estimates that for products like VCRs and TV sets, 30 to 50 percent of the parts for offshore production are still exported from Japan, as local suppliers have yet to be developed for key components.

Note too that the export position of Japanese makers of industrial electronics products is much lower in Asia than in other markets, a function not only of more limited infrastructure and industrial investment in the area, but also of the far more competitive position in the area of Western producers. As will be seen below, while the consumer electronic sector has been largely lost to Asian competition, Western companies are still very much in the game in the industrial electronics sector.

Looking again at consumer electronics and the size of the market, we

•

estimate that the China market now purchases 9 million color television sets annually, which will grow to a 12-million-unit-per-year market by the mid-1990s. Gemini Consulting (Japan) estimates that over 58 million Chinese households are now potential purchasers, with another 13 million households in Indonesia also now a potential market, with current penetration levels at only one-tenth to one-fifth of the total market size.

JAPANESE COMPANIES'
OFFSHORE BASES

Not only is the East Asian market of very great size; it also represents a key investment opportunity as a base for worldwide product sourcing. Japan's Matsushita Group have been leaders in investments in the area. Matsushita is a world leader in air conditioners and is now basing its world sourcing strategy on its investments in Malaysia. "The Matsushita Group has a long-term target of increasing its share of the global air conditioner market to 20 percent by 1995. According to the firm, the world market for air conditioners is expected to grow from 16.5 million units in 1991 to about 21 million units in 1995. Of the current total market, sales in Japan account for about 7 million units, the U.S. 3.5 million units, Southeast Asia 3.44 million units; and the Middle East 0.85 million units. Matsushita is now producing about 2.45 million air conditioners each year, and to realize a 20 percent share of the global market, it will have to increase its production to 4.2 million units by the midnineties. . . . When these plans are realized, Malaysia will surpass Japan as the world's largest exporter of air conditioners. . . . The Matsushita Group is producing 2 million rotary compressors and 5.7 million motors for air conditioners each year in Malaysia."[10]

Matsushita, the world's largest electrical appliance maker, now has 15 affiliates in Malaysia, accounting for about 4 percent of Malaysia's total exports. These are coordinated through Matsushita's Singapore regional headquarters, with major investments in Thailand, Taiwan, Indonesia, and the Philippines. An extreme view of the Japan approach to Asian investment was offered by a Hitachi executive: "We will not be making consumer electronics in Japan anymore. Production will all be in Southeast Asia." Malaysia has been a particular focus for Japanese electronic investments seeking offshore production sites, providing a sup-

●

portive investment climate with a rapidly developing infrastructure of parts and subassembly manufacturers.

Enthusiasm for East Asia investment is not surprising in light of the success of Japan's electronics companies with their investments in the area. As Appendix Table 2 indicates, Asia has been the source of profits for Japan's electronic companies as they have moved abroad, with Europe also attractive but North American investments reporting very heavy losses. The pattern of success is to first build a major position in the Japanese market where new products and new fashions in consumer electronics first appear, with production in Japan for world markets of the most sophisticated of the product line and with production moving offshore as the product moves to maturity in its life cycle. Japan's imports of electronic products from Malaysia increased by more than six times in the five years from 1985 to 1990, less sophisticated products like electric fans and simple air conditioners. The pattern is straight out of the classic economics textbooks—and it works.

The scope of the Japanese consumer electronic programs in East Asia is very great. In the case of Sony, "Sony has factories for audio, TV, and video products and parts, two each in Taiwan, Korea and Thailand, three in Malaysia, and one in Singapore. In 1990 a new semiconductor factory in Thailand and two factories in Malaysia went into operation.

"Sony International of Singapore (SONIS) is Sony's general headquarters for the Southeast Asian region, and Sony's Southeast Asian factories and affiliated companies are connected by a communications network. The Central Distribution Center in Singapore procures parts from around the world to be used by factories in the Southeast Asian region. The CDC also collects products manufactured within its control area for delivery worldwide.

"Starting in 1991, Sony will introduce into its structure a worldwide general information communications system. Through this system, the headquarters will be connected on-line with its 39 domestic companies, nine US companies, 18 European companies and five Southeast Asian companies as well as important cooperating firms. Production and sales planning, which was previously drawn up in monthly units, will change to weekly planning. After two years this plan is expected to reduce by half the required inventory and will cut the time from receipt of orders to delivery by two-thirds.

"Like Sony, other major electronics manufacturers such as Matsushita Electric are considering global logistics that integrate production, sales and distribution. They are planning information communications networks that stretch across the globe to connect Japan, North America, Europe and Southeast Asia."[11] These electronics companies are pioneers in the globalization of Japan's companies, and East Asia is integral to the worldwide system.

AMERICAN ELECTRONICS PRODUCERS

For all of their successes in autos and consumer electronics, Japanese companies by no means have an unchallenged run at East Asian markets and sourcing. The situation in industrial electronics, and in key components areas, is quite different; Western and especially U.S. companies are building major positions in Japan and the rest of East Asia.

IBM—An Early Player in Japan

A case in point is IBM. For all of that company's problems, it has dealt rather effectively with the East Asian challenge. Its operations in Japan, key to any Asian strategy, total about $12 billion in sales, or about 15 percent of the company's total global sales. Because the Japanese economy is about 15 percent of the world economy, effective operations in Japan should in general make up some 15 to 20 percent of an international company's total sales, and IBM meets this objective. Moreover, IBM has for many years organized itself on a regional basis, and IBM's Asia/Pacific Group, Tokyo-based with offices in key locations throughout the region, provides central planning and coordination for the region. The result is that IBM's sales in East Asia are about 17 percent of its world total, reflecting the area's share of the world economy.

IBM is still a powerhouse, at any rate until recently. What about newer players in the computer game? Apple is an interesting case in point. Way back when personal computers were a novelty and the Macintosh a thing of wonder, Apple, along with Tandy, had what there was of a PC market in Japan—a tiny market, with no Japanese-language software provided, and of little interest to the U.S. companies in any case given the explosive growth of the U.S. market. However, with advances

•

in memory capacity and software, the Japanese market became a major one for PCs, with Japan's NEC in solid control of half of the total.

Apple's Pacific Sales Growing

Apple for its part continued to fumble. Presidents of the small Japanese company—all expatriates—changed annually, or so it seemed. One of Japan's great companies, Canon, was involved in Apple distribution, but the combination was never really effective. In the late 1980s, the Apple position in Japan began to change. A veteran Japanese executive was hired away from a competitor. Software in Japanese became available. Sales began to move, as agreements were entered into with Sony and Sharp, among others, for product development and supply. Apple sales in Japan are estimated to be some $500 million in 1993 from a miserable beginning, with a billion-dollar target for the mid-1990s.

With this revolution in position in Japan, Apple has made as well a major thrust into East Asia as a whole. Pacific region sales in 1992, including Japan, accounted for about 20 percent of Apple's total turnover, compared with only 10 percent four or five years ago. Unit shipments in the Pacific were up 70 percent in 1992 over the previous year. One of Apple's four worldwide manufacturing centers is now in Asia, in Singapore. In a strategically critical move, Apple Computer has joined with the Singapore government in a $10 million R&D center in Singapore to focus on the development of computers that "read" and "speak" Asian languages, especially those based on ideograms—which opens the possibility of effective sales in China, taking advantage of China's new copyright law, which provides protection against software piracy.

Clearly, Apple recognized both the opportunity East Asia presents as a market and the potentially fatal threat of East Asia as a source of competitors. Bill James, managing director of Apple Far East, says, "Each Tiger has a strong indigenous PC company. They produce quality products and sell them at very low prices. . . . We have to set ourselves apart to compete effectively. We are aggressive on pricing and have a wide channel of distribution with good retail outlets, system resellers and value-added specialists that offer excellent service and support." The European and U.S. balance of payments would be much improved if more Western companies had responded to Asian competition, as Apple is now doing. The final competitive outcome is not clear, but in any case there is real and continuing competition.

In electronic components too, U.S. firms appear to be moving to more aggressive strategies. East Asia has long been used by component manufacturers as a source of cheap labor, from the early days of semiconductor assembly in Korea and Taiwan, and later sites like Malaysia's Penang. Like Nike, however, these were gypsy operations, with the products, aimed entirely at the U.S. and European markets, not representing real commitments to an Asian position. This appears to be changing.

Texas Instruments' Comeback in Asia

Texas Instruments is an impressive example. One of the founding companies of the industry and a pioneer in technology and markets, TI used its technology to batter its way into a wholly owned operation in Japan in the mid-1960s, and now it has well over a billion dollars in annual sales in Japan, along with a wholly owned R&D center in Japan's science city, Tsukuba. However, TI, like other leading U.S. firms, has been through more recent troubled times. It is using Asia as the platform for its comeback.

"Asia has become crucial to the Dallas-based company as a growing market as well as a cost-efficient production base. The company's sales in the region will total about U.S. $1.5 billion this year. Asia accounts for 30 percent of the company's total non-military turnover. . . . All of the firm's new capacity is being added in Asia, with the exception of a semiconductor plant in Italy. In the past decade Texas Instruments has invested more than U.S. $1.5 billion in the region, and now has 15,000 workers on its payrolls."[12] The semiconductor industry is especially capital-intensive, and TI has long felt at a serious disadvantage in cost of capital relative to its Japanese competitors. TI has attempted to counter that handicap by joining with Asian investors in Japan and Taiwan, taking minority equity positions in world-scale production facilities.

Of special interest is the fact that in Taiwan TI has joined not only with the local computer firm Acer in its venture there but has as its partner the government's China Development Corp. as well. Moreover, like Apple, TI's new production facility in Singapore includes in its equity holders the Singapore government, as well as Japan's Canon and Hewlett

•

Packard from the United States. A recurring theme in many of these positive strategies, by both Japanese and U.S. companies, is the involvement of local partners. The inclusion of governmental investment corporations, especially in Singapore, by the Americans is intriguing. Singapore is heavily committed to multinationals who can provide high technology to a land- and labor-constrained economy, and at the same time it is attractive to high-technology Western firms in search of capital.

AT&T—A Newcomer

AT&T is of interest as a case of late entry to international business in general and to the East Asian area in particular. With specific reference to China, John Pasquali, managing director, AT&T China, Inc., said, "After the breakup of AT&T in the early 1980s, we looked at the world and said, 'Where do we invest?' A lot of people said Eastern Europe. When we looked at the Pacific Rim, we saw that half of the world's communications market potentially lay in Asia, especially China. In addition, given the huge infrastructure needs here, explicitly called for in China's five-year plan, we obviously saw the great potential of the market."

The AT&T Beijing office opened in 1985, with an interest in satellite and line telecommunications and in the sale of equipment. The company has several joint ventures in China, the most important being a 50 percent-held venture in Shanghai manufacturing transmission equipment. China is a minor part of the 16,000-person East Asian position of AT&T, who in a few years have set up manufacturing in Singapore, Thailand, and Taiwan, in addition to two joint ventures in Korea with the Lucky Goldstar Group. In Japan, the long lines business is a money spinner, but AT&T's real Japanese asset—still very much underutilized by the company—is the billion-dollar NCR computer company, traded on Tokyo's first exchange. In a short time, AT&T has a lot of pieces in place in East Asia (including two service ventures with Singapore government agencies). It remains to be seen how the pieces will fit into an overall Asian strategy and major Asian presence.

Other important Western firms in the industrial electronics sector that are moving effectively in East Asia include such companies as Motorola; GE, particularly with its medical diagnostics products; Applied

•

Materials in semiconductor manufacturing equipment; AMP in electronic connectors; and Hewlett Packard in computer technology. It is noteworthy that all of these companies have substantial positions in the Japanese economy that are major drivers of their wider efforts in the rest of East Asia. Moreover, all of these businesses are in newly emerging technologies. Unlike autos, for example, or much of consumer electronics, the competitive base is recently developed and is still taking shape. This technological fluidity provides new competitive opportunities— and plays to the strengths in creativity of the best of U.S. companies.

Success through innovation need not be through high technology. Avon Products, improbable though it may seem, looks poised to achieve a major success in China, starting in Guangdong. John I. Novostad, vice president, Avon Products, says, "We anticipate that our sales will be huge by the year 2000. The plan first year was $1 million but actual sales were 500 percent over target. In five or six years we could be the eighth largest Avon operation out of 30 country operations worldwide." Avon's Novostad offers an intriguing insight. "Direct selling does extremely well in countries with limited infrastructure and transportation; the opportunity is that direct selling bypasses these obstacles and gets quality goods to the market even before infrastructure is in place." Amway, coming off its huge success in Japan, seems to have reached a similar conclusion as it announced entry into the Indonesian market.

JAPAN AS THE SPRINGBOARD INTO EAST ASIA

What seem to be some of the characteristics of Western companies that do well—and badly—in East Asia? One thread running through much of the experience is the critical importance of a Japan position. Japan's economy is, after all, nearly three-quarters of the total economy of East Asia. Japanese capital and technology help drive the area forward. Japanese companies are the major competitors in virtually every field in which Western companies might compete. It is not surprising, then, that companies that have done well in Japan also tend to do well in the rest of Asia. Companies like General Motors that have blown their Japan

●

chances have little market position in the rest of Asia and are not likely to have much there in the future.

One of America's leading pharmaceutical firms illustrates the Japan issue as well. Eli Lilly began exporting product to Japan in 1923, but with its great product development successes in the postwar period, it chose to cash out through product licensing to Japanese companies, rather than through direct entry and investment in the Japanese market. It was not until 1985 that Lilly began its own marketing in Japan, and even now only 5 percent of total sales are in Japan and less than 10 percent in all of East Asia. It is perhaps a measure of Lilly's understanding of and commitment to East Asia that Asia-Pacific headquarters have been located in Indianapolis, Indiana, until 1993.

Question: Are substantial businesses in Japan a precondition to Asian success? Probably, in most industries. Are the kinds of companies that made the necessary effort to be in Japan also the kinds of companies that will have the perspective to build a total East Asian position?

A Philips in consumer electronics that had kept its technology and built its own position in Japan rather than licensing to Matsushita would be by order of magnitude more powerful than a Philips that tries to build its Asian position via Taiwan, Australia, and China but without a major Japan base. Ford and GM made no effort to rebuild their prewar positions in Japan; by contrast, NCR and IBM made full-out and successful efforts to rebuild and will move further forward—and in a politically more sensitive industry. Some of the problem here may well be a fundamental set of views and attitudes toward the world in general, and toward Asia in particular. Managements of some companies, and perhaps the cultures of those companies, were more sensitive to the changes going on in Asia and their effects and more respectful of the competence and potential of Asian companies than were their competitors.

It may be along this dimension that the relative success of Western industrial electronics firms can be explained. Most of these firms—Apple, Hewlett Packard, Applied Materials—grew into major stature during the period that Japan achieved industrial leadership and that Asia began to prosper. Their focus then has not been exclusively on western Europe. Indeed, in most of their businesses, the western European position is insignificant and the real competition comes from Asia. No surprise then that the managements of these companies are bent on building powerful Asian positions.

●

OPPORTUNITIES IN CHEMICALS

It is perhaps this perception of threat and opportunity that helps explain the limited position across Asia of many of the powerful chemical companies of the West. DuPont can hardly be faulted for its technological and market accomplishments, and after a series of limited and risk-averse joint-venture moves in Japan, it has built a very large, wholly owned position in that economy, with total sales well over $1 billion in specialized and high–value-added products. However, Asia as a whole accounts for only 6 percent of DuPont's worldwide sales. Like many of the more risk-averse multinationals, DuPont is focusing its manufacturing in Asia, outside Japan, in Singapore, and now has six manufacturing plants under construction in the Asia Pacific region. Emphasis is on products for the auto and electronics industry.

Nothing seems wrong with the DuPont situation, except that it seems slow and late. A danger in this is that it may allow the building of competitive position by Japanese, Taiwanese, and Korean competitors. The chemical producers of Northeast Asia, Japan in particular, have been small by world standards in what is a scale-driven industry, and have undistinguished R&D performances. It is not surprising then that DuPont, Dow, Hoechst, Bayer, BASF, ICI, and their Swiss peers all have very substantial positions in the Japanese chemical market. However, a failure to invest and grow at least as rapidly in East Asia as the East Asian markets grow will provide an opening for the chemical companies of Northeast Asia to establish scale and eventually world position.

Germany's Hoechst shares leadership in Japan with DuPont in the foreign-owned chemical industry sector. Like DuPont, the Hoechst position in Asia hardly reflects the area's importance; with the Middle East and South Asia included, the area makes up less than 15 percent of Hoechst's worldwide sales. Like DuPont, Hoechst focuses on speciality product sales to the region and products in which it holds some proprietary advantage. The risk is that commodity chemicals are the kinds of chemical products that East Asian markets most need, that will be fastest-growing, and that will not be provided competitively by Western companies. This may well leave the growth opening that East Asia's chemical industry needs.

As an indication of possible developments, the six largest general trading companies of Japan announced in late 1992 a plan to invest $6 billion in an integrated petrochemical complex in China's Liaoning province—Japanese companies' favorite site in China. The complex will be integrated forward from petroleum refining to chemical resins, and will be a joint venture with Chinese government entities, in which the Japanese are to hold a majority position. This will be, of course, a world-scale facility, using inexpensive Chinese land and labor, with the latest production technology that Japan's top companies can command.

The risk for the chemical companies is one that a great many other companies will encounter with respect to East Asia. It is a replay of the Japan issue. Maximizing near-term profit means forgoing investments in East Asia as being lower-margin businesses in difficult business environments. Forgoing investments in East Asia means allowing local companies to seize on the growth and, through it, grow into world competitors of formidable competence, while their Western competitors remain encumbered by obsolete factories that need writing off, labor unions that are politically entrenched, or antitrust laws that date from the nineteenth century.

KODAK'S ISSUES IN EAST ASIA

Eastman Kodak may be a case of this sort. George Eastman had an office in Shanghai in the 1920s; the area is not new to the company. However, it was not until the late 1980s that Kodak established a full-scale operation in Japan, and in the meantime Fuji Photo Film, growing faster with higher profitability, had become a worldwide competitive threat. Still worse, the electronic threat to Kodak's main business of imaging was coming from Japan, an industry in which Kodak had no position. In Kodak's support, it must be said that the measures taken in the late 1980s by its top management to remedy the terrible Japan gap were bold, large-scale, and directly aimed at its problems—a major electronic research facility, control over product distribution through costly acquisitions, and integration of local operations under Japanese management.

Kodak's Robert L. Smith, president, Eastman Kodak Asia-Pacific, describes Kodak's Asian strength: "Kodak has had an Asian presence since before World War II. In most cases, we were the first and only company in our industry at the time of establishment in these countries. This early presence has allowed us to capture and hold leading shares in

•

most products throughout Asia. In most cases, we charge a premium
price for our products throughout Asia. Nonetheless, our products speak
for themselves and are the customer choice. The future in Asia is bound-
less and I am happy to be part of such a dynamic region."

Still, the regional organization of Kodak for Asia came into being
only in 1991. Even though Kodak has a total of ten plants in the world,
not a single plant is located in Asia, nor are there plans currently to locate
one there. Mr. Smith again: "We have not closed our U.S. plants and
moved them to Asia like some of the electronics companies have. If you
ask why Japanese firms are going into Asia and Western firms are not, I
can only answer that we are, in our own way, by developing markets,
strengthening companies where we have them, establishing them where
we don't. Manufacturing will be a function of where we need it."

Kodak's confidence may well be entirely warranted. However, a recent news article noted, "More than a decade ago, Kodak almost mo-
nopolized the Thai market. . . . Fuji only began to make serious inroads
in 1984. Even now, Kodak claims 60 percent of Thailand's total consumption."[13] A 40 percent share loss in a key market in eight years? Why
not close a Western plant in order to be in Asia with integrated operations, including manufacturing? The issue again is one of the weight at-
tached by the Western firm, long-time world leader, to the potential and
risks associated with East Asia's development.

It is certainly the case that the best of U.S. companies, and DuPont
and Kodak are good examples, are reorganizing themselves to focus
management attention more closely on Asia. The best of them are putting senior officers in residence in Asia to manage their Asian business
(and putting them in Tokyo, where the center of the East Asian economy is). Perhaps this is the necessary preliminary to taking the kinds of
drastic strategic measures needed to deal effectively with East Asia over
the coming years.

WESTERN STRATEGIES FOR EAST ASIA

The range of strategic options for Western companies in East Asia is very
great indeed. There is at one extreme the Nike approach: take advantage
of what East Asia can offer in cost and speed of production, and hold the
high–value-added operations of design and marketing in the West. This

assumes a speed of design change and competence in design leadership that not all companies can achieve. It assumes too little interest in the Asian market, or worry about Asian competition. It is a powerful strategy that fits rather few companies.

At the other extreme is the Mabuchi approach, made possible in part perhaps by the company's Japan location: put all manufacturing operations in East Asia and build both manufacturing and marketing position there, and over time presumably R&D capability as well. This is in fact what Matsushita Electric is doing, at a product level, with its air conditioner business by moving to put it all in Malaysia. The very large market in East Asia for its products makes this a viable strategy for these companies—but a strategy that may well apply to an increasing number of Western companies as well, especially those with a strong Japan position.

A third East Asian strategy, and again one that seems still limited to Japanese companies, is to build an entire industry in the growing economies of Southeast Asia. This is the approach of Toyota, which takes advantage of the ASEAN trade arrangements, of Singapore's favorable treatment of regional headquarters, and of the coordination capability offered by the computer and telecommunications. It is pushed by the need to impose scale on what are still a number of small markets. Matsushita Electric and Sony are adopting this approach as well, whereby an entire integrated industry is positioned in Southeast Asia, drawing on resources from Japan (and potentially from the West as well) for technological support.

The Western option is well illustrated by the industrial electronics companies, taking major positions throughout the region, putting world-scale facilities in place in East Asia and sourcing from them for world markets, engaging governments of the area in their businesses for shared development needs, and organizing themselves so that the region is at the very center of corporate decision making. Full advantage is taken of East Asian growth, and East Asian industrial competence, while forestalling the growth of competitors that East Asia's economic success might nurture.

The strategic issue is finally commitment—the willingness to risk in East Asia the capital, technology, and human resources that the importance of the area warrants and that the competitive environment requires.

Why is the position of Western companies in the East Asian economies currently so limited? And given a limited position now, what can be

●

done by U.S. and European companies to take advantage of this sea
change in industrial power?

No doubt a part of the explanation has to do with the views of Asia
held by many Western executives—exotic, distant, poverty-stricken, not
a serious site for business—and in any case there is still time to enter.
Given the recency of the Japan example, where many of these same attitudes led to failure in dealing with Japan's success, one might suppose the
error would not be repeated. Still, a comparison can be made to the
reaction to the opening of eastern Europe and the former Soviet Union.
There was a rush of interest and investment, with the purchase of properties of dubious value throughout eastern Europe, in tiny economies
with no infrastructure and no business or management class or tradition—economies that have since largely quite simply fallen apart.

The conclusion is inevitable that the difference is in some part a cultural one. Most Westerners have little sense of Asian history, and what
sense they do have deals generally only with the relatively brief period
during which the Western powers held economic and political hegemony over the area. One result is continuing surprise at what is seen as
"sudden" industrial success, apparently sudden only because the run-up
to the success has gone unobserved.

No doubt too some part of the cause of the limited position of Western companies in East Asia is a matter of timing. Over the past several
years, while the outstanding performance and future of the East Asian
economies has become increasingly evident, U.S. and European companies, and most especially those from the English-speaking economies of
the United States, Britain, Canada, and Australia, have been going
through very hard times. The manufacturing sectors in these economies
especially have been reducing work forces, closing down obsolete—and
not so obsolete—facilities, cutting back on research and development
budgets, and generally doing what is felt necessary to get through a bad
time. Even with some signs of a not very vigorous U.S. recovery, continental Europe has moved into recession.

On the whole, then, the companies of East Asia have been sheltered
from Western competition in some part because most Western companies feel themselves to be in no position to undertake major new ventures. Still, this has not prevented Western companies from making efforts in eastern Europe—and certainly does not preclude replacing North
Atlantic facilities with new, world-scale facilities in the western Pacific

•

region. The issue is one of priorities, and East Asia is not high on the priority list of all too many Western managements.

Still another factor related to this issue of economic recession and its impact on competitive moves is the failure of capital investment by U.S. companies in particular. With savings rates at the level of a less-developed country, U.S. firms have been confronted with high costs of capital and with the requirement therefore of high profit returns to justify investment. No surprise then that investment in the United States per capita has been and remains about half that of Japan's. No surprise either that U.S. firms find it difficult to undertake competitive investments in the Asian area, where they are at a similar disadvantage. The Asian area, with its high levels of savings and rather high share price levels, makes possible generally lower costs of capital and generates a capacity to accept lower margins on sales than Western companies must achieve.

MEETING THE CHALLENGES OF THE EAST ASIAN MARKET

What can be done to remedy the situation? How do Western companies reposition themselves to deal to their advantage with the historic developments in East Asia? "By the end of the decade, it will be increasingly difficult for firms to be global players if they are not a major factor in Asian markets. To the extent that the participation of American firms in the booming markets of Asia falls behind, they will be handicapped, and the U.S. economy will suffer."[14]

The experience of companies in the area to date suggests some steps to deal with the challenges and opportunities of East Asia:

1. *Grasp, and accept, what is happening.* It is all very well to fulminate about dumping, or government supports, or copying, or cheap labor, and to see East Asia's success as unfair. The plain fact of the matter is that Japan, Taiwan, Korea, and the rest of the economies of East Asia are very important. However they got there, they are not a temporary phenomenon; they are not going away. The map of the world in the minds of the top managements of Western companies must be redrawn to deal with these new Asian realities.[15]

2. *Make sure a Japan strategy is in place.* If you do not have a Japan

•

strategy, you do not have an East Asia strategy—Japan represents three-quarters of the total East Asian economy. Its companies are overwhelmingly the major competitors in the area. It is the source of capital and technology for the area. One cannot imagine a Western Hemisphere strategy that is not based on a major position in the United States.

This does not necessarily mean manufacture in Japan, however. Amway is a billion-dollar Japanese company without Japanese manufacturing capability, as is BMW. DuPont's titanium dioxide plant to compete in Japan is sited in Taiwan, as is PPG's fiberglass operation. It does mean that a carefully thought-through approach to and way of dealing with Japan is required, not least to be integrated into the Japanese community to ensure access to Japanese aid and infrastructure investment throughout the area.

3. *Establish a world-scale facility in East Asia.* Close clapped-out Western plants as necessary to warrant a facility in Asia that has a cost position from which competition can be undertaken anywhere in the world. Remember—East Asian investment is new.[16] Your East Asian competitors do not have obsolete plants. You will be competing with the best. Invest accordingly.

A very real problem is that, leaving Japan aside, these are generally small markets. Some Japanese firms have dealt with this by setting up ASEAN-wide facilities, like the ASEAN car of Toyota. A more manageable alternative is to first close plants in the West as needed to allow worldwide sourcing from your East Asian facility. Second, supply these fast-growing markets with part of the output of the world-scale facility, and in the process preempt the growth of these fast-moving markets. As they become large, so does the position of the established, large-scale competitor.

One way of thinking about strategies for the rest of East Asia is to be sure not to repeat mistakes made earlier regarding Japan. Do not sell to Asian firms the technology that you can use to establish yourself, or that they can use to become effective competitors to you in world markets. Do not miss out on the rise of a major world market whose scale will change the very structure of your industry. And do not forget that competitors breed in the area where the growth is, unless you take the growth.

4. *Reverse the brain drain.* Be more daring. Use fewer expatriate Western managers in Asia. If half of all U.S. science degrees now go to non-U.S. nationals, with East Asians the largest group, take advantage of

the fact. Surely your firm has outstanding Chinese and Vietnamese engineers and staff. Surely they will be more useful in Asia than a Western short-timer with no background. Some imagination and risk-taking in staffing is needed. Remember always the networking patterns in East Asian business circles. Remember too that this reverse brain drain is a U.S. advantage not available to your Japanese competitor.

Be more daring in location as well. Especially if your firm frees itself from the tyranny of the expatriate, locations for operations change. In a recent survey of Japanese and Western executives on the question of the "most promising East Asian nation for investment" the Japanese selected Indonesia and China, with Vietnam fifth after Thailand and Malaysia. The Western executives picked Singapore, Korea, and Taiwan among their top five, sites not even in the Japanese preferred group, but made no mention of Vietnam and ranked Indonesia fifth.[17] In one view the Western selections were perhaps good ones for the 1980s but do not reflect the 1990s. In another view, the Western selections are risk-averse. The safest, however, is not where the future is likely to be, even if it is the most comfortable place for Westerners. Singapore is splendid for foreign families but offers very little by way of a market.

A little more daring, imagination, and future-oriented thought is needed in these location decisions for East Asia and in selecting managers who can integrate the Western company into Asian economies and societies.

5. *Manage for cash.* The focus on reported earnings is a problem for Western and especially U.S. firms everywhere, arising in good part from the nature of Western stock markets and capital markets, reinforced greatly by the use of stock options to reward executives. In terms of Asia, there are three problems with this. First, a great many local competitors and Japanese firms are not under the kind of reported earnings pressure that most Western firms are. They are prepared to take an earnings hit in the early period of investment. You had better be prepared to as well. Second, many Asian competitors are still privately held. Reported earnings are irrelevant; cash is what counts if the family is to do well and if the company is to continue to grow. Third, depreciation charges will be high as investments are made to keep up with growth. These provide cash flow but depress reported earnings. Make sure your company's yardstick of success in Asia is the correct one.

6. *Use local partners to facilitate entry.* The Western company in East Asia will not, initially at least, have available the network of government,

banking, and business links so necessary to success in the area. Granted
that joint ventures in the long run are almost invariably failures—with a
few exceptions here and there—and are clumsy in decision making and
general management. They need not be forever, but can serve for entry
purposes.

One pattern is a link to local governments. Mitsubishi Motors joined
with the Malaysian government to carry out that government's goal of
building a local automobile industry. Mitsubishi Motors and Mitsubishi
Corporation share a quarter interest in the venture, which appears to be
doing well with strong government support, and is even exporting some
products. (Where were the Europeans and Americans when this was put
together?) Singapore's government seems especially accessible, as Apple,
AT&T, and Texas Instruments among others are linked to Singapore
agencies. Singapore seeks to offset its disadvantages of size of market and
population by a focus on high technology. This plays to the strengths of
many Western companies, and a joint effort not only provides local support and market access but can also furnish very useful local capital. One
must remember however, that joint ventures also mean joint or shared
profits and that partners' objectives seldom stay parallel over time. Still,
the joint venture can be a useful entry device.

A further point about joint ventures, as much used by the Japanese,
is that many of the local entrepreneurs and investors are quite willing to
take a less than majority position in an investment. Japan's trading companies and banks in particular cultivate local power centers throughout
the area on behalf of their Japanese clients. Thus the Bangkok Bank and
the Mitsui group are linked in Thailand, the Mitsubishi Group with the
Ayala interests in the Philippines, and Sumitomo Corporation and
Marubeni with the Liem interests in Indonesia.

Joint ventures with Japanese companies where there has been a long
relationship may be possible. As PPG is building its Asian position in
glass, it has turned to its worldwide competitor, who is also a chemical
venture partner in Japan, Asahi Glass, as a partner in major facilities in
Guangdong and Liaoning at Dairen. The shared cost and risk are seen by
PPG as outweighing the hazards of a shared position with a dangerously
powerful competitor. Again, DuPont has set up a venture with Mitsui
and Co. with the intention of jointly exploring possible new ventures in
East Asia and elsewhere through Mitsui's massive network in Japan and
throughout the world. These two cases are unusual; joint ventures elsewhere in Asia between Western and Japanese companies have been very

●

rare. The outcomes will be of real interest to many companies as possibly providing a new pattern for East Asian investment.

7. *Hold the CEO and board of directors responsible for Asian strategy decisions.* The general pattern of divisional organizations and worldwide product strategies militates against dealing with Asia on the basis of the long-term needs of the entire company. A product manager cannot and should not take the kinds of risks associated with a world-scale project in the East Asian market. The product manager cannot from his or her position evaluate the significance of the investment for the company as a whole. The Asian regional manager can be a resource to the top of the company but is suspect as advocate of an investment.

A major investment in the future of East Asia, and in the assurance of the company's position in East Asia's growth, is a decision for the board. It is, moreover, the task of the board to ensure that East Asia does in fact get the attention, and investment, that the company's future demands. A major, long-term commitment, sustained over time, is needed and can be made only at the top of the company.

Effective positioning in East Asia will not be easy or accomplished quickly. But it must be done, and soon.

3
•

JAPAN IN ASIA

The single greatest force moving East Asia from Western hegemony to autonomy has been the rise of Japan. The economic success of Japan is no postwar miracle, for the efforts and investments to achieve industrial parity with the Western world began in Japan in the late nineteenth century. It has been a long and difficult course, however, and by no means direct; there have been many setbacks and detours. Nonetheless, it is Japan, both as example and as driving force, that has put East Asia on its present course to world industrial leadership.

The seeming suddenness of the Japanese economic accomplishment has been no small factor in the difficulty much of the world has had in accepting the facts of Japan's economic might. As recently as the mid-1950s, the Japanese economy accounted for less than 3 percent of the global economy: it mattered little then if it was a closed and protectionist economy—as it thoroughly and unabashedly was—because its size was comparable only to the Italian economy. The Western world, largely ignorant of and generally indifferent to developments in Asia, little realizes the long building process that had occurred in Japan earlier and has led to its industrial success. Because the result seems sudden, it has been the more disorienting. Economic growth as rapid as Japan's highly desta-

●

bilizes established trade relations, supply arrangements, and competitive interaction.

In 1955, Japan's economy was about two-fifths the size of its British counterpart. The Japanese economy today, less than 40 years later, represents 15 percent of the entire world economy. It is now more than three times the size of the British economy, nearly as large as Britain, France, and Germany combined, with the highest per capita output of any of the major nations. Its significance is great now as the largest source of badly needed new capital, as a major factor in all new significant technologies, and as the largest source of development aid to the world.

That the developed world has had great difficulty in accepting Japan's success hardly needs detailing. The efforts abound to explain it away as temporary, achieved through trickery or cheating of some fashion, or to argue that Japan has economic rules and follows economic laws unlike any others.

Part of the problem in accepting the Japanese achievement is that it has occurred in Asia. The rich men's clubs have traditionally been white men's clubs; the industrial world is in the North Atlantic; and the rules of the game have been worked out by western European gamesmen. Suddenly this view is upset as a gross outsider, from a part of the world relegated to peasant poverty, who moves not only to a position of parity but to one of economic leadership. The shock can be measured in the bitterness of the reactions aroused by Japan's competitive successes.

It may well prove to be the case that many of the same factors that worked to obscure the Japan phenomenon from Western attention will also obscure the developments now taking place across East Asia generally. One unappreciated aspect of great importance is the overwhelming position of the Japanese economy in the area, owing to a continued preoccupation of Western observers with the romance of China. The fact is that the Japanese economy now makes up three-quarters of the entire combined economies of all the nations of East Asia, including China.

In fact, Japan has about the same relationship in economic size to East Asia that the United States has to the Western Hemisphere. It is sometimes asked whether Korea or some other Asian economy will be a "second Japan." The question is as grotesque as the suggestion that Canada or Brazil will be a "second United States." Korea is important in its own right as a "first Korea," but it is not and will not be a second Japan. Its economy is less than one-tenth the size of Japan's, and that of main-

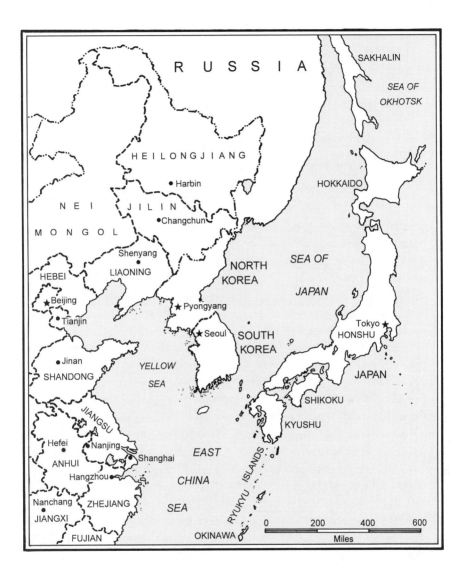

land China is not much larger. The sheer size of Japan's economy over-whelms the rest of East Asia.

Japan's economic success has provided an example for the other Asian economies to follow. Japan has been the first non-Western nation to industrialize successfully, putting an end to the view that economic leadership is a Western prerogative, particularly because its organizational

●

approach to industrialization is unique and derives from its own social system, rather than the West's. The analogue is to Roger Bannister and the four-minute mile, held to be impossible in learned discussions until Bannister ran it, after which a great many found that they could too. So will be the case with Japan and other non-Western industrial systems.

JAPAN TRANSFERS INDUSTRIES
TO EAST ASIA

The Japanese impact on East Asia's economies has been much more than merely providing an example to follow. Japanese government and business leaders recognized early that Japan's continued economic growth and prosperity depended on transferring to developing countries those industries and sectors of industries no longer suitable for a nation with rising wage and education levels. What has been termed the virtuous cycle of growth became a matter of policy.

Y. Ojimi, vice minister of international trade of industry, speaking to the OECD Industrial Committee in June 1970, articulated Japan's policy as follows: "Because of technological exchanges between advanced nations in the 70s, there will be an equalization of levels of technology, and the industrial structures of these nations will become increasingly homogeneous. Also, industrialization in developing countries will stimulate competitive relations in the markets of advanced nations in products with a low degree of processing. As a result, the confrontation between trade protectionism and free trade will become more intense.

"The solution of this problem is to be found, according to economic logic, in progressively giving away industries to other countries, much as a big brother gives his out-grown clothes to his younger brother. In this way, a country's own industries become more sophisticated. A solution of the North-South problem depends not only on internal development for developing nations but also on giving them fair opportunities in the area of trade. To do this, the advanced nations must plan for sophistication of their industrial structures and open up their market for unsophisticated merchandise, as well as offer aid in the form of funds and technology."[1]

To the mutual advantage of Japan and its neighboring economies, there has been a general appreciation that continued increases in income

•

and wealth require corresponding changes in industrial structure. Industries must die—must move offshore to more appropriate locations—as other, more sophisticated industries rise, and labor and capital must transfer to industries where their output is of higher value.

It is one of the ironies of international trade discussions that Japan is seen as protective of industries when in fact its rate of industrial change is unusually high. (Agriculture in Japan—as indeed it is everywhere—is largely an uneconomic exception.) Japan's coal mining industry, probably the largest source of employment in the early 1950s with more than 300,000 workers, has virtually closed down, with only a half-dozen mines and a few thousand workers remaining. The competitive economics of low-cost petroleum and better-quality coal from abroad combined with steadily decreasing shipping costs caused this.

Textiles are a more politically charged sector, recalling the bitterness of the Nixon-Sato negotiations over textile trade between Japan and the United States in the era of the "dollar blouse." The trade conflicts reached a political peak at or even after the peak of the actual trade issue, however, because the labor-intensive part of Japan's textile industry was already winding down when the political battles were most intense.

This part of the textile industry story illustrates well the effect of Japanese industrial change on neighboring economies, for Taiwan and Korea were beginning to gain economic stature just as the textile battles occurred, and became the successors to Japan in that industry, which provided the initial base for their economic growth. In the process, Japan became a major importer of textile products. Unlike that of the United States, Japanese trade policy has not been directed to protecting such relatively low-value industries as textiles, to the advantage of Japan's long-term growth rate. The United States, on the other hand, tends to use its trade negotiating position to protect losers—shoe manufacturers, for example—which creates a drag on U.S. growth and makes the simultaneous protection of growth sectors more difficult.

Another example of shifts in Japan's industrial structure is the steel industry. Japan's very large steel industry is one of the world's most competitive. Japanese engineering, technology, and equipment were critical in the building of Korea's steel industry, which may now be in fact the world's low-cost producer. Imports of Korean steel into Japan are substantial and growing rapidly, largely in the lower end of the line—carbon steel in standard shapes. Japan's steel producers are required not only to become more cost-competitive but also to move downstream to more

•

sophisticated and expensive types of steel. Again, a virtuous cycle has arisen, where both economies benefit from the shift of Japanese industry and technology abroad to a developing economy. Another example can be seen in consumer electronics, as radios, tape cassette players, monochrome television, and hand-held calculators all go out of production in Japan and are sourced from producers, including Japanese companies, located in East Asia, while Japan's industry moves up to camcorders and HDTV sets.

This pattern has often been described as a flying-geese pattern, with Japan developing initially, and the economies of Northeast Asia and then Southeast Asia following in turn. The analogy implies a regularity and neatness that is inexact, however, because the patterns of development across East Asia are becoming much more complex and interactive than the flying-geese pattern would suggest. It does, however, make clear the fact of Japan's leadership position, facilitating the subsequent developments elsewhere in the region.

SHIFTING BALANCES OF POWER

Japan has been critical to East Asia's industrialization in its role as example, by the sheer weight of its economic scale, and by the dynamic impact on Asian economies of the continuing process of industrial restructuring that has occurred over the past three decades. Through much of this post–World War II period, however, the dominant relationship for Japan has been that with the United States. The absorptive capacity of the U.S. market, the technological sourcing from the United States, and the predominant world position of the U.S. capital market all meant that Japan's economic links and key external economic, political, and strategic policies were developed in relation to the United States and its position. East Asia was important, but not in shaping Japanese thinking or policies.

The shift in the Japanese position began with the change in relative positions of the United States and Japan. At the financial level, Japan has become the banker to the world, the supplier of credit and capital. Britain occupied this position for a long time, from the Industrial Revolution to the end of the nineteenth century—as a high saver with large trade surpluses, it was the predominant supplier of capital and a massive over-

•

seas investor. The United States assumed this position at the turn of the century and held it to the early 1970s, when it became the world's largest debtor nation. A momentous shift in financial power has occurred, and it is little wonder that the fact is often resented in the West.

At the same time, and not coincidentally, the strategic position of the United States in East Asia began to diminish. The two major wars involving the United States during the postwar period were in East Asia, and in both the United States fared badly, with stalemate in Korea and defeat in Vietnam. With this began a diminution in the United States's overall strategic position, symbolized most recently by the loss of air and naval bases in the Philippines. With the collapse of the Soviet Union and continued severe financial pressures at home, a steady reduction in the U.S. presence in East Asia is in fact underway and no doubt will continue.

Concurrent with these changes in fundamental financial and strategic position has occurred a less remarked but long-sustained shift in U.S. trade policy. Beginning with the textile affair of the 1960s, U.S. trade policy has moved in an increasingly protectionist direction. American rhetoric still emphasizes free trade, but its actions do not, beginning with textile restrictions and moving to quotas on steel imports, consumer electronic products, auto imports, and most recently on machine tools. These are the highlights of a considerable apparatus of restrictive changes that has been constructed and is aimed primarily at Japan and secondly at other Asian sources.

These long-sustained trade tensions have made Japan the target of fevered criticism that has been given intellectual credibility by books hostile to the country. The "revisionist" school argues that Japan operates outside the normal patterns of economic and political behavior, thereby justifying special measures to deal with it. Not surprisingly, this "Japan bashing" has resulted in a swing of U.S. public opinion against Japan, with Japan seen increasingly as the "enemy" and the "greatest danger."[2]

As might be expected, the shift in U.S. views toward Japan, widely reported in detail in Japan's press, has caused hostile reactions in Japan as well. Thus, for some time not only the substance of but also the feelings about the relationship have changed for the worst.

With the diminution of the U.S. position, Japan's position has greatly expanded. Technology relations provide a good example of this. Until the late 1970s, Japan's economic growth depended on technology

●

inputs from abroad, especially from the United States. In the reassess-
ment following the oil crises and the consequent search for new sources
of economic growth, there developed a widespread conviction in Japanese business and government that the future required major initiatives by
the Japanese private sector to build an independent technology development capability. R&D budgets expanded greatly, to the point where
nongovernmental, nonmilitary expenditures on research in Japan now
exceed those in the United States. In a number of key fields, such as
superconductivity and optoelectronics, the Japanese position is now
strong and Japan's long dependence on the United States as a source of
technology has ended.

These are very great changes indeed. This is not to say that the U.S.-
Japan relationship has in any sense ended: a considerable degree of interdependence still exists, arising out of mutual trade and cross-investment;
the postwar security treaty remains in place; and there is a steady flow of
people between the two countries. The United States remains a great
military power with considerable wealth, but its relative position has substantially diminished. The United States is pulling back from Asia, in
many important respects, as it makes the necessary adjustments to its
commitments appropriate to its reduced power base.

JAPAN'S FOCUS ON EAST ASIAN
INVESTMENT OPPORTUNITIES

With the change in the Japan-U.S. relationship there are parallel changes
in Japan's position with respect to East Asia. While U.S. economic
growth slows and the economy stagnates, East Asian growth has continued at very high levels. One result is that in 1991, Asia replaced North
America as Japan's biggest export market, with Japanese exports to Asia
totaling $116 billion, compared with $107 billion to North America.
Asia accounted for about 40 percent of Japan's total trade, compared
with about 30 percent for North America and about 20 percent for Europe. This is a dramatic change in only a few years; as recently as 1986
North America took 44 percent of Japan's exports and Asia only 28 percent. This shift will continue, given the differences in growth rates in
East Asia and North America.

●

As with trade, so with investment. With massive trade surpluses, Japan became a major overseas investor in the 1980s, with annual direct investment abroad increasing tenfold in the decade. For much of the period nearly half of this annual investment, which reached $200 billion in 1990 alone, went to the United States. However, "Japanese investors sliced spending to establish or acquire manufacturing operations [in the United States] from 1988's record $10.7 billion to $4.4 billion the following year and $3.9 billion in 1990. . . . The rapid growth of corporate Japan's U.S. manufacturing presence has come to an end."[3]

Japan's investment will shift to East Asia, where the profits on overseas investment have been most attractive for Japanese firms. MITI reports losses for Japanese investments in the United States and only modest returns in western Europe. In each of the nations of Southeast Asia, Japan, together with Korea and Taiwan, provides the great majority of new direct investment, with new investment from the United States a small and rapidly declining proportion of the total.

The Japanese shift to East Asia is now being reinforced by the increased attractiveness of China as an investment site and market. For most of the postwar period, Japanese traders and investors have approached China with extreme caution, more skeptical about the stability of the government and about the climate for business than most Western businesses. Japanese investment in China is still only 1 percent of total offshore direct investment.

This is now changing. The broad swing away from the West and toward Asia by Japanese business and industry was put in sharp relief by the 1992 totals of new businesses established abroad by Japanese companies, as indicated in Table 3–1. There has been an abrupt drop in new companies established in North America, and more than half were located in Asia. The main driving force in the shift has been the sudden jump in numbers of companies newly established in China, where the 1992 total reached 82, nearly a match for North America, where 84 new firms went into business.

The amounts of investment in China reported by Japanese firms are still limited. Caution is still the watchword. However, barring a major shift in Chinese economic policy—always a possibility in what is still a Communist country—or an economic crisis in China from inflation or internal disorder, Japan's companies will lead the move by Japan to close economic relations with the key coastal provinces of China.

•

Table 3–1   The Shift to Asia: Japanese Direct Investment Abroad (percent)

| | Number of Companies | |
	1952–92	1992 only
North America	27.4	14.2
Europe	21.7	24.8
Asia	38.6	51.6
Other	12.3	9.4
TOTAL	100.0	100.0

Source: Data from S. Takahashi and Y. Watanabe, article in *Shukan Toyo Keizai* (Tokyo: Toyo Kiezai), April 10, 1993, p. 92.

FOREIGN AID PATTERNS

Official development assistance from Japan is an even larger source of funds to the area than is direct investment. Japan is now by a good margin the largest provider of economic aid to the world, and over half of that large and still growing total is expended in East Asia. In each of the main recipient countries of East Asia Japan is by far the largest supplier of aid funds (see Appendix Table 3). While the proportion of Japan's total aid to East Asia has been dropping, the rapid increase in its total aid funds—an increase since 1970 of 24 times in U.S. dollars—means a continuing dominance of Japan as Asian aid donor.

Official development aid, perhaps more than any other indicator, presents a clear case of U.S. withdrawal from the area. In 1970, nearly 60 percent of all U.S. ODA funds were allocated to Asia. By 1980, the share was only 13 percent and the amount was one-third of the decade earlier total. By 1990, only one-tenth of U.S. aid went to Asia. Even Germany, certainly more remote from Asia economically and strategically, allocated a full fifth of its growing aid funds to Asia, proportionately twice the U.S. allocation.

In a comparison of U.S. and Japanese aid programs in East Asia, a recent analysis noted, "East and Southeast Asia's share of total U.S. Official Development Assistance (ODA) disbursements dropped from $16.4 billion in 1973 to $1.4 billion in 1989. This decrease contrasts with most of the major Development Assistance Committee (DAC) countries, which are increasing or maintaining their assistance to the region.

"The decline in U.S. aid to the region can be traced largely to a shift of security concerns to the Middle East and Central America. . . . In contrast to U.S. policy, the Asia region remains a Japanese priority. . . . At least half of Japan's Official Development Assistance has gone to the Far East in the last 20 years."[4]

The contrasting messages to East Asia from Washington and Tokyo are quite clear. It is not only funds from Japan's private sector that are helping to drive the economic development of East Asia but also government funding in even greater amounts and proportions of total funds. It is important also to note that one-third of Japan's aid funds support infrastructure investment—capital-intensive projects in the fields of telecommunications, transportation, and energy. Critics of Japan suggest that this is an example of Japanese aid used in Japanese economic self-interest as Japanese firms are well-positioned to supply the required equipment. It might also be noted, however, that it is precisely in the area of infrastructure that East Asia's economies have their most serious bottlenecks to further economic growth. Aid in support of infrastructure development has a powerful multiplying effect on overall economic development of the recipient nations.

When aid and investment totals from Japan, the United States, and the European Community to Southeast Asia are compared, Japan's flow of aid and investment funds is 50 percent greater than the combined flow from the developed economies of the West. Japan's aid and investment together were nearly $10 billion in 1990, compared with just under $4 billion for combined aid and investment from the EC and the United States.

An important further indication of the shift of Japanese interest and commitments toward East Asia, and of the massive position Japan is building as supplier of funds to East Asian economic growth, is in the shift in commercial banking away from Western borrowers toward Asian customers. "Japanese banks are de-emphasizing the United States and Europe and turning to their own backyard. At present, Japanese commercial banks' loans to the rest of Asia amount to around US$6 billion a year, 20 percent of their international lending.

"But sources at the Bank of Japan . . . say that Asia will be allocated 'the major part' of new commercial lending from now on, while lending in the United States and Europe will stagnate or decline. The return on assets is generally higher and loan defaults lower in Asia. A source at BOJ [said] that the 'international activity of Japanese banks is at a turning point.' . . . Japanese securities houses face the prospect of meagre revenues from a depressed Tokyo stockmarket. They too are turning to Asia, where they believe they can profit from boosting corporate Japan's fund-raising on local stockmarkets—especially in ASEAN."[5]

POLITICAL SHIFT TOWARD ASIA

The turn toward Asia in economic and business terms is increasingly reflected in political affairs as well. There is a keen desire to see a settlement of the conflicts in the Indo-Chinese peninsula, and the Japanese government has taken an active role in the efforts to find a peace settlement in Cambodia. Japanese political figures have been involved in Korea as well, in efforts, to accelerate discussions between North and South Korea. The most dramatic shift in policy, however, has been the enactment of legislation to allow Japanese troops to go abroad for the first time since the defeat in 1945, and to take an active part in United Nations peacekeeping operations. This legislation marks the beginning of a new era in Japanese international policy.

Another indication of shifting priorities was the announcement in the autumn of 1992 that the government of Japan would renew economic aid to Vietnam. Japan is filling the trade vacuum left in Vietnam by the collapse of the economies of eastern Europe. For a long time Japan deferred to U.S. policies that imposed an economic embargo on Vietnam, but that deference has finally ended as pressure built to work toward the integration of Vietnam into ASEAN and the Asian economic system.

These specific examples are of special importance because of a general reluctance on the part of Japanese political leaders to make broad statements of overall strategy. For the Japanese it is more a matter of "consider what I do, rather than what I say." In the West, grand policy statements are the norm, honored as much in the breach as in the keeping perhaps, but still expected as signals of changes in policy. In the Japanese case less rhetoric is employed, and therefore specific policy moves become all the more significant as indicators of real change.

This swing toward Asia has been termed a "New Asianism," in con-

•

trast to the nineteenth century Japanese leader Fukuzawa Yukichi, who advocated a "Quit Asia" philosophy for Japan and special respect for the West, its ideas, and systems. In this vein, Japanese opinion long held Japan separate from, and superior to, the rest of Asia. As this changes, younger Japanese businesspeople, like the Wharton-educated and very Western-mannered chairman of Fuji Xerox, Kobayashi Yotaro, state, "I believe the primary task in Japanese foreign policy is to direct the nation toward 're-Asianization.' . . . Perhaps the term 're-Asianization' conveys too strong an image of a Japan barricading itself in Asian confines or taking a seat in a 'Fortress Asia.' What I mean by it is nothing so closed or self-contained. Just as Gorbachev once declared that Russia's home was in Europe, so it is only natural for us to say that Japan's home is in Asia, not in the United States or Europe."[6]

JAPAN'S IMAGE IN EAST ASIA

As Japan's changing role in and approach to Asia is discussed, Western reaction very often focuses on the question of Asian attitudes toward Japan. There is a widespread view, amounting to a conviction, first that Japan as a nation and Japanese in general are very much disliked and mistrusted throughout Asia, and second, as a corollary, that the dislike of the Japanese will prevent the businesses and the government of Japan from playing a major leadership role in the area.

Much of this view is based of course on Western views of Japan's part in World War II and the events leading up to that war, especially in China. Periodic incidents reinforce this view—the demonstrations in Thailand and Indonesia in the early 1970s, when the Prime Minister Tanaka visited those countries, rows with Korea and China over Japanese history texts, and efforts to obtain compensation for actions by Japanese troops in World War II. "Its callous, selfish and cruel past behavior towards neighboring nations still haunts it in its relations with the region."[7]

It cannot be denied that Japan, like all the other great powers, has some ugly passages in its history of relations with neighbors that continue to color relations. Germany's actions against its European neighbors and the activities of the United States in Latin America offer similar examples. These facts have not prevented considerable economic and political

•

initiatives, however, nor stood in the way of subsequent constructive relations.

The first question, then, is how much do attitudes of peoples toward each other matter in economic affairs? There is no doubt about the mutual antipathy between Japanese and Koreans. All opinions polls at all age levels report mutual distaste in considerable degree, which does not seem to abate with time or greater contact. Yet Japan and Korea are each other's second-largest trading partner. Korea especially might prefer affairs to be different, but the efficiencies of purchasing from Japan overwhelm all other considerations, and Korea runs a considerable, increasing trade deficit with Japan, even while Japan buys in large amounts from Korea.

Even at, or perhaps especially at, individual company levels Japan-Korea relations are often close. Hyundai depends for its auto position in good part on Mitsubishi Motors. Nippon Steel designed and engineered the production facilities of Pohang Steel. Samsung has ventures with Japan facilitated by the fact that its chairman is a graduate of Waseda University in Tokyo. That there are unhappy ventures and experiences is true, but on balance the conclusion must be that economics can and frequently do override attitudes and feelings, in Asia as in Europe and North America.

It is also the case that attitudes toward Japan vary from country to country. In Taiwan, where most of the population viewed the Japanese occupation period quite positively, there seems to be little problem. Curiously, however, Taiwan is especially restrictive of Japanese imports, in a futile effort to reduce its trade imbalance. (Like Korean businesses, Taiwan firms find the quality, price, and delivery of Japanese machine tools, parts, and other components highly competitive against all other suppliers, notwithstanding the Taiwan government's efforts to step up purchases from America.)

It is not always possible to measure public opinion in China. It is clear, however, that the Chinese government, like the Korean, is prone to make skillful use of anti-Japanese themes in government negotiations and to embarrass the Japanese government in consequence. How much this reflects public attitudes is quite simply impossible to say. It seems likely though that the north of Asia, or more properly, continental Asia, as represented by China and Korea, sees Japan more often as a rival and as a threat than is the case elsewhere in East Asia. Both nations have been under direct Japanese military occupation in modern times—and in Korea's case in earlier history as well.

To the southeast, the issue of attitudes toward Japan seems to be seriously distorted in most Western discussion. For example, the foreign press corps in Tokyo quite clearly anticipated some serious, and highly newsworthy, negative reactions to the visit of the Japanese emperor and empress to Thailand, Singapore, and Indonesia in 1992, the visit symbolizing transition following the death of the wartime Showa emperor. In the event, there was no news, or at any rate none to be reported in the Western press, because the visit passed without incident.

The Foreign Ministry of Japan, hardly indifferent to attitudes toward Japan, commissions periodic surveys of public opinion in the five main ASEAN countries of Thailand, Indonesia, Malaysia, the Philippines, and Singapore. The most recent was carried out in 1992, using many of the same questions as in previous surveys undertaken in 1987 and 1983. By examining the results of these surveys, we have useful data, extending over a decade, on views of Japan in Southeast Asia.

The answers to the first question are on the whole indicative of many of these data. First, attitudes toward Japan have not changed very much over the decade, with Indonesia by some margin the most positive in response to Japan, and Singapore the least. From the answers to the survey as a whole, it appears that the answer to the question of which country one knows best is in part a surrogate for which country one likes best (see Appendix Table 4).

A key question asks about present feelings concerning Japanese actions in World War II. As noted in the Foreign Ministry report, the survey was carried out as the fiftieth anniversary of the war was being widely discussed, which no doubt affected responses. Feelings were distinctly more negative for Malaysian and Philippino respondents in 1992 than in 1983. Still, in each country, the proportion replying that World War II events are not at issue now or simply do not matter makes up much the largest group, with only 20 to 40 percent of respondents, depending on the country, reporting World War II issues as unforgettable (Appendix Table 4).

A new question asked in 1992 had to do with whether Japan is using its economic power in a reasonable fashion internationally, whether it is doing its part economically in the world. Only the Singapore group raised negative issues, with nearly 90 percent of the Indonesians respond-

●

ing that Japan is using its economic power properly, and nearly 60 percent of the Thais and Malaysians agreeing.

There is a general attitude that Japan is not importing as much as it should, with feelings strongest in Thailand and Singapore. However, when asked if Japanese factories are welcome in their economy, in every country more than 80 percent stated that they are welcome, with the largest proportion of dissenters oddly enough in the Philippines and Thailand—but less than 15 percent in each case.

Asked about national relations with Japan, they are described by all the samples surveyed as friendly, at the 100 percent level in the case of Indonesia and over 90 percent for all the other nations studied.

These kinds of public opinion polls are of course not definitive but surely can be taken as indicative. There are differences in attitude in these surveys from country to country, and there are clearly topics and issues on which Japan is viewed with some skepticism and distaste. However, it is hard to read into these results a real problem for Japan in attitudes toward it in Southeast Asia. In fact, it is rather more a mystery as to why the view persists so strongly that there is hostility toward Japan, when so little data support the view. Is it comforting to Westerners to think that somehow they are more liked? Does this help compensate for a loss of position? If so, it seems a dangerous illusion, for it can lead to mistaken conclusions about policy directions.

The Western view of a general dislike of Japan in Southeast Asia is the more curious in light of the fact that at least two of the nations involved have quite explicitly advocated Japanese approaches as policy in their own countries. Lee Kuan Yew of Singapore, while critical of Japanese policy on many occasions, has held up Japanese business policies as models for Singapore. His neighbor, Prime Minister Mahathir of Malaysia, was even more explicit in pressing a "Look East Policy"—a policy of turning away from Western models in matters political and economic to Eastern models of proven superior performance, such as Japan and Korea.

As a footnote to this issue, it must be noted that throughout East Asia, where legislation allows foreign ownership of retail shops, Japanese department stores and supermarkets, making no secret of their identity, have been highly successful and are widely patronized—hardly an indication of anti-Japanese sentiments on the part of the shopping public.

The shift in focus of Japanese business toward Asia is not and will not be the stuff of high drama. The commitment to Western markets is con-

•

siderable, and their attractions will not suddenly vanish, nor will the existing investments that are continuing. Rather, the balance will continue to shift, attracted by higher profits and higher growth in Asia, and driven by increasing barriers in the West.

ECONOMIC SUCCESS, THE KEY
TO POWER

The transition will be reinforced by the worldwide shift from military power as the basis of relations to economic power and the marketplace. The collapse of the Soviet Union has not had the same kind of impact in Asia as in the West. For one reason, elements of the cold war continue in Asia. By late 1992, there was still no peace treaty between the Soviet Union or successor governments and Japan ending World War II for these nations. The division of the Korean peninsula remains, with very real tensions and U.S. troops still deployed in forward positions. And the Indo-Chinese peninsula has not yet achieved stability after the defeat there of the French and the United States.

Still, East Asia itself, absent interventions by outside powers, is focused on economics and building the markets of the region. Minor territorial questions exist, but ideological differences do not strain relations, nor does any country interfere with its neighbors. Military expenditures are on the whole quite small, with only Singapore, Taiwan, and Korea spending as much as $100 per capita on defense and with military budgets declining over the 1980s in China, Indonesia, and the Philippines.[8]

As a result, Japan's role in the area can and does focus on business and economics. Japan in any case cannot play sheriff, or Lone Ranger, in international affairs. A country that must import to live, and is thereby dependent on maintaining good relations with all potential suppliers, is in no position to act as policeman or sheriff—even if it had some interest in doing so. The Japanese government will gradually play a more active role in United Nations programs, under neutral leadership, as witness the decision to send unarmed troops to take part in peacekeeping operations. The people and government of Japan show no interest in interfering in the affairs of other peoples and governments, in many respects an admirable trait.

International investments are not protected by military force—wit-

●

ness the expropriation of U.S. properties in Cuba and Chile at a time when the United States maintained the largest naval power in all history. Rather, trade routes are maintained by international agreements, and a considerable Japanese military power, added to its already massive economic power, would quite likely render a Japanese presence unacceptable in many of East Asia's host countries.

Thus a happy combination of Japanese self-interest and national policy militates against military buildup, at a time when military power seems less and less relevant with the end of the superpower confrontation. Japan's government cannot be indifferent to defense, however, because nuclear weapons are still deployed in Asia, with the possibility of even more. Regional disputes will occur as the superpower confrontation ends. But the assumption that military power inevitably will derive from great economic power, a cliché offered by Euro-centered commentators like Henry Kissinger, could well prove in error in the Japanese case.

As economics dominates government policies in East Asia, the role of the United States will continue to diminish, owing in no small part to the inability of the U.S. economy to generate investment funds in sufficient amount and at competitive cost to maintain its world position. Table 3–2 provides one review of the past several years in East Asia in terms of direct investment by foreign businesspeople. It is quite clear that in the four main economies of ASEAN, U.S. investment is being overwhelmed by the massive flow of investments from Japan and the four NIES—Korea, Taiwan, Hong Kong, and Singapore. As East Asia invests

Table 3–2   Foreign Direct Investment in ASEAN, 1986–91 (percent)

Source	Malaysia	Thailand	Indonesia	Philippines
Japan	26	42	26	29
NIEs	45	29	18	25
United States	7	12	5	14
Rest of World	22	17	51	32
Total	100	100	100	100

Source: Data from Ad Hoc Economic Group, "Vision for the Economy of the Asia-Pacific Region in the Year 2000 and Tasks Ahead" (Tokyo: Asia Pacific Economic Committee, August 10, 1992), Appendix 23.

•

increasingly in East Asia, the relative position of U.S. companies in these marketplaces will diminish accordingly.

Much U.S. comment on the shift taking place in relations in East Asia takes a self-flattering view that a diminution in U.S. presence is negative for the area—the term most often used is "destabilizing." For example, "the relative weight of the American economic presence in East Asia is waning—a potentially destabilizing long-run trend that is far more apparent to Asians than to Americans."[9] Again, "Japan's emergence as the economic nerve center of the region and its growing political influence may suggest a continuing need for significant U.S. economic, political and security involvement as a regional balancer."[10]

THE U.S. AS A BALANCE TO JAPAN

Some support for this rather self-serving U.S. view that continued U.S. power in East Asia is necessary comes from statements by some Asian political leaders declaring their desire for a balance to the power of Japan. "Singapore's Prime Minister Lee Kuan Yew [said] . . . that the NIEs welcomed European cooperation 'because they are keen on an economic order in Asia that is not dominated by Japan.' Lee and other Southeast Asian leaders have expressed anxiety about being 'left alone' in the region with a dominant Japan."[11]

It is rational for political and business leaders in East Asia to want more than one player at the bargaining table. Their position improves when there is competitive bidding, whether for factory sites, aircraft landing rights, or military alliance. The position is understandable but should not be overestimated as a factor in the longer-term relations of the nations of East Asia.

In fact, world economic and political relations are changing massively, and not the least of the changes are those occurring in East Asia. Nostalgia is only natural for an older order that for much of East Asia was stable and secure, not least because of the U.S. strategic commitments in the area. Too much has changed, however, to permit a continuation of traditional roles.

With the success of East Asia, the economic role of the United States has much diminished relative to its earlier position. The export trends shown in Table 3–3 describe one aspect of this. Aid programs are another

•

Table 3–3   Changing Trade Patterns in Asia

	Share of Exports (percent of total)	
	1985	1991
Asia to Rest of Asia	33.8	42.6
Asia to United States	32.3	24.2
United States to Asia	21.9	26.3

Source: Reprinted from C. H. Kwan, "The Asian Economics in the 1990s," in Tokyo Club Foundation for Global Study, *The Economic Outlook Toward the Year 2000*, June 1992.

aspect, as seen above. Direct investment in the area is still another sector where Asian investment in Asia is dominant. To some degree, the reduced position of the United States in Asia reflects the relative decline of U.S. economic power as a whole. To a considerable degree, however, it is also a reflection of a general U.S. failure to keep pace with Asian growth, losing market share and political position in the process.

With the continuing reduction in relative economic position has occurred a considerable reduction in the strategic commitments of the United States in the East Asia area, signaled most sharply by the closing of the great air and naval bases in the Philippines under domestic Philippine political pressure. Reductions in troop numbers in Korea and Japan continue, and there is a considerable likelihood that these reductions will accelerate. Although this ongoing withdrawal of strategic resources may well be—indeed, almost certainly is—both necessary and appropriate, given the changing world and U.S. situations, it does form an integral part of a vastly changing power structure in East Asia.

With this U.S. reduction and the virtual absence of Russia as a factor of any sort in East Asia, and as economic power has come to take precedence in world affairs over military power, the future of relations in East Asia and the question of the role of Japan in Asia's new order become issues of central importance. One aspect of the problem is symbolized by the terms used to describe the area and by the groupings of nations that exist now and are proposed for the area.

In the United States, the term "Pacific Rim" has been in vogue. Given the vast size of the Pacific, it might be thought difficult to perceive a meaningful rim. Nonetheless, Pacific Rim serves the purposes of including the United States in the area. The term has no currency in Japan,

•

where *Nishi Taiheiyo* is used—West Pacific, including Australia—or *Ajia Taiheiyo*—Asian Pacific, which leaves out Australia and in both cases omits the Western Hemisphere. The World Bank and other agencies increasingly use East Asia, as does this book, to take in Japan, China, the NIEs, and ASEAN.

Politically, the question of who is part of Asia Pacific is decided in one way by APEC, the Asia Pacific Economic Conference, which includes the broadest definition of Asia Pacific, with the United States in a lead position, and takes in potentially all countries with a Pacific Ocean frontier. The East Asia Economic Group or Caucus, proposed by Prime Minister Mahathir of Malaysia and strongly opposed by the United States, includes only East Asian nations, without Australia, the United States, or Canada.

In these brouhahas over debating society memberships, which is what APEC and Mahathir's caucus appear to be, Japan's position has been difficult. When then Prime Minister Hawke of Australia first proposed what has become APEC, he was reacting to Australia's isolation from Asia and did not include the United States or Canada as members. It was the government of Japan that insisted it would take part in the grouping only if the United States were also a member. Similarly, Japan has been officially cool to the Mahathir proposal, in part for the same reason.

JAPAN AS AN INTERNATIONAL LEADER

The situation illustrates both the reduced position of the United States in the area and Japan's dilemma in formulating its position and policies in East Asia. Japan is part of East Asia; East Asia is of increasing importance; Japan's position in the area is expanding steadily. Yet Japan's interests are by no means regional—they are global. Japan imports half its food supply from sources around the world. Japan imports the majority of its energy supply, mostly from outside East Asia. So with raw materials, and so too with Japan's export markets. Japan's markets and supply sources are worldwide.

The consequences are that Japan's policies must necessarily be unheroic. Dependence on nearly all corners of the world for existence demands an effort to remain on good terms with nearly all the world. Although East Asia is important, and its importance is rapidly increasing, Japan must maintain far wider and close ties, not least with the United States, which remains a critical component in Japan's security arrangements.

Japan's position has many parallels to that of Germany, especially in a reluctance to take independent initiatives in foreign policy and an adamant refusal to commit to any manner of military undertaking. For both, World War II, its causes and consequences, remain constraints that are only beginning now to abate, as Japan's parliament, for example, reluctantly approves participation of Japanese military personnel in nonmilitary United Nations peacekeeping operations.

A slow response to changing world conditions is more pronounced in Japan owing to the weaknesses of the Japanese political system and its leadership. The nation has been managed for the most part by bureaucrats—highly trained, highly competent and dedicated—who by position and training are not capable of taking policy initiatives or moving in directions discontinuous from past policies. The redefinition of Japan's role in East Asia, and a change in policy commensurate with the changes in the environment, demand political initiatives.

Here is a major problem for Japan. Japanese society has undergone extraordinary changes over the past four decades—in life expectancy, education level, income levels, family structure from the extended to the nuclear family, family location from villages to great cities, corporate organization, science and technology, even in such homely matters as individual body size. What had not changed in four decades was the Japanese political system and system of political parties, dominated by rural representatives and by an antediluvian conservative party led by tired old men of the immediate postwar generation, without a credible or even marginally competent political opposition.

The political system is now changing as well; the conservative Liberal Democratic Party in 1993 lost control of the parliament for the first time since its founding in 1955. The new coalition government represents the beginning of a new era, with political redistricting and other political reforms underway. Whatever combination of parties emerges after a likely period of instability, the leadership will be comprised of younger men and women, less focused on relations with the United States, seeking to define a larger role for Japan in international affairs.

Yet Japan, in any case not much given to high political drama or noble political speeches with splendid visions of the future, remains a

●

reactive rather than proactive nation in world affairs. It is what the Japanese call a low posture, unheroic and subdued, appropriate to the dilemmas inherent in Japan's economic position, and appropriate to the legacies of history and lags in political development that still shape Japan's policies.

STABILITY, A JAPANESE PRIORITY

What does all this mean for Japan in East Asia? One conclusion is that Japan will not seek to be on the side of rapid change. Where Japan can be a useful intermediary and agent of stability, it will take initiatives. Examples are the role Japan is taking in the United Nations program in Cambodia and its moves in late 1992 to bolster the economy of Vietnam. There is no evangelical tradition in Japan. The Japanese are—pleasantly enough—not given to urging peoples to change their governments no more than they are given to missionary work on behalf of religions. Rather, forms of government are the business of the people of each nation, in the Japanese view, to be dealt with without outside interference.

A case in point is the issue of China. There is no indication that Japan seeks to change the government of China, nor to interfere with the policies of that government. There is every indication that the government of Japan places a very high value on stability in China. An unstable China can be dangerous. An unstable China can threaten the stability of East Asia as a whole. An unstable China might bring about the ultimate Japanese nightmare—tens of millions of unemployed Chinese taking to boats to seek a better life in Japan. Policies toward China are one of the areas in which the United States and Japan might approach a collision course as the United States in its self-assurance puts economic and political pressure on China to bring about change in Chinese internal policies, pressures with which Japan will feel bound to disagree.

The basic thrust of Japanese policy is likely therefore to support stability in East Asia through aid and investment. This leaves the question of trading blocs and the probable Japanese attitudes toward the formation of something like Mahathir's proposed East Asia Economic Group. Certainly all of the economic data indicate a shift of Japanese interest and involvement toward East Asia, as we have seen. Asia is receiving attention in Japan at a level quite unlike earlier periods, and the attention is

•

positive. The increased hostility toward Japan expressed in the West in general and in the United States in particular reinforces the economic shift toward East Asia. But Japan will not join in an exclusively Asian trading bloc in the foreseeable future.

The seeming contradiction arises from a simple calculation of Japan's self-interest as a major world industrial power. For Japan, and in fact for Asians in general, including Prime Minister Mahathir, an Asian trading bloc—meaning not simply a trading area of close economic relations but an area that is also exclusive of outsiders—is the least desirable of world trade patterns. Asia, including Japan, will have a trading bloc only if driven to by the establishment of blocs in the major marketplaces of the world that exclude Asian products and companies. An Asian bloc in the proper meaning of the term will be reactive to the policies of the rest of the world.

Japan will support and, without jeopardizing other relations, take part in East Asian regional groupings, programs, and joint policies. It will increasingly take leadership positions in programs that promote the stability of the area. Whether Japan in East Asia turns to leadership of an East Asian bloc will depend on the policies of the United States and western Europe. Japan's self-interest and Japan's choice is open trade in a multicentered world.

East Asia will need to undertake security arrangements with limited U.S. involvement on a regional basis. Western Europe is attempting to establish regional security arrangements for much the same reasons—the end of the cold war, the increased incidence of local tensions and disputes, and the reduced position of the United States. East Asian nations have not had an immediate crisis to spur their own efforts to work out regional security plans and programs. This is no doubt an area where an initiative by Japan would still be inappropriate, and one by the United States could be of great value. It is another area, like medical research, space exploration, production technologies, and programs to defend the environment, where Japanese-U.S. partnerships could achieve great good for the world.

4

●

ASIA'S NEW ECONOMIES

THE CHINA FACTOR

Of the winds of change sweeping across East Asia, none is more dramatic or unexpected than the development of new economic areas that cross political boundaries and take on the characteristics of major economies in their own right. To the southern end of East Asia, the Growth Triangle centered on Singapore that includes parts of Malaysia and Indonesia is a focus of public and private investment. More impressive, nearly the entire reach of the China coast is a series of regional economies, drawing capital, technology, and entrepreneurial skills from Hong Kong, Taiwan, South Korea, and Japan in turn. To the north, there is talk in Japan of a Japan Sea Rim economic area, reinforced by the United Nations Development Programme proposals for a Tumen River development project on the Japan Sea where China, the Russian Far East, and Korea meet.

The development of these new economies in East Asia is so recent and has been so rapid that there is as yet no standard term to describe them, nor standard names for each of the areas. These economies challenge the conventional paradigm of national markets. They cross the political boundaries of the area, linking comparative advantages of adjacent territories in different countries into rapid flows of cross-border trade and

•

investment. And because investment and trade flows tend to cluster around production sites, these regional economies do not trigger large-scale movements of cheap labor across borders—a potential catastrophe for countries lying adjacent to China's 1.3 billion people.

These were not, and still largely are not, creatures of government planning or fiat. The flow of money and goods moves without bureaucratic encumbrance, and throughout East Asia the successful growth areas are those where economics has overridden politics, and where the pace of development has been more rapid than governments can deal with. And now, with the enormous success and advantages of the areas becoming evident even to unreceptive officials, the governments of China, Taiwan, Korea, and Japan are facilitating their development.

These areas were described early in the 1980s by Asian-based economists, notably Toshio Watanabe, who has pioneered much of the study of regional economies.[1] He uses the term *regional economic zones* to describe them. Another analyst, Lee Tsao Yuan of Singapore's Institute of Policy Studies, refers to these areas as *subregional economic zones,* to differentiate them from the broader regional designations that are also much used.[2] The Asia Development Bank discusses "growth triangles," but several of them require much imagination to be seen as really triangular in pattern. Perhaps the term *regional economies* will serve instead as reasonably descriptive and brief.

However they are described, the rise of these regional economies demands a new level of analysis in corporate strategy formulation and business planning. For example, it is no longer sufficient to speak of a single Chinese market—if indeed the term was ever valid. China is now a political entity that includes within its political boundaries several distinct regional economies that must be dealt with individually if business plans are to conform with economic reality.

Each of these regional economies has different patterns of investment and sources of technology. Each has language and social structures that are unique to its own area. And each is of sufficient magnitude in terms of area and population to become a major economic entity in its own right, however the specific political configurations of entities such as Hong Kong, Taiwan, Korea, and mainland China might evolve.

These regional economies are the logical, indeed with hindsight, the inevitable result of the rapid growth of Japan, Asia's NIEs, and now the Southeast Asian area. The forces that have steadily driven development

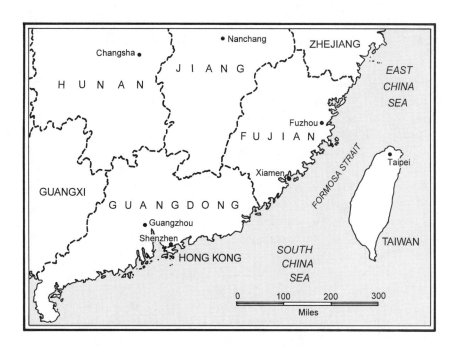

in the region to areas of less expensive land and labor to maintain growth have, as a natural progression, also driven the economic development across national boundaries. This is not "borderless" activity: national borders remain real and important. But the borders of Asia, in the south especially, are more porous than most of the world's political boundaries, and in any case the movement of capital—if political risk is accepted—is relatively free of constraints.

As these regional economies continue their extraordinary economic growth, they will have an increasingly significant impact on the political structure of the area. Their emergence raises real questions about the future of the government of China absent some form of decentralization, and may well bring about political regroupings in the region, not only in China but in the northeast, in Korea and Russia, and in the southeast, with Singapore and its neighbors as well. To appreciate the enormous impact on the world that these new East Asian regional economies are having and will continue to have, they must first be examined in some detail individually.

•

HONG KONG ABSORBS GUANGDONG

The first to arise and currently the most dynamic is what might be called the South China regional economy. It includes Hong Kong and the adjacent Chinese province of Guangdong, and is on occasion extended to include the island of Hainan. While most of the provinces of coastal China are doing well economically, Guangdong is the fastest-growing, and moved in the decade of the 1980s from tenth to first place among China's provinces in economic size—far outpacing the historic leader, Shanghai. The Japanese ratings indicate a continued preference for the northeast, the province of Liaoning, familiar to the Japanese from their imperial past. Even the Japanese rate Guangdong second, however—and have established more companies there than in any other Chinese province. (The overall performance and ranking of China's coastal provinces are set out in Appendix Table 5.)

Guangdong's development has until recently depended heavily on Hong Kong for investment and trading, with companies from Taiwan, Japan, and the West also investing significantly in the last three years or so. Businesspeople continue to express concern about the consequences of the scheduled political absorption of Hong Kong into China in 1997. These concerns notwithstanding, the fact is that Hong Kong is in the process of economically absorbing Guangdong. The Hong Kong dollar is a major currency in the province. Provincial officials—sometimes in direct disregard of Beijing—are changing tariffs and other regulations to conform to Hong Kong investment needs. The flow of money, goods, and people between what is still a separate crown colony and the adjacent mainland occurs without hindrance, forging real interdependence that many see as irreversible.

The impact of these developments on world economic patterns is not generally appreciated. The South China regional economy of Guangdong and Hong Kong comprises the largest economy in Southeast Asia (see Appendix Table 6). Its total population approximates that of Germany, about 70 million people. Its GNP is larger even than that of Indonesia, two to three times the size of the economies of the Philippines and Malaysia. And the South China regional economy is a massive trading area, with exports and imports three to four times greater than any other major Southeast Asia economies. This fast-growing regional economy is already a significant player in world terms.

Two major forces came together to trigger the extraordinary growth of the South China regional economy, one political and the other economic. On the political side, with the return to power of Deng Xiaoping, the Chinese government began a controlled experiment in economic reform. Three "special economic zones" (SEZs) were established in Guangdong province, which officially welcomed overseas investment, and specifically investment by Overseas Chinese. At the same time, government investment was greatly increased in the area to build a minimum infrastructure to support increased investment.[3]

The political moves might have been futile if the economic ground had not proved exceptionally fertile. Throughout developing Asia, the costs of labor and land were becoming major problems. By the end of the 1980s, Hong Kong had virtually no unemployment, while Japan and Taiwan were experiencing labor shortages as constraints on growth. The SEZ of Shenzen, the star growth area in Guangdong, had, by the end of the 1980s, manufacturing labor costs less than 20 percent and factory space costs about one-tenth those of Hong Kong. Moreover, a flood of migrant labor from the hinterland of China into Guangdong will ensure both ample and inexpensive labor supply well into the future.

Working concurrently with the political and economic forces moving the South China economy, and perhaps equally important, have been cultural forces. The common Cantonese language and family connections are critical links; because 90 percent of Hong Kong's population are émigrés from nearby Guangdong, there have been no barriers to the quick establishment of business relations. Moreover, Guangdong has historically been distinct, and for long periods politically separate, from the Mandarin-speaking north, centered in Beijing. "That venerable Chinese saying—'The mountains are high, the emperor is far away'—applies neatly to the situation today in Guangdong province."[4]

MANUFACTURING MOVES INTO GUANGDONG

Politics and culture have helped, but economics has been the driving force. Patrick Wang, managing director of the Hong Kong–based Johnson Motors, whose chief competitor is the Japanese company Mabuchi Motors, which also has a large plant in the north in Dalian, states,

•

"It is a question of survival for many of us. I could not manage production if not for Guangdong—not in terms of costs, labor or delivery time. We would have to cut back drastically if not for our China production." Mabuchi Motors executives would no doubt express the same sentiments.

Throughout the 1980s, more than $20 billion of foreign investment moved into Guangdong. A total of 95,000 projects and thousands of small and medium-sized manufacturers shifted production operations from Hong Kong to Guangdong. They brought with them the machines, tools, and semifinished goods to set up factories to handle orders from their offices in Hong Kong and Kowloon, building their warehouses and assembly lines along the rivers and coasts adjacent to the SEZs.

Hong Kong manufacturers' rationalization of their production processes to cheaper sites in Guangdong has played the key role in linking Hong Kong and Guangdong. The most common method, known as value-added process manufacturing (VAM), requires moving the labor-intensive sections of production to Guangdong to maximize the benefits of cheap land and labor there. (The Chinese call it *sanrai yibu*, literally, "three inputs and one finished product for export.") Two-thirds of Hong Kong's imports from China and three-quarters of its local exports to China are for VAM.

The impact of all this change is by no means limited to China and, more specifically, Guangdong. Wages and land prices continue to rise in Hong Kong, and with this there is a massive shift out of industry into services, now more than three-quarters of the Hong Kong economy. As road and rail links are increased, an estimated 30 million persons crossed the border between Hong Kong and Guangdong in 1991, and it is suggested that the labor force engaged in the region by Hong Kong manufacturers, now about 2 million people, will reach 10 million by the year 2000. Moreover, Chinese government agencies and state enterprises are investing heavily in real estate, manufacturing facilities, and service operations in Hong Kong.

As Hong Kong and Guangdong grow ever closer, they are pulling other areas into their economic orbit. Nowhere is this more clearly seen than in Hainan, a large island off the South China coast immediately south of Guangdong province. Hainan was made a SEZ in 1988, and like Guangdong has a reputation for acting independently of Beijing. Beijing has approved the establishment of a free-trade zone in Hainan, and the

•

creation of a "second Hong Kong" is being discussed, with proposals to develop the port of Yangpu on the island.

This proposal is of special interest because the organizer of the Hainan project is Kumagai-Gumi, the Hong Kong subsidiary of the major Japanese construction company of that name, which holds 35 percent of the Hong Kong company's shares. It is an interesting case that Western construction companies would do well to study and emulate: a foreign construction company has moved directly into the field of infrastructure investment and development in East Asia, where the demand for infrastructure expansion is very great.

In any case, Kumagai proposed a 15-year project to develop a segregated industrial and port city at Yangpu to be undertaken by a consortium of companies from Japan, Korea, and the United States, in which Kumagai would take lead position. Hainan is of interest as an extension of Guangdong but remains itself a marginal area, barring a shift of trade and investment from Hong Kong/Shenzen in search of still cheaper land and labor. The concept of Hainan as a significant part of the South China regional economy is intriguing but still some way in the future.

DENG'S REFORMS

In its effect on China, an initial consequence of the South China regional economy's success has been to reinforce the reforms initiated by Deng Xiaopeng. The program of SEZs was expanded in the mid-1980s from the initial 4 cities to include 14 more, and zones have been added more recently on China's inland borders with Vietnam, Russia, and Myanmar. The victory at the 14th Party Congress in late 1992 of Deng and his associates, who assumed greatly increased power at the expense of the hardliners, is no doubt due in good part to the successes of the regional economies.

In broader terms, an important issue is the impact of the regional economies, and South China in particular, on the economic and political structure of China as a whole. The 14th Party Congress reaffirmed China's move toward a socialist market economy, whatever that may prove to be, and parts of China are beginning to look more capitalist. Communist China now has stock markets, however one might rationalize the existence of corporate share ownership and share trading with

●

communism. Shenzen, in Guangdong, was not the first such market in China—Shanghai was—but Shenzen quickly became the scene of the heavy trading activity, as more and more Chinese companies are listed on the exchange, and foreigners are allowed to purchase "B" shares—specially issued shares that allow foreigners to hold equity positions in listed Chinese companies.

The surge of consumption in the South China regional economy is a conspicuous part of a wider move toward wealth, industrial power, foreign exchange earnings, and economic autonomy. Household incomes in the Pearl River Delta region, where Avon, Victoria's Secret, and Procter and Gamble are vying for consumer attention, are estimated to average $5,000 by 1991. Can a centrally governed, Communist party–controlled government continue unchanged as these regional economies move forward? Before attempting to address this issue, we will find it useful to look further at these regional economies.

At the time the three SEZs of Shenzen, Zhuhai, and Shantou were established in Guangdong in 1979, the city of Xiamen was designated as the fourth SEZ in neighboring Fujian. The political goal behind this step was the "peaceful reunification" of Taiwan with mainland China, just as integration of Hong Kong was no doubt a major aim in setting up the SEZs in Guangdong. Xiamen, formerly the treaty port of Amoy, is directly across from Taiwan, and although not the capital of Fujian province, it is a major center of commerce and industry and the major port for the province.

THE FUJIAN-TAIWAN LINK

Fujian and Taiwan together make up a second regional economy on the China coast that might be called the Taiwan Straits regional economy. The combined populations of Taiwan and Fujian are about 50 million, compared with South China's 70 million, again as large as a great many major nations, Britain included. The GNP of the regional economy totals nearly $200 billion but is overwhelmingly located on Taiwan, where per capita incomes are nearing $10,000, while Fujian incomes officially average less than $400. Nonetheless, these economies are drawing together for the same reasons that have brought about the South China regional economy.

The pattern of development is quite different, however. Beijing's 1979 Xiamen SEZ initiative was initially greeted with cool suspicion by both the private and public sectors in Taiwan, as the mainland still publicly threatened to recover Taiwan by force. As the economic straits of manufacturers squeezed by rising costs in Taiwan worsened, businesses there looked with an increasingly interested eye at Fujian. The Taipei government remained adamantly opposed to the idea, however, and threatened fines and even jail sentences for those caught illegally trading or investing in the mainland. Despite Taiwanese officials' opposition, economics began to work powerfully on behalf of closer relations across the Taiwan Strait.

By the mid-1980s, Taiwan, like Hong Kong and Korea before it, was catching the "NIEs disease"—a chronic and potentially crippling combination of rising costs and labor shortages that afflicted labor-intensive, land-intensive manufacturing and threatened to spread throughout the economy. Taiwan's own success was also its downfall in this regard, as workers left the factories for white-collar or service jobs, pushing up manufacturing wages to some five or six times those in Fujian. Land prices ballooned, and increasingly stringent environmental protection measures in Taiwan contributed further to costs. The final blow was the 40 percent appreciation of the Taiwanese currency that occurred after 1985, as Taiwan was accumulating the highest foreign exchange reserves in the world.

Against this background, politics came second to economic survival for many in Taiwan. As the economic picture worsened, small- and medium-sized manufacturers, the backbone of Taiwan's double-digit growth in the 1970s, began to pressure the Taiwanese government to allow direct trade and investment with the mainland. The ruling Kuomintang (KMT) strongly resisted, fearing that trade and investment links would lead to dependency on China.

KMT RELUCTANCE TO TRADE

The KMT had its own struggle for survival: Taiwanese, now richer and more internationally savvy after 15 years of trade with the West, were beginning to demand political freedoms commensurate with their new prosperity. A new political party, the Democratic Progressive Party

●

(DPP), arose in the non-KMT cities of the south and called for Taiwan's independence from China. Younger mavericks in the KMT also pressured the party elders to "get off the pot," a sneering reference to the hard-line KMT octogenarians whose paralysis in the face of growing economic relations across the Taiwan Strait was an embarrassment to them.

Finally, in late 1985 the KMT bowed to reality and acknowledged they would not interfere with exports to China if they were indirect. Taipei's grudging recognition of indirect trade with the mainland led to further concessions. The final figleaf fell from Taiwan's official "three no's" policy ("no cooperation, no negotiation, no compromise with the mainland") when the KMT permitted family visits to the mainland in 1987, and businesspeople from all over Taiwan used the occasion to develop investment contacts in China.

Since the collapse of KMT efforts to restrict trade with the mainland, growth of the Taiwan Strait economy has been extraordinary. Two-way trade has increased at an annual rate of 32 percent since 1985, doubling about every three years. Less than $100 million in 1979, the total in 1992 is likely to be $7 billion, about 80 percent of which is Taiwan's exports to China. Despite the fact that the trade, except for some smuggling, all passes through Hong Kong, Taiwan became China's sixth-largest trading partner by 1991. In talks with the Hitachi management in Taiwan, they reported that they still buy parts from the same Taiwanese supplier, but they now come from Fujian via their buying office in Hong Kong for use in assembly in the Hitachi Taiwan plant.

Taiwan's investment in China, especially in Fujian, has jump-started much of this trade, as manufacturers ship machinery, tools, raw materials, and semifinished goods to production sites springing up on the mainland. The Hong Kong government estimates over half of all trade across the straits is production-related. The Asian Wall Street Journal recently used the term "China fever" to describe the preoccupation of Taiwanese businesses with trade and investment in China. In investment terms, Taiwanese officials report some 2,500 companies registered as having investments in China—usually through shell and third-party companies. The same sources suggest that the actual total might be 3,000 or so, including informal and unofficial entrants to China. Most of these are small- and medium-sized companies, no doubt working through and with family connections and friends on the mainland.

Just as the number of Taiwanese companies in China by the early 1990s is uncertain, so the amounts of investment are not clear. It appears that investment amounts were doubling annually in the late 1980s, to a total in all of China of somewhat under $3 billion, nearly all invested since 1985. A number of observers estimate the actual total to be perhaps twice that amount but no one really knows. It is clear, however, that the growth of investment has been very rapid, a great many Taiwanese companies—perhaps most—are participants, and the amount is already rather large, all this despite official barriers and discouragement from the Taiwanese government side.[5]

In terms of the development of the Taiwan Strait regional economy, there is a general consensus that about one-half of the investment moving from Taiwan to China is into Fujian province. The Chinese government reports approval of some 3,000 projects into Fujian since the 1979 economic reforms, with about $1.3 billion of investment in place. Taiwanese investments into other areas of China—Guangdong, Shanghai, Tianjin, and elsewhere—continue to increase as well. A new tendency is for larger companies, such as Taiwan Plastics, to push for governmental approval of large-scale projects, particularly in Fujian.

One result is that all of China's provinces the rate of increase of total trade has been greatest for Fujian, at an annual rate of 27 percent compounded from a very low base in 1979, outdoing even Guangdong's impressive 23 percent.[6] Continuing investment from abroad will no doubt support further growth. It must be noted, however, that unlike the South China situation where Western and Japanese investors play a substantial role, the integration of Fujian and Taiwan is almost entirely a Chinese matter, with investments from Japan and the United States each less than 1 percent of the total in Fujian, and by only four or five companies from each country. This is a Chinese affair.

The affair will probably intensify. China has announced its intention to make Xiamen a free port, and Taiwanese businesspeople traveling to Xiamen can pick up visas there on arrival. Plans for a stock market exist as well.[7] At the same time complaints of red tape and corruption in Xiamen are pushing investors to move elsewhere in Fujian.[8]

A MASSIVE SOUTH CHINA ECONOMY?

As they now are constituted, the regional economies of the South China coast have a number of common features. First, they are dominated by Overseas Chinese in terms of foreign investment flows. Second, they are

●

heavily involved in producing for export, with products flowing through
Hong Kong channels for the most part (with Taiwan still blocked for
political reasons). Third, small- and medium-sized companies have led
investment, generally in light industry first. Bigger companies have followed in their wake, as the barriers to investment fall and infrastructure
develops. Thus, while China as a whole is about equally divided between
heavy and light industry, light industry is two-thirds of the total industrial
sector of Guangdong and Fujian provinces.

This is not surprising, because the main attraction of the area to investors from Hong Kong and Taiwan has been the lower labor and land
costs in the mainland provinces. As Table 4–1 makes clear, the great
difference in labor supply and costs between Hong Kong and Taiwan, on
the one hand, and Guangdong and Fujian, on the other, has not only
continued but has in fact widened. Labor shortages and the consequences
of rapidly increasing labor productivity in Taiwan and Hong Kong have
driven wage rates up by 10 to 25 percent annually. While rates in China
have also risen, the pace of increase has been slower, so the wage gap has
become even greater. Thus, the appeal of the mainland provinces as a site
for labor-intensive manufacture continues and strengthens. Products like
shoes, luggage, toys, and fabrics are Hong Kong's largest China-sourced
exports.

Table 4–1   Labor Costs, 1985 & 1991
Average Monthly Wages in Manufacturing (US$)

	1985	1991	Increase (percent)
Hong Kong	$400	$810	+109%
Taiwan	319	918	+188
Guangdong	39	55	+42
(Shenzen)	65	79	+22
Fujian	29	39	+33
(Xiamen)	37	58	+57
China, National	32	38	+20

Note: Exchange rate with U.S. dollar: Hong Kong unchanged, Taiwan +32%, China
−81%.

Source: Data from *China Statistics Yearbook 1992*, ed, by National Statistics Bureau (Beijing: China
Statistics Publishing Company, 1992).

•

Not surprisingly, as these two regional economies of South China and the Taiwan Strait have flourished in parallel, their integration into a massive South China economy that would incorporate both of them is a possibility. The combination would be a formidable addition to the economic map of the world. If the economic terms Guangdong, Fujian, Hong Kong, and Taiwan were considered a single entity, they would form an economy with a population of 120 million, approximately equal to Japan's in an area of similar size.

The combined GNP of this Greater South China regional economy would be about the size of all five ASEAN nations (leaving out Brunei) added together. The real growth rate of the area would be on the order of 10 percent annually, averaging the 5 percent or so of Hong Kong with the 7 percent or so of Taiwan and the 10 plus percent of the mainland provinces—a growth rate similar to Japan's during its period of high growth in the 1960s. Per capita incomes would be on average seven or eight times that of China as a whole, doubling in approximately seven years or so. This would effectively add another Japan to the world economy over the next decade.

It is an interesting scenario, and the numbers shown in Table 4–2 are formidable. If economic events were to run their course with little or no political intervention, the concept could well become an economic reality—indeed, it is on its way to realization even now. It requires a degree of political flexibility and rationality that may not exist, however. The impending integration of Hong Kong and Guangdong is a major step—

Table 4–2   Greater South China Regional Economy, 1991

	Population (million)	Area (thousand sq. km.)	GNP ($ billion)	GNP per capita ($)
Greater South China Regional Economy*	121	3.4	307	2,526
ASEAN 5	329	30.5	334	1,015
China	1,158	96.0	371	320
Japan	124	3.8	$3,386	27,323

*Guangdong, Fujian, Taiwan, and Hong Kong.

Source: Data from *China Statistics Yearbook 1992,* ed. by National Statistics Bureau (Beijing: China Statistics Publishing Company, 1992).

•

but the barriers to the political integration of Taiwan into the area remain very great. Still, this massive South China economy could be a
reality in the next decade, and business planners need take careful note.

Whatever the political shifts, it would be difficult to extricate these
mainland Chinese provinces from their international involvements. Between one-quarter and one-third of the GNP of Fujian and Guangdong
is now dedicated to exports, which are growing 20 percent annually.
Foreign companies account for about one-fifth of industrial output. Any
Chinese government attempt to reverse the international thrust of these
economic developments would be risking the political consequences of
a disastrous drop in incomes in the provinces.

A possible weakness in the long-term development of South China
is that the technologies flowing into the two regional economies are low
to middle range, rather than leading technologies, owing to the cheap
land/labor focus of investment. Similarly, the level of capital intensity of
production is relatively low. In these respects, developments in the South
China area contrast with the pattern of regional development that seems
to be emerging to the north, where heavy industry plays a larger role.

ECONOMICS FIRST, POLITICS AFTER

In the north on the China coast, notably the provinces of Shandong and
Liaoning, the foreign sources of capital, technology, and management
are Korea and Japan rather than the Overseas Chinese community.
Much of this difference in pattern of industrial development is due to
historical developments, but it may well be too that the central government of China encourages this differentiation in economic structure,
with the more capital- and technology-intensive developments taking
place nearer to Beijing's reach.

The developments to the north have not had the same spectacular
rate or scale as the South China and Taiwan Strait regional economies,
because the political boundaries there are much less porous. Both Japan
and Korea have histories of strong nationalism, and the whole area remains caught up in the divisions and tensions of the cold war to a considerable degree. Furthermore, there is not the same cross-boundary degree of language, kinship, and origin ties that link the southern provinces
with Hong Kong and Taiwan.

●

Still, the same economic driving forces are operative—the search for lower-cost land and labor and the interest in expanding trade with a growing China on the part of Korean and Japanese businesses; rapidly strengthening currencies that make exports more difficult and investment abroad more attractive; and substantial accumulations of foreign exchange reserves that provide the funding base for investment abroad. From the Chinese point of view, the success of the developments to the south in pulling in investment and technology that generates rapidly increasing outputs and incomes suggests the value of parallel approaches to the development of the northern coast.

Thus we saw the startling moves by Beijing and Seoul leading to diplomatic recognition, despite ideological differences, Chinese intervention in the Korean War, and the consequent isolation of China's long-time ally, North Korea. Marx was indeed correct; economics is determinative, or so at any rate this case would demonstrate.

In fact, the move to full diplomatic relations was less abrupt than it might have appeared. After the key cities of Qingdao in Shandong province and Dalian in Liaoning province were opened by China to foreign trade in 1983, Korean trade with China nearly tripled from 1983 to 1984, although it is still very limited. Quite remarkably, however, once started, China–Korea trade grew nearly 50 percent each year thereafter from 1984 through 1991—and doubled again from 1991 to the end of 1992, with the removal of all political restrictions. South Korea became China's fourth-largest trading partner in 1991, after Hong Kong, Japan, and the United States, with more than five times the trade of North Korea with China.

With diplomatic relations established, major changes in the South Korean position in the Chinese economy are taking place. The earlier, limited Korean trade and investment in China had been partly indirect, through Hong Kong and Japan, and investments had been small, focused on trade and labor-intensive businesses, such as toys and apparel. With the normalization of relations, Samsung announced a VTR joint venture in Tianjin, Pohang Steel a tin plate joint venture in Shanghai, and Samsung with C. Itoh an ethylene plant in Jilin province—all very large investments. Discussions of cement plants and auto assembly began at once. For China, in need of heavy investment, the payoff on this diplomatic move was immediate.

The normalization of relations can also be expected to encourage Korean businesses to move more actively into China's northeast prov-

●

inces, even without a solution to the North–South Korea issue. The ethnic Korean presence in the three northeast provinces is substantial, with
1,200,000 ethnic Koreans in Jilin province, 450,000 in Heilongjiang to
the extreme north of China, and 230,000 in Liaoning.[9] Although the
Chinese government's interest seems more directed to attracting Korean
investment to Shandong, ties of affinity are likely to make the northeast
attractive to Korean business as well.

In spite of all the developments along the China coast, Japanese
companies have been exceedingly cautious about investments in China.
Total direct Japanese investment in China through March 1991 was less
than 1 percent of all of Japan's overseas direct investment. Japanese companies have remained highly skeptical of the stability and reliability of the
Chinese government, having had more experience than most with the
painful consequences of sudden, unpredictable, and drastic changes in
Chinese leadership and policies during the Communist era.

This seems now to be changing, signaled, it seems, by the willingness
of the Japanese government to arrange a visit of the emperor and empress
of Japan to China in late 1992, despite concern that the Chinese would
raise the embarrassing issue of war reparations or ask Japan to publicly
apologize for Chinese suffering during the Japanese occupation in the
1930s. The visit went off without incident, and by what may have not
been a coincidence, the leading trading companies of Japan announced
their plans for an enormous, $5 billion petrochemical investment in
Liaoning province.

TIES BETWEEN JAPAN AND LIAONING

Liaoning and its main city of Dalian are familiar areas to Japan's
businesspeople. This was Manchuria, the beachhead for Japan's invasion
of China. It was at Port Arthur on the Liaoning Peninsula that the Japanese Imperial Army ended Russian expansion in Asia in 1905, and with
the Russian defeat, marked the beginning of Japan's colonial dominance
over Korea and north China. Home to hundreds of thousands of Japanese before the war, Dalian and environs remain a comfortable location
for Japanese, with a Japanese school, a mayor fluent in Japanese, and a
joint Japan-China Industrial Park that is now being expanded by a Japanese-
led consortium to handle more Japanese companies investing there.

JETRO, in its ratings of the economic potential of China's provinces, rated Dalian's Liaoning above all others in attractiveness, including Guangdong, Shandong, and Shanghai. Liaoning was rated especially high in terms of its industrial base and matched Shanghai in terms of infrastructure, which, like those of Taiwan and Korea, was originally put in place by the Japanese. However, while Guangdong was moving from tenth to first place in GNP from 1978 to 1990, Liaoning fell from third to fifth in terms of GNP.[10]

The Japanese in Dalian and elsewhere in Liaoning are generally focused on high value-added or capital-intensive investments rather than luggage or toys. They include Onoda Cement, Toshiba, Canon, Mabuchi Motors, Asahi Glass, and Nisshin Oil Mills, along with banks and trading companies. That it is familiar territory to many senior Japanese is evidenced by the remarks of President Tasuku Takagaki of the Bank of Tokyo about his grammar school days in Dalian. Other current Japanese leaders share his experience; the late Foreign Minister Saburo Ohkita was another Japanese leader born and raised in Liaoning.

Asked about the large number of prominent Japanese who spent their childhoods in Manchuria, President Takagaki remarked that in the late 1920s and early 1930s, ambitious young Japanese in search of greater freedom and more opportunity went West—in this case, to Dalian and elsewhere in Manchuria. Exceptionally able in many cases, their families have supplied equally exceptionally able offspring, to the advantage of northeast China as it seeks Japanese investment.

The task in northeast China is formidable. It is a sprawling area with a population of 100 million bordering mainly North Korea and the Russian Far East. It is largely landlocked except for a passageway through Liaoning and its major port on the Yellow Sea, Dalian. The Stalinist inheritance of state-owned heavy industry remains strong. Despite these obstacles, the Chinese government has shown some thought and skill in trying to recreate the "South China miracle" in the northeast and Shandong through strategic placement of industrial sites, tax breaks for investors, and the like. Particularly if the Korean Peninsula issues are resolved, and the Russian provinces are integrated into the economic orbits of Japan and South Korea, progress in the north and northeast could take on something of the vigor of the southern coast.

The success of Chinese government efforts at sparking trade and investment in the northeast is not assured, however. The characteristic common to development along all parts of the China coast is that it has

occurred without government subsidies or formal barriers to the movement of goods and capital. The driving forces have been economic, and
the actors have generally been Overseas Chinese private businesspeople.
In the northeast, the Chinese government is obviously hoping South
Korean businesses will link with local ethnic Koreans, and that their industrial parks will ignite massive investment and trade as has happened in
the south.

THE GROWTH TRIANGLE AS A
SINGAPORE SOLUTION

At the geographic extremes of East Asia, regional programs of a somewhat different nature are underway. The most remarked, and much the
furthest advanced, is the Growth Triangle of Singapore, the Riau Islands
of Indonesia, immediately adjacent to Singapore, and Johor, the largest
and southernmost state of peninsular Malaysia. Development is focused
on the island of Batam, about two-thirds the size of Singapore, adminis-
tratively separated as a development zone where the Indonesian government had earlier attempted to set up an industrial zone.

For Singapore, a breakout from its limited territory is a necessity if
growth is to continue. Singapore is suffering a labor shortage; its labor
force is expected to grow only about 0.5 percent annually, while those of
its neighbors will grow more than 2 percent. The shortage of both land
and labor drives costs up and draws investment to neighboring economies, instead of into Singapore.[11] Well before the Growth Triangle, labor
was sourced from Johor, just across the causeway between Singapore and
Malaysia, as is water for Singapore.

The Riau Islands and Indonesia, which are to supply the low-cost
labor and land, are only a one-hour trip from Singapore, where capital-
and knowledge-intensive operations would be sited. Medium-skill and
higher-cost labor and land would be supplied by Johor. The Singapore
and Indonesian governments have not only cleared away formal barriers;
the Singapore government is the major source of funds for the Batam
Industrial Park, with its Indonesian partner, the Salim Group from Indonesia, which brings close connections with the Suharto government.

The expansion of Singapore's labor and land supply is a welcome
development for many international businesses that want to take advantage of Singapore's many attractions as an operating center but are put off

●

by rising costs there. There are problems of infrastructure in the Riau Islands, but these will yield to continued investment, and several multinationals are investing in manufacturing facilities there.

There must be a question of the long-term economic attractiveness of Batam, Bintan, and the other Riau Islands in terms of cost of transport and infrastructure. Unlike the China provinces, these islands have no massive hinterland from which to draw additional labor, nor a potential market for some part of production—Indonesia is not open to products from the triangle except as ordinary imports. Singapore's Growth Triangle is a valuable industrial site. It is not, and will almost certainly not become, a regional economy in the China coast sense. The political issues involved in defining the triangle alone will prevent early realization of anything like a regional economy in this area. Both Indonesia and Malaysia have considerable reservations about the balance of advantages to them of the concept.

Still, with wages one-quarter Singapore's level, a rapidly growing population now at more than 100,000, an international airport on the way, and Singapore government support, Philips, Thomson, AT&T, Bowater, and Sumitomo Electric are all committed to investing in Batam. Perhaps it is better noted as a very interesting investment site rather than an example of regional development.

THE BACK OF THE BEYOND

Still further from real substance, but presently the stuff of development dreams, is the Tumen River Area Development Program (TRAD). The Tumen River, not visible on many Western maps of the area, forms the China–North Korea border as it empties into the Sea of Japan, although the last 15 kilometers are in fact the border between Russia and North Korea. Development of the area would involve the improbable combination of North and South Korea, Japan, China, Russia, and Mongolia.

In fact, this odd group met in 1992 under United Nations Development Program auspices to discuss a development that has been wildly described as "the future Rotterdam of the Far East," and more accurately as "the back of the back of beyond."[12] Still, these disparate nations did assemble and established a TRAD Council, which will be the project's board of directors, working on a 20-year, $30 billion plan for area development, to include building a city of 500,000, railways, an airport, and a

port. All of this will be accomplished jointly by the governments concerned with UNDP support, with the plan to be ready by the end of
1993. China has already declared its key city of Hunchun a special economic zone to attract investment into the area. China very much wants the
access to the Sea of Japan that the Tumen development would provide.

The concept is a grand one. It also fits well the complex of complementary resources in the area—Japan's capital and technology, the labor
and raw materials of northeast China and North Korea, with energy supplied from Russia and northeast China. It also fits very well and indeed
is a special case of the Japan Sea Rim concept that interests a great many
Japanese. Northeast Asian development has focused since World War II
on the Pacific coasts and the Yellow Sea coasts, while northwest Japan,
northeast China, and eastern Korea have fallen out of the race. Both
economics and politics dictate more attention to the Sea of Japan/north-
ern Korea/Russian Far East/northeast China area.

In a very general way, a recent Japanese government publication
summed up the situation: "In the region 'the Sea of Japan rim,' there has
not yet been adequate use made of the wealth of available resources. If
we were to add to Japan's capital and advanced technology the still underutilized rich resources of the Russian Far East, China's labor power
and the middle range technology of South Korea, we can expect very
rapid economic growth of the coastal nations. Can we not say that the
21st century will become 'the era of the Sea of Japan Rim?' "[13]

Whether so ambitious a scheme as the Tumen River Development
materializes, it is a measure of the increasing confidence and reach of East
Asia that the plans are being formulated and discussed. It is also a measure
of political maturity that so disparate a group of nations can meet for the
discussion. There is a tendency in the West to disparage these efforts, just
as the potential of ASEAN as a regional grouping has been disparaged.
But the consistent underestimation of Asian developments should by
now have taught the West a lesson—the economic potential of East Asia
is now being realized, and the end to this great process is not yet in sight.

CHINA'S REALISTIC PROSPECTS

No overview of Asia's new economies would be complete without consideration of China's future as a whole. China's coastline has emerged as
the breeding ground for some of Asia's most dynamic regional econo-

mies: South China, Taiwan Strait, and perhaps one in the north. The future of these regional economies is still closely linked to larger developments in China, however, because despite their considerable economic clout they have no political weight. Questions naturally arise, then, about China's future as a nation-state. How will its development affect the regional economies? What are the prospects for continued reform in the post-Deng era? Whatever the answers, surely the Chinese Communist party will play a key role. Thus it is important to look at this key institution in the context of China's economic achievements.

This is not an easy task. Even for experienced China hands, China presents a snarl of paradox and contradiction: a great economic success while the majority of its people are still very poor; an aging and feeble 1930s-style Stalinist gerontocracy presiding over the world's most dynamic and fastest-growing economy; a highly centralized state tugged apart by regional economies and highly vulnerable to changes in leadership. It is praised for its promising future, damned for its human rights record. The temptation for a corporation to take a substantial position in China is nearly irresistible, yet at present there are still few instances of multinational corporate success and profitability.

The Chinese economic achievement, especially over the past 15 or so years, is stunning. Comparison with the former USSR is inevitable and appropriate. As the USSR was breaking into pieces, many actively hostile to each other, China's central government steered a course through a series of crises, often rather brutally but without secession. And as the remnants of the former Soviet Union shrink drastically in economic size, suffering explosive inflation and general breakdowns of their markets, China stunned the West by posting the world's highest growth rates in the period 1980–90 and continuing into the 1990s as well.

The statistics on China's growth since the reforms of late 1978 are remarkable indeed (see Table 4–3). The economy's real growth, at nearly 9 percent per annum for more than a decade, has more than doubled per capital output. Trade is doubling every five years, more than quadrupling over the period. Inflation has on average been a moderately high but manageable 6 percent, with capital investment also very high. Exports have been aided by a currency depreciating relatively rapidly against the U.S. dollar, while foreign reserves exceed those of France and Britain.

All this has been happening in an economy that includes one-quarter of the world's population in an area about the size of the United States. Naturally there is high enthusiasm about China's prospects. "Each year,

●

Table 4–3   China's Economic Growth Rates Since Reform

		Annual Average Increase 1979–91 (percent)
GNP		8.6
GNP per Capita		7.1
Food output (tons)		2.8
Industrial production		12.2
Fixed asset investment (1981–1991)		18.6
Consumer price increase		6.0
Exports		16.6
Imports		14.5
Exchange rate	1978	1.68
(Yuan:$)	1991	5.32
Foreign reserves	1978	$1.6 billion
	1991	$42.7 billion

Source: Data from Zhu Yan, "Chugoku no keizai kaikaku to Sona Tenbo," *Fuji soken Ronshu,* No. 111 (July 1992), p. 30.

on average, for the past 14 years China's real GNP has grown 6.5 percentage points faster than America's. If that difference persists, a little after 2010 China will have the world's biggest economy."[14] This view requires taking a very positive view of China's present situation and projecting the best of possible futures. A more conservative projection suggests that China's average growth might be around 6 percent annually to 2010, where its economy would be about one-fifth the size of Japan's and about one-eighth the size of the North American economy, somewhat more than three times its present size, $1.15 trillion.[15]

It is in no way a denial of the achievements of China's economy to note that for all the great increase in Chinese trade, Taiwan's 20 million people trade one-third again as much as China's 1.5 trillion. With a combined total population of about 65 million, Korea and Taiwan have a distinctly larger national product than China, even taking into account its growth over the past 15 years. And China's economy remains a bit more than one-tenth the size of Japan's. Although it is all very well to describe the immensity of China in terms of land mass, population, cultural influence, and potential, the fact is that China as a whole is not yet one of the world's major economies—nor is it within reach of becoming one soon.

●

FOREIGN INVESTMENT ESSENTIAL

China's leaders have pursued policies that have allowed its regional economies to become major players in the world's economy. Their agricultural reforms that freed rural villagers from collectivism and central control have, like land reform in Japan, Taiwan, and Korea, increased farm output and productivity dramatically, allowing surplus money to flow from the countryside to fund industrial growth. China's leaders—or at any rate, Deng Xiaoping—have done their homework on Asian development economics. The lessons learned include an appreciation of the role that foreign capital and technology can play in growth and the need for free and open trade. The practical applications of these lessons have been extremely successful, especially in attracting foreign investment to the regional economies.

Beijing has not confined itself to attracting foreign investment to the regional economic areas and SEZs. Presently officials are negotiating with Hong Kong's Wharf (Holdings) Limited, which has an ambitious plan to turn the hinterland provincial center of Wuhan, once known as the Detroit of China, into a container port and transport center for the transshipment of goods to Hong Kong. Philips and NEC have joint venture fiber-optic operations in Wuhan, and Peugeot has an auto assembly joint venture there. Still, most of the relatively few foreign investments have been made by small companies from Hong Kong and Taiwan. Bureaucratic tangles increase with distance from the SEZs, and the quality of infrastructure—roads, airports, rail transport—decreases. Wuhan's boom is probably still in the future.

Overall foreign investment in China continues to increase. Numbers are deceptive because actual investment and Chinese government reports differ considerably. Nevertheless, in 1992, U.S. and Japanese investments were up threefold over the year before, while still only a small fraction of the amounts pouring in from Taiwan and especially from Hong Kong.

Beijing's actions have not always supported foreign investors, however positive the general trends of the last decade have been. Beijing's sudden and frequent policy reversals in the past have left a bad taste in the mouth of many Japanese firms. Thus while Japanese direct investment in China is somewhat greater than U.S. direct investment—perhaps 14 percent of China's total compared with 10 percent for U.S. companies—only a minuscule 0.9 percent of Japan's total foreign direct investment

•

goes to China. But loan funds from Japan and funding by Japan's Export-Import Bank have been very substantial. Japan has a great deal at stake in China and is prepared to pay a price to help ensure its stability. Thus, of total foreign funds officially reported to have moved into China from 1983 to 1991, 31 percent came from Japan, one-quarter from Hong Kong, and only 5 percent from the United States, largely owing to Japan's massive loans to China as aid and Ex-Im Bank funding—a total for the period of about $14 billion.[16]

TRADE AND CONTINUED REFORM

In trade, Beijing's leaders have been careful to preserve Hong Kong's key role of entrepôt center for China's interaction with the world economy. Trade patterns for China over the decade of the 1980s underline this (see Appendix Table 7). Both exports and imports with Japan are down over the period, and trade with ASEAN remains at a low level—probably because of the similarities in the ASEAN and Chinese economies. Nearly half of China's exports are to Hong Kong, and a good part are then reexported to the United States, whose consumption patterns continue to be a key source of Asian growth. Europe is important but not critical to China's trade, although again, no doubt, a part of the Hong Kong figure reflects transshipments to Europe. Of some interest is the low proportion of China's trade with the former Soviet Union. China stood clear of the Soviet economy—and was fortunate to have done so. The Soviet collapse hit Vietnam heavily (and surely North Korea as well) but had little effect on China.

As a player on the world economic stage, China remains a medium-sized economy with low levels of income but with spectacularly growing and increasingly prosperous economic enclaves along its Pacific coast. The reforms put in motion in 1979 have had an electrifying effect on the performance of the economy as a whole, and with the opening of key cities to international trade and investment, foreign capital and trade are supporting continued growth of the total economy. The critical question is, Can this political stability and economic growth continue over the next decade as well?

It first must be said that it would be a mistake to see China's agricultural reforms and opening to trade and investment with the West as a

•

sudden conversion to capitalism and market economics. From its beginning, economic reform has had a hard, practical political logic behind it.

For example, economic reform was widely recognized as the only
available means to bring China back from the disastrous Cultural Revolution of 1966–76, which exhausted and weakened it both internally and
externally. Deng and his supporters saw that restoring China's rightful
place among great nations could not be achieved without help from the
West. China's embarrassing drubbing in its 1979 border war with Vietnam reconfirmed this.

Economic recovery has justifications closer to home too. China's
leaders fear mass emigration from the countryside to the cities and the
instability this would bring. It was thus natural in 1979 to allow farmers
to own their own land and participate in a market economy, no matter
how difficult the ideological acrobats might be, as a means of preventing
this.

The economic reforms had, and continue to have, geopolitical un-
derpinnings as well, specifically to speed political reunification with Taiwan, Hong Kong, and Macau. Although in the long term the course of
events may not turn out as Beijing has planned, certain of its key objectives are already being met: Hong Kong and Guangdong are irreversibly
linked through the South China regional economy, and a similar process
may be happening between Taiwan and Fujian, despite vigorous opposition from the KMT.

Perhaps most important is the belief by Deng and his reformist fol-
lowers that economic success means continued political power for the
Communist party. It would be absurd to suggest that in 1979 Deng fore-
saw the collapse of Eastern Europe and the Soviet bloc. But Deng has
succeeded in convincing many in the party, with help from the Soviet
bloc's 1989 collapse, that economic stagnation can cripple the Commu-
nists, while economic growth can only fortify their grip on power. Thus
Deng, as recently as April 1992, exhorted Chinese to "continue to walk
the capitalist road with socialist characteristics and spread reform across
China"—it is a matter of intense political self-interest, no matter
how badly the canons of Communist doctrine are bent in the process.
The same political imperatives behind the 1979 reforms are operative
today: an outward-looking economic development will continue to be
seen by China's leaders as a means to internal stability, international prestige, and most important, continued political power for the Communist
party.

•

THE CASE AGAINST OPTIMISM

Against these forces for continued stability and economic reform lie formidable obstacles. There are management issues: state enterprises still occupy more than half the industrial base and are massively inefficient, supported by subsidies and price controls at considerable cost to the entire economy. Half of China is still rural, and the unemployed—perhaps as many as 160 million persons—are concentrated in the countryside but as migrants could put very great pressure on the cities. Infrastructure needs, environmental issues, housing and education requirements will all need careful handling if progress is to continue.

Still, even larger issues are likely to be the decisive ones. Succession is at the top of the list. There is no visible successor to Deng Xiaopeng, in a country that arguably has an "in-built penchant of the Chinese people for one-man rule or a personality cult."[17] Nor is a successor guaranteed to have the same commitment to economic reform that Deng has held. Not all of its leaders share Deng's views. Moreover, it is a country that has in the past swung suddenly and even violently from one position to another—witness the Great Leap Forward, the Hundred Flowers, the Cultural Revolution, and most recently, Tiananmen Square. Few doubt that when Deng dies there will be turmoil, maybe even blood spilled.

Even if the succession issue is dealt with reasonably, with perhaps a period of uproar and uncertainty but no sustained discontinuities in economic policy, two broad issues can be argued to be potential sources of major problems. The first is the presumed conflict between increasing market freedoms and continued tight political control. Increased economic prosperity and freedom of choice seem to lead eventually to a desire for political freedom, although Asia's development suggests that prosperity can buy a good deal of political tolerance and loyalty in the meantime—witness Singapore, Taiwan, and Korea, for example.

A second issue is that of regional economic successes and centrifugal forces in China versus the need for central controls in a Communist regime. Deng and his associates avoided the Soviet collapse by moving to reform ahead of economic crisis and accelerating economic reform in response to success. However, China is an immense country physically and diverse in many aspects of its culture, especially on its north-south axis. As the explosive growth of the southeast provinces allow them to generate foreign exchange and engage in foreign trade, the natural pres-

●

sures for decentralization—especially if the process of succession to Deng is protracted—might well threaten to tear China apart.

The centrifugal forces might be dealt with by repression—as was the case with the Tiananmen demonstrations. Another possibility is a move to some form of de facto decentralization or federalization. Something like that already seems underway as local authorities are allowed more autonomy in decisions regarding foreign investment, for example.

The deciding factor for repression or continued reform will probably be whether the regional economies and coastal provinces continue to respect their tacit contract with Beijing: proper, but do not challenge the dominance of the Communist party. If this was explicitly worded in four commandments, they might read like this: respect the central government's control over diplomacy; do not meddle in military affairs; keep a balanced (foreign exchange) budget; and work for political unity of China under the Communist party.

It is likely, although not certain, that as long as the sanctity of these commandments is preserved, China will continue its pragmatic approach toward the regional economies. Thus, good advice to corporate CEOs would be to consider China, for the next five to ten years at least, as a geographic mass of several separate major markets, with a central political structure. This political structure—the Chinese Communist party—is no Soviet Union, frozen in bureaucratic and ideological incompetence. It is instead a force that sees trade and foreign investment as the key to China's prestige, internal stability, and ultimately its own survival. Although China's issues and problems are very considerable, the prospect of continuing pragmatism, at least over time, seems a fair bet.

POSITIONING THE WESTERN COMPANY IN CHINA

It has been little more than a decade since the reforms began in China, and an even shorter period since foreign investment came to have significant potential. The experience base for strategy recommendations is limited. A few major themes are emerging, however.

Focus on the provinces, not the center. The significant developments are taking place in the coastal provinces, where the growth rates are high and local governments increasingly have decision-making au-

●

thority. The center remains exceedingly powerful and must be cultivated and dealt with. However, business will be in a specific province, with its own history and culture. Moreover, the long-run relations between China's center and periphery are not at all clear. A strong base in a major province is a needed insurance against possible decentralization of the nation.

Relationships are key. Among the rather few aspects of China on which there is general agreement, the importance of relationships is invariably, and correctly, emphasized. An experience base in Hong Kong or Taiwan is of special value, and companies like DuPont have built on their Taiwan staffs to manage their way into the mainland markets. In any case, Hong Kong and Taiwan intermediaries can be a critical asset in the early stages of China operations, while more direct relationships are being established.

Minimize initial exposure. The risks associated with China remain very considerable, as leadership succession is in question, long-term economic policy continuity is by no means assured, and very serious problems of economic management are all too visible. In any case, the company without experience or relations in China would do well to minimize equity exposure, starting small and building position gradually. This fits both the company capability and the Chinese reality. Toyota's small truck success has been achieved with no equity exposure as yet, working through licensing and other fee arrangements to realize and export profits, and is an example of what can be accomplished without major capital investment.

Use partner arrangements. The two issues of the importance of relationships and the desirability of limited exposure suggest the usefulness of some form of joint venture as an initial mode of entry into China. The hazards of joint ventures—difficulties with decision making and control, differences in objectives between partners—are familiar, but a properly formulated joint venture with Overseas Chinese interests may well be the appropriate vehicle for initial positioning in China, with independent and larger operations to follow as warranted by increased corporate competence and by what one hopes will become a more secure Chinese environment.

In the final analysis, a China strategy must be built on an appreciation of China's limitations over the decade, with a minimum of romanticism about the country's potential. China's modern economy is an important part, but only a part, of East Asia's powerful position in the world.

5

•

TAIWAN AND KOREA

NEW DIMENSIONS, DIFFERENT DIRECTIONS

In magnitude and rate of economic change, Taiwan and Korea have no parallel in world history. Each has moved in only four decades, less than two generations, from being impoverished ex-colonies—bad risks from nearly every perspective—to powerful and important members of the community of industrial nations. They have far surpassed even the speed of Japan and Germany in those nations' moves to industrialization.

The pace has been extraordinary. For two decades these economies have been growing at more than three times the world growth rate. Output per capita, as each country's population growth has slowed, has been increasing at more than four times the world rate (see Table 5–1). Little slackening of these rates is occurring in the early 1900s, despite the sharp turndown in world markets and their heavy dependence on trade. Expectations that the recessions in America, Japan, and Europe would halt this growth have simply not taken account of their basic economic strengths nor the increasing self-sufficiency of the East Asian area.

Taiwan and Korea are among the world's top dozen economies in scale of import and export trade, and among the leaders in production of a wide range of industrial goods. Per capita output in 1992 was nearly $10,000 for Taiwan, an economy with a total product of about $180

●

Table 5–1   Growth and Inflation, 1971–1990 Taiwan
                 and Korea (percent per annum)

	GDP		GDP per Capita	
	1971–80	1981–90	1971–80	1981–90
Taiwan	9.3	8.5	11.4	11.0
Korea	9.0	9.9	10.3	11.0

Note: World GDP growth, 1965–1980 = 4.0%, 1980–1990 = 3.2%.
World GDP per capita growth, 1965–1990 = 1.5%.

Source: Data from Asian Development Bank, *Asian Development Outlook* (Hong Kong: Oxford
University Press, 1992), p. 288 pp.; The World Bank, *World Development Report* (New York, Oxford University Press, 1992), p. 222 pp.

billion. Assuming growth continues at something like the rate of the past
20 years or so, the economy will double by the end of this decade. Taiwan would, by the year 2000, be a good deal larger than Sweden or the
Netherlands today, with per capita income approximating the current
French level.

Korea is now an economy of about $280 billion, or about equal to
that of Australia, with per capita output of about $6,500. Assuming a
slowing of growth so that the economy merely doubled by the year
2000, it would then be about the size of Canada today, with per capita
output at about the current Spanish level. Given the records of Taiwan
and Korea over the past three decades, the momentum of their growth,
and the supporting effect of broader Asian growth, the assumption of a
doubling by the year 2000, putting these two economies into the major
leagues, seems only reasonable.

It is time to give these economies full consideration in their own
right. It is not helpful to describe them as "Asian tigers" or "little dragons," as though they were members of some interesting sports team—
alike and similar to Hong Kong and Singapore as well. That sort of implied condescension is only misleading because these economies are very
different in critical ways. More important, the directions in which they
are moving are very different, as Taiwan rapidly becomes integrated with
the economy of mainland China and Korea a major power on the Asian
mainland.

A brief review of the similarities in the development process of Taiwan and Korea is useful for perspective. However, consideration of the

•

weight they should be given in global corporate strategies requires that
each be examined separately to understand the unique dynamics at work
and to predict their development over the coming decade.

HISTORICAL PATTERNS
OF DEVELOPMENT

The first common pattern for the two economies was their rapid shift out
of agriculture into industry. Around 1950 more than 90 percent of
Taiwan's limited exports were agricultural products— bananas, pineap-
ples, sugar, and the like—that had been the mainstay of colonial exports
to Japan. By the late 1980s, agriculture accounted for only 6 percent of
GDP, while manufacturers produced nearly one-half, the highest in the
world at the time, with total exports more than half of GDP.[1]

Similarly with Korea. From a later start, in the early 1960s, agriculture dropped from 40 percent of GDP to less than 10 percent by 1990,
while industry grew from one-quarter to one-half of the economy over
the same period, and exports were valued at 40 percent of output.

Some common factors generating this growth are clear enough. First
are the external threats faced by each. Both Taiwan, from mainland
China, and Korea, from North Korea and the Communist bloc, have
been under very real threats for a considerable period. This stimulus to
industrial growth is similar to Japan's when the country was confronted
by the military power of the West when it opened its doors to the world.
Industry became the means of ensuring independent survival. External
threats do not inevitably generate growth, but they do provide an effective rationale for stringent measures to enforce savings and investment,
and a powerful motive for group effort and sacrifice.

Concurrently with these policies went thoroughgoing land reform
in both economies—in Taiwan in 1949, and Korea in 1954—again par-
alleling the Japanese experience of the immediate postwar period. The
leveling effect on the social structure and the consequent increased mo-
tivation to raise agricultural output were critical to the growth of both
economies—and the lack of land reform persists as an issue in those East
Asian economies like the Philippines where hacienda/plantation-style
land ownership remains a major barrier to social and economic progress.

In sharply contrasting ways, both Japan and the United States were also critical factors in their development. Speaking of Korea, but in terms that could be applicable to Taiwan as well, Tony Michell notes, "For a country located close to Japan there can have been no more favorable time to enter the world economy than in the early 1960s. Japan had passed the 'turning point' in the labour market and companies were seeking to export labour-intensive manufacturing processes. In 1960 the various indirect barriers to trade with Japan were removed."[2]

Both Taiwan and Korea were once colonies of Japan. They thus shared the advantages of a relatively advanced infrastructure and educational system left over from the colonial period and proximity to Japan as a development model. Korean hostility toward Japan, in contrast to Taiwanese attitudes, coexists with an explicit adoption of Japanese economic experience and government and business methods.

Japan's continuing relationship with both countries is as a supplier. For both, the principal source of imports is Japan, which accounts for one-third of Taiwanese imports and over one-quarter of Korean imports. These consist of machinery items for the most part—the tools, parts, and subassemblies on which both economies depend to maintain their industrial output. At the same time, both countries place the most severe restrictions on imports from Japan. In disregard of any international conventions, Taiwan's government periodically publishes long lists of items prohibited or restricted from purchase from Japan, along with visa restrictions on Japanese offices in Taiwan wanting to bring staff in from headquarters.

Korea for its part also places elaborate limits on Japanese imports. A Japanese-made auto in Korea would be a rare item because the auto market is closed. For all of this, Korea is, after the United States, Japan's largest export market. The quality, price, and delivery of Japanese industrial goods overwhelm prejudice and preference. And so too with Taiwan. Cutting off key industrial purchases from Japan would quite simply cut off a good part of their industrial output, a problem experienced by the United States when members of Congress sought to eliminate Toshiba's access to the United States, only to find that too many producers depend on Japan to make the embargo feasible.

The effect of all this is that in recent years Japan has enjoyed considerable trade surpluses with Korea and Taiwan, about which both countries quite strenuously and futilely object. But their deficits with Japan have been largely balanced and funded by their own trade surpluses with

●

the United States: Taiwan continues to have a trade surplus with the United States, whereas Korea's has only lately diminished.

The importance of the United States in the development of Korea and Taiwan should not be underestimated. The United States supplied funds first through military and other aid programs, considering Taiwan and Korea on the frontiers of communism. As this funding decreased, the U.S. role as an absorber of goods increased. Through America's profligate 1980s both Korea and Taiwan benefitted massively from the U.S. appetite for goods and made significant contributions to the U.S. balance-of-payments deficit.

ACTIVIST GOVERNMENTS

In both Taiwan and Korea, following the Japanese model, the government played a major role in the initial stages of development, providing protection for infant industries, controlling fund allocations, initiating certain industries through direct government ownership, and generally providing direction to industrial development.[3]

Governments played critical roles in all of these Northeast Asian economies in the dangerous and formative period right after World War II. The nature and extent of government participation changed steadily and dramatically in Japan as the economy grew and changed, just as government's role is now changing in Taiwan and Korea to reflect their changing needs. An unsurprising conclusion is that growth is most rapid and effective when government plays a directing role in support of a strong private sector—the key, as is so often the case, is in the mix and in the timing of application of policy.

In a confession of the inadequate state of current analysis, a senior World Bank officer recently suggested, "The East Asian NICs and their successful emulators are a powerful argument that a more activist, positive governmental role can be a decisive factor in rapid industrial growth. An urgent task for the World Bank is to perform more research into East Asian approaches to trade and industrialization, including the experience of Japan. What is replicable and transferable must be brought to light and shared with others."[4]

Theories aside, much comes down to the roll of history's dice, it appears. "In the 1960s several conditions came together to produce at one and the same time relatively favorable access to industrial country markets, dramatically increased access to international finance, and increasing relocation of production by multinational corporations to low-wage sites. Location and geopolitical importance are also relevant. Hence part of the success of 'governed market' policies in East Asia is due to the favorable historical and international conditions in which they were implemented. To the extent that these factors are different at other times and places, this throws doubt on the possibilities for other countries at other times to emulate East Asian success."[5]

In the case of Taiwan and Korea, as with Japan, industrial success has brought with it ever higher labor costs; increasing labor shortages; escalating land prices, with environmental controls also contributing to factory costs; steadily appreciating currencies, making acquisition of foreign assets both desirable and less expensive; and trade surpluses that allow the funding of foreign investment. And now their economies are moving to new levels of sophistication in terms of technology and value-added products. Both economies are investing abroad, initially heavily in the United States to defend their market positions there from protectionism, but increasingly in Southeast Asia. However, here differences between the two economies are very great, as is discussed below.

DIVERGENT ECONOMIC STRUCTURES

The elements common to the success of Taiwan and Korea—external threat, domestic social upheaval, U.S. funding and markets, Japanese inheritance, technology and methods, the role of government—are diminishing rapidly in their importance as these economies become industrial powers with their own special interests and problems and as the two countries—in quite distinct geopolitical circumstances—move in different directions.

In contrast to Korea, Taiwan is not, for most governments and international agencies, a "country," but rather an economy. Owing to Chinese protests that "Taiwan and Hong Kong are not countries," Japan no longer refers to NICs—newly industrializing countries—but rather, to the NIEs—newly industrializing economies. Taiwan is an island of émigrés, largely Hokkien from what is now Fujian province in China,

•

though at the end of World War II, several millions came from other parts of the mainland, refugees and officials from the collapsed Kuomintang government. Taiwanese have known many masters over the centuries, so they arguably have no special sense of nation or separate cultural identity—in notable contrast to Koreans.

It seems likely that emigrant Chinese patterns and the small size of the Taiwanese economy have worked together to limit company size. The Taiwanese economy is made up of a great many very small businesses and very few large ones, as entrepreneurial and family-owned businesses are the modal types.[6] Perhaps refugees are more independent than settled citizens. Another explanation has been offered: "These smaller units of production, though based on the indigenous structure of Chinese/Taiwanese business, were encouraged by the Taiwanese government in a deliberate attempt to prevent alternative power centers, such as the *chaebol* in South Korea, from emerging. . . . In Taiwan, where 3 million mainlanders, holding political power, regulate the economic activities of 10 million Taiwanese, the government could not risk upsetting its power-base; the Korean government, whose power-base is more secure, had no need to diffuse the units of production."[7]

The difference is considerable and impacts the structure of the economy, resulting in more competitors in Taiwan, with a more limited capacity to penetrate large-scale, capital-intensive industries or undertake large R&D efforts—without substantial government support. Another characteristic of Taiwan is the small size of its domestic market, with a population of only 20 million. In considering the future direction of the Taiwanese economy, it is useful to think of the development of other smaller industrial nations—Sweden, Switzerland, the Netherlands. Taiwan shares their "small economy problem" and like them will find solutions through trade and investment abroad. (South Korea's 43 million, together with North Korea's 20 million, is a different sort of market.)

This small domestic platform is limiting in ways besides market size. Unemployment in Taiwan is barely over 1 percent, and laws are changing to allow immigration of labor despite the density of population. Land is scarce—and environmental pressures are building as air and water pollution truly foul Taiwan's cities. Continued growth is confidently forecast (the 1992–96 plan calls for 7 percent annual growth, which will likely be exceeded), but that growth will require accessing labor and land abroad to make more productive use of limited local resources.

Also of major significance is Taiwan's hugely favorable trade posi-

•

tion. In 1992 Taiwan managed to reach a total of $94 billion in foreign reserves, up from more than $80 billion in 1991. These are the highest levels of reserves, excluding gold, in the world. They have been built from enormous and continuing trade and current account surpluses. "In 1986 . . . the current account surplus had grown to nearly 20 percent of GDP—probably the largest current account share of GDP ever recorded, with the possible exception of some oil producers during the heyday of OPEC."[8]

It should also be noted that the Taiwanese economy has been on the whole quite open, especially to foreign investment. There has been a steady increase in foreign investment throughout the 1980s, first from Overseas Chinese and now from the United States and Japan. (see Appendix Table 8). Not only is this foreign investment now important as a potential source of technology imports, but it betokens a business community quite accustomed to open interaction in both trade and investment.

Taking all these characteristics into account—continuing high growth, a highly entrepreneurial private sector, rapidly increasing domestic costs with an appreciating currency, a drive to hold share in current markets while moving to more sophisticated products, a readiness to interact internationally, and above all an enormous supply of funds—it should be no surprise to find that the dominant theme in the Taiwanese economy today is overseas investment.

Taiwanese Outward Investment

Official Taiwanese government data indicate that total investment abroad increased about 40 times from 1985 to 1990, with the share to the United States falling from an initial level of 86 percent to 28 percent more recently. As with all Taiwanese foreign investment data, problems exist with these statistics in terms of understating Taiwanese flows to East Asian economies. Malaysia reports Taiwanese companies as having been the country's largest investors in the 1986–90 period, with a total for the five years of $1.4 billion, nearly a much as Taiwan reports as its total foreign investment.

Reports by the governments of Malaysia, Indonesia, and Thailand indicate that from a 1986 total of $26 million, Taiwanese direct invest-

•

ment had increased more than 85 times to $2.3 billion by 1990. Even with the tiny earlier numbers, Taiwan's total investment over the five years in these three economies was very much more than that of the United States, and about 40 percent that of the main investor, Japan. (see Appendix Table 9).

Still larger investment figures have finally recently been released by the Taiwanese government, reporting that a cumulative total of more than $12 billion has been invested in Southeast Asia by Taiwanese companies. Malaysia reports that the previous five years' total of $1.4 billion was matched in 1991. At the same time, Vietnam is the newest investment destination, with investment approvals there totaling more than $500 million in 1991.[9]

The impact of this rapidly increasing investment from a new source has been a major factor in the continued growth of the economies of Southeast Asia, as we see in Chapter 6. It is shaping the new circumstances that are making possible the rapid economic growth of the next group of East Asian economies. However, the need and capacity of Taiwanese companies to invest abroad has by no means been satisfied or exhausted by the wave of investment into the ASEAN economies. From 1990, Taiwan succumbed to "China fever."

"CHINA FEVER"

In the last four or five years, Taiwan's economy and that of the adjoining provinces of mainland China are fast becoming integrated, with flows of capital and technology overwhelming political barriers. The isolated and beleaguered small-island stage of Taiwan's progress is being left behind as "China fever" transforms both countries.

Technically, a state of war still exists between the Republic of China and the People's Republic of China. There are no direct shipping, aviation, or communications links between Taiwan and the mainland. Goods and people must move through third countries, and investment is, by law, required to move through firms registered in third countries—although all of these restrictions are under criticism and pressure for change. For all the restrictions, there has been a quite sudden and spectacular level of exchange between these presumed enemy territories.

An early move by Taiwan toward exchange, despite hostile relations,

•

was the lifting in late 1987 of the ban on family visits, provided the visits occurred through third areas. By 1992, in only four years, 4 million from the total Taiwanese population of 22 million had visited China for a variety of reasons, not least of them business. (The return flow from China to Taiwan, not surprisingly, has been rather less—perhaps 30,000.)

The driving forces are familiar—low-cost labor and land made highly accessible by the deep ties of kin and friends, language and customs that still bind the two sides of the Taiwan Strait. The small businesspeople of Taiwan, with an ever-stronger currency and cost pressures in their often low-technology businesses, have every reason to seek out associations, particularly in Fujian province.

For example, the Taiwanese company supplying Nike's footwear moved its production to a joint venture set up in Fujian. As a result, about 4,000 workers are now replacing the supply that previously came from Taiwan. "Indeed, Taiwan's footwear industry has moved virtually en masse to China. The industry association in Taipei estimated that by the end of 1991 some 400 of the grouping's 891 members had set up factories in China, employing about 100,000 workers. A further 200 had simply gone out of business. . . . The Taiwan Toy Manufacturers Association said that 70–80 of the island's toy makers had invested [in the mainland] and that most of the remaining 500 firms would eventually follow." [10] Taiwan's labor force will move to electronics, pharmaceuticals, and other higher value-added sectors, and will not be making toys or shoes.

Taiwan's economy, with its massive foreign reserves, permits the large flows of funds into China, and to ensure continued growth must move labor- and land-intensive businesses offshore. China, for its part, needs the employment opportunities these businesses represent. As a result, and despite the apparent political biases against investment, estimates are that a total of $3 billion has been invested in some 3,000 companies by Taiwanese firms moving to China in only three or four years. In the first half of 1992 alone, an additional $1.3 billion moved from Taiwan to China in direct investment, a threefold increase over the same period of the previous year, according to the Chinese government.

The Taiwanese government can and has blocked investment by large firms. As an example, the $7 billion petrochemical complex proposed for Xiamen by Formosa Plastics was vetoed by the government. However, it is simply not possible, even if desirable, to block the investments, often informal and unofficial, of Taiwan's many small and family-

●

owned businesses. It may well be that the actual investment flows are much greater than the official mainland announcements indicate and Hong Kong gossips would suggest. The flows in any case are sizable and are changing both economies profoundly.

The flows of trade are increasing as rapidly as the flows of capital, despite the fact that goods can flow—leaving aside smuggling—only indirectly between the two countries. The explosive increase in Hong Kong trade with China over the 1980s continues. What is less well appreciated is that a significant and increasing part is trade between China and Taiwan that flows through Hong Kong (see Table 5–2).

Taiwan's grandiose proposal to invest $300 billion over a six-year period in infrastructure, technology, and environment makes a good deal more sense—indeed, becomes imperative—if the economy is to leap forward into higher technologies and services. There is little time to make the transition. Taiwan must import technology, first by continuing to repatriate its U.S.- and Japanese-trained engineers and scientists. Second, it must encourage Japanese, American, and European firms to invest in Taiwan with technologies appropriate to Taiwan's higher cost/higher technology status. Third, it must invest its own funds in R&D as it proposes to do, despite the handicap imposed by the relatively small size of most of its business firms.

From the foreign firm's point of view, Taiwan is now an alternative to Japan as an East Asian site for sophisticated product development and manufacture. It is also an interesting option for moving into the mainland market through a Taiwan-supported Fujian base. The perception of

Table 5–2   Chinese Trade with Hong Kong and Taiwan

	1980 ($ billion)	1991 ($ billion)	Annual Growth Rate, 1980–91 (percent)
Hong Kong trade with China	5.7	64.5	11.4
Of which, China–Taiwan trade via Hong Kong	0.3	5.8	18.2

Source: Data from a report by Fuji Research Institute Corp. on p. 11 of *Fuji Times*, October 1992. Both Fuji Research Institute Corp, and *Fuji Times* are subsidiaries of Fuji Bank, Tokyo.

•

Taiwan as economically fragile is obsolete, as is the view of Taiwan as a source of efficient, low-rate labor.

Concerns over Taiwan's political stability will no doubt persist, fed from time to time by reminders of its independent sovereignty, such as the purchase of F-16s from the United States weapons of course aimed at the mainland. Taiwanese policy will no doubt continue to be a Hegelian interaction between integration with the mainland and complete independence as a nation in its own right. The outcome of the Hong Kong experience of integration with China will be watched with great interest. Taiwanese identity will be used increasingly in all manner of international meetings from sports events to Asian Development Bank conferences. And the course of political events in the mainland itself will be critical. But with all of the economic integration that is increasingly driving both systems, sudden breaks in pattern are very unlikely. Rather, a slow and extended process of rapproachment seems likely, as evidenced by the "one country, two governments" formulation offered recently by Taiwan.[11]

DRAMATIC POSTWAR GROWTH
IN KOREA

The economic growth of Korea has been even more dramatic than that of Taiwan. The Korean War meant that Korea's starting point was later and even more impoverished than Taiwan's a decade earlier: "In 1960 the Republic of Korea had a per capita income of $82 (current). This approximates to estimates of the Japanese per capita income in 1868 (at 1960 prices). The industrial structure, in terms of industry's share in the GNP and of the labor force corresponded to that of Japan in 1900 or of England as far back as 1700."[12]

From the $80 per capita GNP of 1960's 25 million Koreans, the economy had grown to $6,500 per capita GNP for 43 million Koreans, at current prices by 1991. A $2 billion economy had in a bit more than a generation become a $280 billion economy. "The year 1992 marks the beginning of Korea's Seventh Five-Year Plan under which the growth rate of GNP is projected to be 7.5 percent per annum . . . At this rate of growth, Korea's GNP at current prices will be $493 billion in 1996, making it probably by then one of the 15 largest economies in the world."[13]

•

Korea is reckoned now to have the world's fourth-largest textile industry, second-largest shipbuilding industry, seventh-largest steel industry, ninth-largest auto industry, and third-largest semiconductor industry. Focusing on exports to drive growth, Korea, like Taiwan, increased its exports over the last three decades at rates three times and more the world averages (see Table 5–3). Like Taiwan, Korea trades even more than China and such highly developed economies as Sweden.

Korea's market displays the changes as well. "With an average annual urban household income of $19,000, the Korean market looks attractive. The French fashion magazine *Elle* has licensed a Korean-language edition. British-owned Haagen-Dazs is setting up premium ice cream shops in the affluent sections of Seoul despite the high cost of land. Convenience stores, many of them under license from Japanese concerns, are starting to effect [retailing] change. The number should double in 12 months."[14] Affluence reaches the Korean peninsula.

The parallels of Korea's development to that of Taiwan, and by somewhat strained extension to those of Hong Kong and Singapore, have been widely noted. They include the factors discussed above—limited resources, dense and homogeneous population, urgent external threat, U.S. military and economic support, Japanese colonial inheritance and Japanese model and support, high values on education, strong government, and Confucian values. "There is a consensus that the Confucian culture, the high desire for education, the homogeneity of the nation and the status according to government officials have been of great assistance to the development of the Republic of Korea. However, if successful development had not taken place, it would have been possible to account for this [failure] by an equally relevant set of characteristics,

Table 5–3   **Trade Growth, 1965–90 Taiwan and Korea (percent per annum)**

	Exports		Imports	
	1965–80	**1980–90**	**1965–80**	**1980–90**
Taiwan	18.9	12.1	15.1	10.1
Korea	27.2	12.8	15.2	10.8
World	6.6	4.3	4.6	4.5

Source: The World Bank, *World Development Report* (New York: Oxford University Press, 1992), pp. 244–45.

●

including revenue for farming in an overpopulated country, the emphasis on learning by rote in education, emphasis on personal prestige rather than economic ability, and over-bureaucratic minds."[15]

Whatever conclusions might finally be reached concerning the complex causes of Asian economic development—and the answers still seem largely unsatisfactory—it is clear that the continued grouping of the disparate economies of East Asia into categories like "dragons" and "tigers" has become actively misleading. As these economies of East Asia have achieved economic success, the differences become plain. Korea has a clear and powerful national identity—a very long history with its own heroes and villains, legends and literature, its own traditions of art, cuisine, and architecture. Korea is a continental nation of beef eaters, with physiques like the other peoples of the great Asian land mass. Korea's business is not led by émigrés from China. Instead, Koreans have emigrated to China and form a sizable minority group in that country.

Comparisons of nations and economies can be very misleading. For example, it has been said on occasion that Korea is a second Japan. Of course, it is not. It is a first Korea and in no fashion a pale reproduction of Japan, however much it may draw on Japan's example for planning and organization. Nor is it a dragon or tiger, to be grouped with the small populations of Taiwan, Hong Kong, and Singapore, each in a somewhat different way an island of Chinese émigrés and descendants with little history or identity as separate nations. Korea as a nation will seek and establish its own destiny, while the destiny of the Chinese islands will be determined in good part by modern China. Looking at the direction in which the government and economy of Korea appear to be moving, we see it is evident that Korea must be considered in its own right from the perspective of international business planning.

THE *CHAEBOL* AS ENGINES
OF GROWTH

A first characteristic of the Korean economy that sets it apart from Taiwan is the degree of concentration of industry in a few very large groups of companies, family-founded and largely family-controlled, called *chaebol*. The founding entrepreneurs generally came from small business and retailing backgrounds, and received government support and fund-

•

ing as their companies became the chosen instruments for economic growth in the 1960s. The precise number of *chaebol* is uncertain, because the term can in fact refer to any large company with subsidiaries. Legislation in 1992 singled out 30 of the biggest *chaebol* for credit restrictions to promote specialization of the groups' investments, so perhaps 30 will serve as an approximation of their number.

The largest are Hyundai and Samsung, estimated by Fortune to have had sales in 1991 of $51 billion and $49 billion, respectively. These are hard estimates to come by because the *chaebol* include a great many companies and, in turn, those companies' subsidiaries. In the case of Hyundai some 30 companies are in the first line of organization, 14 publicly traded. Because they are not consolidated, sales totals are necessarily unconsolidated estimates. Undaunted, Fortune states that the top five, including Lucky-Goldstar, Daewoo, and Sunkyong, with Samsung and Hyundai, "account for nearly 62 percent of GNP."[16]

The *chaebol,* with government support, have achieved scale that has allowed them to compete internationally with the world's major companies in many industries. They command the kinds of cash flows that allow major investments, and thus, for example, Samsung, arguably the most professionally managed of the *chaebol,* is a leader in the enormously capital-intensive manufacture of megabit semiconductors. Hyundai's efforts in autos are well known and include investment in plants abroad to deal with increased protectionism. So with Lucky-Goldstar and Samsung in consumer electronics, with investments in Europe, Mexico, and China as well as the United States in order to be positioned to compete worldwide.

The scale of the *chaebol* also provides capacity to invest substantially in R&D. Korean success has been built on imported technology—as was Japan's growth, but autonomous research and development will be increasingly a requisite for continued advances in productivity and wealth.

As the *chaebol* must get credit for a major role in Korea's success, so they must take blame for weaknesses and problems in the Korean industrial structure. A substantial problem is political, owing to the extreme concentration of economic power that the *chaebol* and their present ownership present. Although Korea has a capital market of increasing scale and open access, the government reports that the 61 largest groups (with at least $550 million in assets) have sold shares to the public of only about 250 of nearly 1,000 affiliated companies. Not surprising, controlling families yield control grudgingly and their power invites political attack.

Perhaps the problem will be solved as the founders pass from the scene, as interests within owning families diverge. The longer-established *chaebol*—Samsung and Lucky-Goldstar, for example—are now into their second generation in top management and have increased nonfamily professional management. Interest in diversifying family holdings, plus the need for large inputs of capital for continued growth, will push more *chaebol* shares onto the public market and mitigate criticism of concentration of ownership.

BRAKES ON DEVELOPMENT

The *chaebol* are, however, both symbol and cause of some rather basic problems in the Korean economy that are steadily becoming more severe. Korean companies make up half of the 100-largest companies in East and Southeast Asia in terms of sales, and 9 of the top 10.[17] But the economy lacks that deep and diverse base of middle-sized and smaller companies that provide the flexibility and creativity that characterize in much greater degree the Chinese-based NIEs of Asia—Taiwan, Hong Kong,a nd Singapore.

Korean firms must look to Japanese suppliers for critical parts and subassemblies—engines for automobiles, recording heads for VTRs, magnetrons for microwave ovens, circuitry for PCs. Indeed, a good deal of the value added in goods from Korea is in fact of Japanese origin, assembled in Korea by the companies of the *chaebol*.

Taiwan has few giant corporations. But it has a great many smaller firms, focussed on niche businesses rather than mass production, seeking to compensate for lack of scale and capital through quick reaction times and ingenuity. The emphasis on scale made it possible to drive the Korean economy to a strong position in heavy industry—steel, shipbuilding, petrochemicals, and the like. It leaves the economy at a disadvantage as growth in these sectors slows and as profits in these heavy industries erode. Japan's industrial winners have not been the *zaibatsu* companies' successors. They have been the Hondas, Canons, Sonys, Toyotas—the highly innovative upstarts of the postwar period, and it is these that have driven Japan's success. Korea needs now to find ways of nurturing independence in a massively oligarchic system.

Indeed, the *chaebol* are a symbol of a more basic Korean characteris-

●

tic: "The Korean government has a more centralized management structure, which assigns precedence in industrial policy to the Ministry of Trade and Industry and the Economic Planning Board. Top officials of these agencies can exercise broad control from a single position, acting through command hierarchies and relating to business groups as leaders rather than equals. The Taiwan government, on the other hand, is less centralized, with power over industrial policy issues dispersed amongst more ministries and agencies. Officials have a narrower scope for the exercise of their authority, and use it more circumspectly in their dealings with private firms."[18] Korea's has been more a command economy than Taiwan's, with the strengths and weaknesses that must go with heavy central control.

It is perhaps inevitable that a controlled system will be on the whole a closed one. Again in contrast to the Sino-states among the NIEs, Korean limits on imports and foreign investment have been severe—and are becoming a disadvantage. In trade terms, a single example will perhaps convey the situation. The Korean auto market is more than twice as large as that of Taiwan and continues to grow rapidly. There are no auto imports into Korea and only three passenger car producers. Imports make up one-quarter of the Taiwan market, and there are seven local producers. Arguably Korea is better positioned to have a world-competitive industry, but clearly Taiwan's is the more open and domestically competitive.

Foreign investment in Korea is similarly limited. About half of total foreign direct investment is from Japan and nearly one-third from the United States, for a total of three-quarters from these two countries with which Korea has a "special relationship." Foreign investment in Korea continues to be very limited, in 1990 about one-quarter of the flow into Taiwan. Foreign direct investment is an insignificant part of Korea's plant and equipment investment, now and historically (see Table 5–4). In most of East and Southeast Asia, however, foreign investment is actively encouraged and is a major source of plant and equipment funding. U.S. and Japanese companies in some numbers found it necessary to withdraw from Korea as conditions became increasingly difficult.

The problem this poses for Korea, aside from bad press and awkward negotiations, is difficulty in accessing foreign technology. The Koreans are the first to complain that the Japanese withhold technology. They choose not to note that technology tends to flow with investment, and that Taiwan seems to experience fewer problems in attracting new tech-

●

Table 5–4   **Foreign Direct Investment as Percent of Total**
Plant and Equipment Investment, 1985 and 1990

	1985	1990
Korea	2.0	0.9
Taiwan	6.0	6.7
Hong Kong	28.2	21.3
Singapore	5.4	9.3
Thailand	9.8	51.1
Malaysia	4.1	46.6
Indonesia	4.3	18.8★
Philippines	2.7	11.2

Note: Hong Kong, Singapore, and Malaysia manufacturing only.
★1989.

Source: Data from "Sekai to Nihon no Kaigai Chokusetsu Toshi," annual report of Japan External Trade Organization (JETRO), (Tokyo: January 1992), p. 47.

nologies. The government of Korea does encourage licensing, but with Korea's economic success, licensing is seen as risking creating future competition. There are about 700 cases annually of technology transfer to Korea, the largest number from Japan, followed by the United States. As with foreign investment, these two economies supply three-quarters of the total transfers. By comparison with the annual flows of 2,000 or more cases into Japan, the Korean totals are in fact small.

The issue is of special importance as the Korean economy attempts to restructure through new technology. Here too, industrial concentration and central control may be a factor in limited technology development. It appears that Taiwanese residents apply for and get five times as many patents in the United States as do Korean residents. It seems likely that Taiwan's smaller, more flexible firms, seeking out sectors of competitive advantage, do in fact produce more technology of value than is produced in Korea's much larger but more ponderous economy.[19]

Perhaps these differences come together to help create what is now the largest difference between Korea and the Sino-NIEs and the principal reason why grouping these economies together is very misleading— the huge differences in trade performance of these economies. Korea's total foreign reserves of about $15 billion are equal to Taiwan's trade surplus in a single year. Taiwan's foreign exchange reserves of $80 to $90 billion make it, after Japan, the world's most important source of new

•

capital. It bids to become a Switzerland of East Asia, as the economy shifts manufacturing offshore and focuses on services, especially financial services. Taiwan has the resources to launch massive infrastructure investments while at the same time becoming the largest investor in East Asia, after Japan.

From 1986 to 1990, while Korea invested a total of $2.15 billion in Indonesia, Thailand, Malaysia, and the Philippines, Taiwan invested nearly $6.50 billion. Japan's total was more than $16 billion, with the U.S. total less than Taiwan's, at $4 billion. This money means influence and access to raw materials and low-priced labor. Korea lags badly. After a brief period in the late 1980s of trade surplus, the Korean economy has returned substantial deficits in the 1990s, and annual deficits on the order of $7 billion to $8 billion threaten to continue.

What are the problems after so great a success? One is in the very structure that made for success—the focus on heavy industry and the forced feeding of very large corporations. The loss of flexibility has been costly. With success the won has appreciated, hurting export prices, and the long-suffering Korean work force in the late 1980s, finally, lost its patience and demanded a fair—at least increased—share of the fruits of its labor. Despite management and government efforts to suppress them, strikes were widespread, and wages rose 15 to 20 percent annually in 1988, 1989, and 1990. The long emphasis on exports has also left a pent-up domestic demand that has found some satisfaction from increased imports, as U.S. pressure has helped open the domestic market.

It is important not to overstate. The Korean economy is today one of the world's fastest-growing economies. It is a massive trader, as export growth again exceeds import growth. The *chaebol* are formidable economic machines and will thrust forward into electronics, aerospace, and new materials. However, the economy is now facing another restructuring period, as do all rapidly expanding economies periodically.

NORTHEAST ASIA AS AN ECONOMIC CENTER

Korea, to repeat, is a continental economy, a nation. It is not a Sino-culture or society, despite its profound cultural links with China's past. Korea is part of Northeast Asia and sees itself as a major power in the

region and the world. It is in all these respects very different from the
Sino-NIEs.

New patterns of relations are developing in fluid and fast-changing
Northeast Asia. First, and most critical, Korea and China have entered
into full diplomatic relations; Korea ignores the distress of Taiwan at this
step. The reasons for the overture to China are quite clear. China seeks
the kind of investments in Shandong province and in its northeast provinces that only Korea (and Japan) can provide. Korea can be the engine
to start development in those areas in the way that Hong Kong and Taiwan have been the engines for Guangdong's and Fujian's development.
Investments in China doubled in 1991 over 1990, even before diplomatic relations were established.

Relations have also been established with the Russians, whose president in his turn ignored his presumed allies in North Korea in seeking
funds and offering military technology, among other things, to the South
Koreans. Korean business has already seen an opportunity to outflank the
Japanese by pressing forward with relations with the Russians, while the
Japanese continue to hold back from a rapprochement with them. There
are Korean joint ventures already in the Russian Far East and more are
being negotiated.

In contrast to Taiwan, facing south and toward China, Korea seems
aimed at building a national space in Asia's northeast. It seems consistent
with this to expect Japan and Korea to seek ways of building a better
relationship, as memories dim and new priorities develop.

The overriding question about the future of Korea remains, however, that of unification. It is quite impossible to read the minds of the
North and its leaders. But the South seems confident now and determined to push ahead on a phased integration. The German example is at
hand—but one must remember that East Germany never invaded or
devastated West Germany, so the analogue can be drawn only with caution. Emotions are not entirely parallel in the two cases.

In any event, a staged process seems likely: trade across the border,
flows of goods, carefully screened flows of people, investment, then
what? There are two obvious preoccupations, at least on the part of the
South: one, the political hazard of integrating 22 million of what appear
to be brainwashed automatons into the brawling democracy that the
South is becoming; two, the economic hazards of integrating very different economies, as has been dramatically demonstrated by the German
experience. Still, these are one people who share a common history, lan-

•

guage, and geographical space. The combined population of 65 million would comprise a large nation indeed, with the mining, hydropower, and heavy industry of the North, together with the modern industries and finance of the South.

Unification of the two Koreas will certainly take place. The great worry is whether North Korea can manage peacefully the transition from Kim Il Sung and continue moving toward a détente with the South. This worry is made greater by fears of nuclear armaments developments by the North. There could be a rough passage to unification. Still, the North is without allies, as even the Russians have swept past them to offer military technology to the South and the Chinese have entered into diplomatic relations with the South. Without allies, without foreign exchange, in a stagnant and even retrogressing economy, the North has no future without the South.

There are real issues for South Korea as well in its current positioning as a Northeast Asian continental power. As South Korea looks around, it sees North Korea on one flank—no help or support there. Russia might have been a market and supply source—but it offers little hope for some years of serving as economic hinterland for Korea. The parts of China abutting Korea are by no means the most populous or prosperous. And relations with Japan, which might well bolster the Korean position through trade and investment, are awkward at best.

Korea is in a cul-de-sac in a way. While cash-rich Taiwan has the entire South China regional economy to exploit in furthering its future growth, Korea has no equivalent now or in the near future. Perhaps unification will provide the arena for a release of capital and technology to build a twenty-first-century power.

For the foreign firm, Korea continues to present major problems as an investment site. Direct investment in Korea has never been great, only a fraction of the amounts from abroad that have been invested in the other economies of East Asia. Alone in East Asia, Korea makes little effort to appeal to foreign investors and often makes a considerable effort to add to investors' difficulties. Not surprising than that in 1992, with a slowed economy, foreign investment in Korea dropped by a third while disinvestment increased five fold.

"Over the past two years, some of the world's biggest multinationals . . . have abandoned plans to build . . . facilities in Korea or terminated existing joint ventures. The exodus could make Korea the first big loser in Asia's increasingly competitive bidding for outside capital and tech-

●

nology. Foreign businessmen have tolerated Korea's contorted, opaque regulations only for the sake of its highly trained, educated work force. But viable alternatives are now mushrooming throughout Asia."[20]

Korea is a major market, still rapidly growing. However, the nation is both by policy and by position to one side of the main directions of East Asian development. The contrast with Taiwan in policies toward foreign investment, in positioning as a platform for involvement in the great changes in East Asia, and in attractiveness as an investment site could hardly be greater. Only major Korean policy changes toward integrating with the world economy and the rest of East Asia are likely to restore Korea to an economic position of interest in the larger strategic concerns of the world's major corporations.

6
•

THE CHALLENGE OF SOUTHEAST ASIA

The great tide of economic growth that has carried Japan to world industrial leadership and has, in turn, swept Korea and Taiwan onto the path to economic power and wealth, is now reaching Southeast Asia. The entry of these economies into the arena of world trade and the concurrent growth of their markets to competitively significant size make East Asia now critical to international competitive success.

Southeast Asia includes the members of the Association of Southeast Asian Nations (ASEAN), which is made up of Singapore, Indonesia, Malaysia, the Philippians, Thailand, and the principality of Brunei. Vietnam and Laos are moving to become full members of the group, with Cambodia and Myanmar (Burma) still isolated.

The pattern of the area is that of Asia generally, large populations with low levels of income. The population of the five major ASEAN members total well over 300 million, or about that of the European Community, while the total GNP of the five nations totals only a little over $300 billion, or not very much more than that of Australia, with a population of less than 20 million. Average per capita GNP for Southeast Asia is therefore only about $1,000 (see Table 6–1).

In population size alone, the nations of the region are very diverse.

●

Table 6–1   **Southeast Asia Population and GNP,**
                  1991 and 2000

Country	Population[1] (million)		GNP[2] ($ billion)	GNP per Capita[2] ($)
	1991	2000	1990	1990
Indonesia	186	209	107	570
Malaysia	18	22	42	2,230
Philippines	63	74	44	730
Thailand	57	64	80	1,420
Singapore	3	4	35	11,160
Total	327	373	308	

Source: Data from Asian Development Bank, *Asian Development Outlook 1992* (Hong Kong: Oxford University Press, 1992), p. 313; The Word Bank, *World Development Report 1992* (New York: Oxford University Press, 1992), pp. 218–19.

At one extreme, Indonesia is the fourth most populous nation on earth with a population expected to reach 200 million within this decade, whereas Singapore, a city-state, has a total population of less than 3 million. Both Thailand and the Philippines have populations on the order of the European nations, around 60 million each. Malaysia, by contrast, includes fewer than 20 million people, a population size similar to that of Taiwan; its government policy is aimed at increasing the population, because its relative size is seen as an economic handicap.

In economic size, the range is also very great among these ASEAN countries—Indonesia and the Philippines are at the low levels associated with developing countries, while Thailand and Malaysia are achieving NIC status, as newly industrializing countries, taking their places beside Korea and Taiwan. Singapore stands as an island of wealth, operating at European levels of output and income, one of what the World Bank calls "high-income economies."

There are other sources of great diversity among the nations of ASEAN. The religion of Indonesia and Malaysia is Islam, and Thailand is Buddhist, Singapore eclectic, and the Philippines devoutly Roman Catholic. Singapore is largely Chinese, its neighbors Malay. The colonial experience of the ASEAN countries was variously Dutch, British, and American, with Thailand a rare case of freedom from Western imperial control. Thailand has a king and Malaysia its sultans; problems of succession to leadership exist in much of the area.[1]

Along with this diversity, these nations were long seen as economically competitive with one another, producing similar products, with economies based on agriculture and extractive industries—tin, oil, nickel, and the like. Each had surplus low-cost labor and sought foreign investment with similar programs.

THE MOVE TO A REGIONAL
ECONOMIC GROUP

Against this background of social and political diversity and economic competitiveness it is not surprising that the concept of ASEAN as an economically integrated grouping of these states was received with a

•

good deal of skepticism. Founded in 1967, for many years it acted more as a political grouping than an economic one, held together in part by a common concern over the situation in Vietnam and Cambodia. Trade barriers between the ASEAN nations were only modestly reduced.

Two great forces are now working to bring the nations of Southeast Asia together into an integrated economic area. The first is the astonishing and unexpected economic growth of these countries in general, and the second is the larger world context in which the ASEAN countries now find themselves.

From the mid-1960s through the 1970s, the economies of Southeast Asia grew at an average real rate of more than 7 percent per annum, doubling in the first decade and redoubling again. Growth slowed somewhat in the 1980s to slightly over 5 percent but is expected to continue at a 6 to 7 percent rate over the next two decades (see Appendix Table 10).

For the region three main factors are at work driving growth. First these are new nations, relatively free of entrenched special interests, with increasingly competent governments focused on encouraging economic growth through savings and investment. Drawing on the experiences of the economies of Northeast Asia, these governments look to support growth through export trade rather than through protectionism and import substitution.

Second, there are continuing massive flows of capital and technology into these economies, from Northeast Asia especially, as Japan, Korea, and Taiwan recycle trade surpluses through capital exports, and as Japanese, Korean, and Taiwanese companies seek raw material sources, less costly land, and cheaper labor supplies to support their continued growth. The appreciation of the currencies of the economies of the Northeast reinforces these flows.

Third, with rising levels of education and with savings accumulations, a risk-taking entrepreneurial class has made its appearance in the region, made up largely of Overseas Chinese, who have provided the spark for domestic growth by building business structures that take advantage of the favorable political and economic environments to create a vigorous private sector, replacing and going far beyond earlier colonial businesses.

With these great changes in the economic performance of the area, there has been as well great change in the larger environment of these

●

economies. The developed countries, key export markets for these nations, have been moving rapidly to organize trading areas, as the EC moves to greater integration and the North American Free Trade Area (NAFTA) has been negotiated. There is a real concern in the area that these economies will be excluded from the benefits of global free trade and from the flows of foreign direct investment. NAFTA especially is seen as a competitor for Northeast Asian direct investment as local content and other exclusionary rules make investment in Mexico and the United States necessary to obtain market access.

At the same time as these world trade areas take shape and pose problems of access, the increasing importance of a fast-growing China is becoming an issue as well. China presents a very large potential market, greater than each of the markets of these nations separately and a low labor cost investment site competitive with each of these nations.

Thus as the GATT-based world trade system is in some trouble and as potentially exclusive trading areas form, ASEAN's members find that they need to plan to group to achieve needed negotiating strength relative to other original groupings like the EC and NAFTA. These are, after all, small economies, taken individually. Even together they account for slightly over 1 percent of the world economy, rising toward 2 percent as the early 2000s approach—only about one-tenth the economy of Japan. It is not surprising then that the ASEAN grouping should be proposed as a way to improve negotiating position in world trade discussions and to achieve economic scale and importance that is not possible for each nation acting separately.

Thus, the meaning of ASEAN is deepening. In 1992, the member countries announced the AFTA program, the ASEAN Free Trade Arrangement, with the goal of reducing tariffs on manufactured goods to a maximum of 5 percent by 2008, 15 years from the 1993 starting date. A group of products, including such important categories as chemicals and electronics, are to receive "accelerated tariff reduction" through earlier action.

This is a high-tariff region. Thailand has average tariffs of 44 percent, the Philippines 26 percent, Indonesia 22 percent, and Malaysia 16 percent.[2] It is not surprising then to find that the AFTA program has escape clauses and provisions for delay. Still, the agreement is a critical first step in creating a free-trade zone in Southeast Asia parallel to the zone in North America and the creation of a wider European Economic Area.

•

Both the solid economic progress and success of the economies of Southeast Asia and the needs of these nations in international affairs are driving them together toward a massive new economic zone of their own.

GROWTH, A RECENT PHENOMENON

The question of why these nations quite suddenly and unexpectedly began to grow so rapidly has no simple answer. A great many factors are at work over the region as a whole and in each of the individual nations concerned. Perhaps the most important factor is that growth is a recent phenomenon, only one generation old. It was in 1965 that Singapore separated from Malaysia to become, reluctantly, an independent state. The failed coup in Indonesia in 1965 ended the Sukarno era as Suharto moved to power and began a new era in Indonesian economics. In the Philippines, Marcos took office that same year. The second Indochina war, with the United States as the main actor, began in 1965, and ASEAN was first organized in 1967.

Thus we can see that a concatenation of great events took place in the mid 1960s, at the same time that Japan's double-digit GNP growth was resulting in trade surpluses and Korea began its drive to industrialization. The emergence of new governments and indeed new nations, the massive intrusion of the United States into the area, and the beginning of Japanese involvement all coincided in a very short period. These events need not have resulted in an economic success story, however, for all of their impact on the region.

At a fundamental level, the region's economic growth serves as another example of the thesis advanced by Mancur Olson regarding the rise of nations. Excepting Thailand (every Southeast Asian rule seems to have an exception), all these nations have been established after a long period of colonial rule—witness the Dutch in Indonesia fighting a bitter retreat in the late 1940s; the British in Singapore/Malaysia yielding with some grace to the inevitable in the 1950s; and the United States's partial withdrawal from the Philippines.

It is the brief of Olson that growth is most rapid after a period of great discontinuity and instability during which established hierarchies and power centers are destroyed. "Countries whose distributional coalitions have been emasculated or abolished by totalitarian government or

•

foreign occupation should grow relatively quickly after a free and stable legal order is established. This can explain the postwar 'economic miracles' in the nations that we defeated in World War II. . . . Countries that have had democratic freedom of organization without upheaval or invasion the longest will suffer most from growth-repressing organizations and combinations. This helps explain why Great Britain, the major nation with the longest immunity from dictatorship, invasion, and revolution has had in this century a lower rate of growth than other large, developed democracies."[3]

FACTORS IN GROWTH: TRADE

As Olson hastens to point out, however, release from established structures and special interests in itself does not make for growth but only offers the opportunity. In the case of Southeast Asia, a general openness to trade has clearly been another important factor. The importance of exports for these economies is often noted; their export orientation contrasts with the import substitution policies that were popular with developmental economists for a long time and that helped prevent the growth of economies like that of India. Following the clear and powerful examples of Korea and Taiwan, the nations of Southeast Asia have generally focused instead on export stimulation.

With success, as Table 6–2 makes clear. The ASEAN economies account for a disproportionate share of world trade. Although their total economic size is about 1.2 percent of the world economy, they account for about twice that share of world exports. Singapore and Hong Kong as entrepôts have multiples of their GDP in trade, as goods flow through their economies to other destinations. The other economies of Southeast Asia increased their exports at double-digit rates in the late 1980s, and except for the Philippines, this kind of rapid export growth is expected to continue. These are export-led economies but, that being said, it must also be noted that imports into all these nations have grown as rapidly. Thus, they are no less markets than they are market suppliers.

Perhaps the region is best described as relatively open to trade, both exports and imports, in contrast to most developing areas. In the late 1980s, exports grew by nearly 20 percent annually and imports by nearly 30 percent. Interestingly, exports to the United States, Japan, the Asian

●

Table 6–2   **Export Growth Rates, 1985–2000 (Percent, Real)**

	1985 to 1990	1990 to 2000
Japan	2.7	2.1
Singapore	16.8	11.7
Hong Kong	18.2	10.8
Taiwan	18.6	10.0
Korea	8.9	7.8
Malaysia	16.4	13.3
Thailand	20.6	13.3
Philippines	11.5	5.4
Indonesia	11.4	10.0
China	18.3	12.5
World	5.2	4.7

Source: From Tetsuo Adachi, "Arata na Furonteia no Hatten ga Ajia no Jizokuteki Seicho wo Unagasu," *Toyo Keizai Sokei Geppo* (Tokyo), May 1, 1992, p. 18.

NIEs, and the EC each measured about 20 percent of the total, a remarkable dispersion and balance of risk across markets.

Still, the United States has been a major source of cash, as the U.S. trade balance with ASEAN has stayed heavily in the red, as has the trade balance of the EC. The moneys gained from the surpluses with Europe and the United States have—no surprise— gone largely to Japan, which is much the largest supplier to the area. Just as growth is furthered by exports, so growth requires machinery, parts, and equipment that come principally from Japan, helped by the fact that Japanese direct investment in the area also pulls in plant and equipment from Japan.

FACTORS IN GROWTH: FOREIGN INVESTMENT

Foreign direct investment has also been an important driver of growth in these economies, which have on the whole been open. The one exception is Indonesia, which was rather restrictive of foreign investment but, since about 1989, has moved rapidly to deregulation. The amount of direct investment in these countries from abroad in recent years has been considerable, as has been the rate of increase, more than five times in five

●

years. Although the rate of growth will no doubt slow or even stop because of the world economic slowdown, a continuation of high investment patterns in this region seems a certainty, given the increasing appreciation of its importance and potential.

The first wave of direct investment in Southeast Asia was the result of the need for raw materials, first on the part of Japan, then in turn Korea and Taiwan, which encouraged investment, particularly in Indonesia. This was, however, very much in the traditional fashion of investment in extractive industries, with little impact on the overall economy of the host country—witness the positions of the international oil majors in the area, with little follow-on impact.

The breakthrough on foreign investment came with the massive yen revaluation/dollar devaluation of 1985–86, when Japan was already experiencing labor shortages that were propelling investment abroad in search of less expensive labor. The doubling of the value of the yen against the U.S. dollar had a compounding effect. Japanese export prices rose as foreign assets were suddenly inexpensive, while Japanese labor continued in short supply at ever-increasing prices. At the same time, a continuing massive surplus in the trade account created a need to recycle that surplus, again encouraging investment abroad.

To compound the effect, Korea and Taiwan, with a time lag, underwent much the same experience on a somewhat smaller scale. Their currencies began to appreciate and they were in a position of trade surplus; Taiwan, in particular, seemed to sink under the weight of its dollar surplus, which equaled that of Germany or Japan. Both countries, but Taiwan more acutely, encountered a domestic labor shortage and rising wage levels, and both are poor in raw materials, another spur to investment. So throughout Northeast Asia the need and capacity for investment abroad was considerable.

The results are evident. East Asian investment is now an East Asian matter. The United States as a source of investment in Southeast Asia now ranks fourth in importance, after Japan, of course, but also after Korea, Taiwan, and Hong Kong or Singapore, depending on the recipient country. (See Appendix Table 11.) As an example of the sourcing of funds, foreign direct investment in Malaysia in the 1989–91 period totaled more than M$15 billion (about US$5.6 billion). The largest source was Taiwan, supplying one-third of the total; then Japan, with one-quarter; and the rest of East Asia, nearly one-fifth. Britain, its long-time colonial master, supplied only 5 percent of the total, as did the United States.[4]

•

The large flows of foreign investment into the economies of Southeast Asia have steadily moved toward the lower-wage level economies. The shift of labor-intensive manufacturing—shoes and simple textiles, for example—steadily southward to, now, Indonesia, is in response to changing wage levels and the search for cheaper but still effective labor supplies. It is noteworthy too that with Indonesian wage levels a bit higher than those in parts of China, there is concern that some of the Korean and Taiwanese investments will move to China away from Indonesia, a considerable worry to the Indonesian authorities (see Table 6–3).

This line from north to south in East Asia has been the growth line, the line along which investment has been moving, and the line along which wage rates move down as well. Put more positively, a virtuous cycle of investment and output growth is working to pull wages up progressively throughout East Asia.

FACTORS IN GROWTH: SAVINGS

Foreign direct investment, like trade, is a critical factor in facilitating economic growth. It pales in importance, however, next to domestic savings and investment when domestic savings reach significant levels. Savings rates are something of an economic mystery: in mature economies there

Table 6–3   Monthly Wages in East Asia, 1991
(US$, change from 1990 in paren.)

	Wages of General Workers
Singapore	$615–846 (8–10%)
Hong Kong	$769–1,000 (10–15%)
Taiwan	$639–1,231 (7–21%)
Korea (starting salaries)	$515 (17%)
Malaysia	$208 (8–12%)
Thailand	$162 (5–6%)
Philippines	$123 (2.7%)
Indonesia	$54–77 (19%)
China-Beijing	$39 (12%)
China-Shanghai	$54–77 (10–15%)

Source: Reprinted from "Labor Costs Rising Throughout Asia," *The Nihon Keizai Shimbun/The Nikkei Weekly* (Tokyo), November 30, 1991, p. 3.

•

seem to be characteristic levels of savings that persist over a long time. Thus Japan, not a notable saver pre–World War II, has very high savings levels that have not much diminished with economic prosperity. Similarly, Germany has high savings rates, with France not far behind, while savings rates in Britain and America are very low—and go far to explain the economic problems of those two countries.

Savings in Southeast Asia have moved very rapidly to high levels (see Appendix Table 12). The remarkable level of gross savings at 46 percent of GDP for Singapore is explained in good part by the compulsory savings system—Singapore's Provident Fund—which solves the problem by taking the money before the wage earner can spend it. That does not, however, explain the high rates in Indonesia, Thailand, and Malaysia, all now twice or more U.S. savings levels and dramatically increased over mid-1960s levels. Perhaps it should be noted here that savings, usually thought of as household or individual in nature, are also accumulated by those rare governments that manage a fiscal surplus and by companies that retain earnings rather than paying them out in dividends. The low U.S. savings rate is compounded by fiscal irresponsibility, high dividend payouts, and low household savings rates. In much of East Asia, this pattern is reversed, with resultant high savings levels. One must assume that these savings levels are a tribute to the stability of governments and to the competence of financial authorities in these countries, else surely savings would be low.

This appears to be the key change in the economics of these nations. As seen in Table 6–4, the change is especially dramatic for Indonesia when the base year 1965 is used. The shift to a gross savings level of more than one-third of GDP is indeed remarkable.

The exception is the Philippines, where the savings level has declined over the period and the level of investment has remained unchanged. It may be that the Philippines is at a low point now in its economic progress, with problems of government incompetence and instability compounded by natural disasters, or it may simply be that the Philippines is the odd man out in East Asia. We need to return to that question shortly.

The root cause of the move to higher savings and investment throughout Southeast Asia over the past several decades cannot, as noted, be fully explained. No doubt rising real incomes are a factor, with individual savings rising as expenditure lags income. No doubt too the region's governments, committed to economic growth, provide incentives to save, if only indirectly from the general political stability of the

●

Table 6–4   Southeast Asia, Economic Growth

	GNP per Capita Annual Percent Real Growth, 1965–90	GDP Annual Percent Real Growth, 1965–80	GDP Annual Percent Real Growth, 1980–90
Indonesia	4.5	7.0	5.5
Malaysia	4.0	7.4	5.2
Philippines	1.3	5.7	0.9
Thailand	4.4	7.3	7.6
Singapore	6.5	10.0	6.4
Japan	4.1	6.4	4.1
Germany	2.1	3.3	2.1
United States	1.7	2.7	3.4

Source: The World Bank, *World Development Report 1992* (New York: Oxford University Press, 1992), pp. 218–221.

region and responsible management of the financial systems. No doubt too the Olson thesis of the ability to reach general consensus on goals and methods when the power of special interest groups is limited also plays a part.

With general political stability and governments focused on economic development and prosperity as their central task, the trigger for growth in the region has been to a very considerable degree the Chinese entrepreneurs resident in each of the nations of the region. The position of the immigrant or Overseas Chinese in each of the nations of the region is different and must be examined separately. In general, however, the Overseas Chinese have led the private sector of these economies—and tend to dominate it. Their extensive familial networks are also an integrating factor in the area. And as China moves forward economically, the Overseas Chinese will be a major channel for flows of capital and goods into and from China as the economies of Southeast Asia and China move to greater linkages.

SINGAPORE: THE ENTREPÔT

Looking not at the region as a whole but at its component countries, we see that Singapore has been the most successful of these nations and has

•

also been key to much of the overall success of the region. Under the exceptional, and often dictatorial, direction of long-time Prime Minister Lee Kuan Yew, Singapore has moved in only one generation to the top group in the world in terms of income. Singapore has taken full advantage of its strategic location at the crossroads of trade to build its entrepôt role, with exports and imports together nearly four times its own GDP. Singapore authorities have sought to deal with the problem of a limited labor force by driving wages to a level that would discourage labor-intensive industries in the country, while investing very heavily in labor force training to make possible a steady shift of the limited labor force to higher value-added, more sophisticated jobs.

At the same time, a forced savings program has ensured a considerable flow of domestic capital of industrial investment, while foreign firms with advanced levels of technology have been strongly encouraged to invest. To encourage the highest level of electronics, the government recently took a 49 percent position in a venture with Apple Computer to develop product at the most advanced edge of commercial electronics, as one example of direct government involvement in the execution of a well-though-out industrial policy. The Singapore government is not reluctant to invest and otherwise directly support businesses in sectors its considers vital to the nation's economic future.

In the region, Singapore presents a paradox. In a great many respects, it has been a critical source of strength for the region. It provides an infrastructure—in terms of communications, trade and transport, and banking and finance— that has been largely beyond the capabilities of the other countries in the region. Thanks in good part to the vision and force of Lee Kuan Yew, Singapore has been a major factor in regional policy-making and in speaking for the region internationally. It is difficult to conceive of Southeast Asia as it has taken shape, and of the institutions like ASEAN that are emerging, without the role of Singapore in conceiving and helping form the regional system.

Yet Singapore is an outsider to the region as well. It is a small Chinese island in a Muslim sea. In his sympathetic portrait of Singapore, Regnier speaks of "anti-Singaporean feeling" and states, "Many regard entrepôt activity as parasitic, profiting from uncomplicated movements through a port of goods produced in both neighboring and distant countries, with a minimal input of labour. The view of Singapore as the 'Jew of the Orient' is firmly established wherever, throughout the region, there is hostility to the Overseas Chinese. While necessarily taking this radical position, numerous decision-makers in Indonesia and Malaysia seek to reduce the commercial monopoly enjoyed by Singapore and the income it derives from this situation, which gives it the highest living standards in Asia after Japan and Brunei."[5]

On the face of it, Singapore would seem to be well placed to act as the go-between for the increasing integration of Malaysia and Indonesia. Nothing could be more remote. Not only do the two large nations see each other as rivals, despite a common religion, but they share a suspicious and skeptical view of Singapore. No doubt as these nations increase in economic strength, they will focus more on the advantages of Singapore as entrepôt and infrastructure center, with less concern for Singapore as competitor, in other words, Singapore as a Switzerland in Southeast Asia. (Comparison is sometimes made, wrongly, to Venice as being another city-state of wealth and influence, forgetting apparently the considerable imperial ambitions that Venice exercised and that are no part of Singapore's thinking.)

The city-state nature of Singapore makes comparison with Hong Kong inevitable, which, until recently, was not in Singapore's favor in many respects. Singapore has not managed, despite considerable effort, to rival Hong Kong as a financial center, even though financial activities in Singapore have increased. The tight controls of the Singapore government and the consequent sterile atmosphere of the city have worked in Hong Kong's favor as well. International firms have preferred Hong Kong as a site for area headquarters over Singapore, despite tax and other advantages offered by Singapore in exchange for regional headquarters' locating there.

As matters develop now, the more important Hong Kong advantage over Singapore becomes clear, and that is the immediate presence of a massive hinterland offering a continuous supply of land and labor, as well as potential markets. The end of Hong Kong's status as a British colony and the Chinese takeover in 1997 have been seen as a major handicap for Hong Kong. In the event, Hong Kong seems to be in the process of taking over Guangdong, as the growth of the South China economic region gathers strength.

Singapore has no hinterland, and therein lies its problem. Both land and labor are in limited supply. A future as a service center only, as airport, phone booth, and bank window, is a sterile alternative to a full range of economic activities with research laboratories, production of the products of advanced technology, and vigorous industrial competition.

•

The Growth Triangle concept initiated by Singapore's current Prime Minister Goh, by which Singapore would extend its economic reach to the Indonesian islands off Singapore and to Johore in the south of Malaysia, is offered as an alternative by which the current land/labor constraints might be overcome. Given the continuing tensions between Singapore and its neighbors, however, this does not yet constitute a hinterland of the sort that Guangdong offers Hong Kong or Fujian offers Taiwan.

Singapore's future then appears to depend critically on its government's ability to move the regional, ASEAN concept forward and make the region Singapore's hinterland.

THE PHILIPPINES: THE POOR MAN IN ASIA

At the other extreme of economic performance in Southeast Asia is the underperformance of the Philippines. Owing to a combination of a rapid increase in population and poor economic performance in the 1980s, the rate of increase in per capita GNP in the Philippines has been far below those of its regional neighbors (see Table 6–4). A considerable part of the problem has been the political instability in the country, a problem of longer standing than the decade of the 1980s.

The economic problems are pervasive. Gross savings in the Philippines, alone in the region, are actually below the 1965 levels, with the rate of gross investment flat over the period. (See Appendix Table 12.) Export growth has been far below that of Malaysia and Thailand in the past several years and projections have export growth continuing at this low level. Foreign direct investment in the Philippines was negligible in 1985, a year of political crisis, but the Philippines received less than 5 percent of the total FDI received by ASEAN nations in 1990. Malaysia, with one-third of the population of the Philippines, received nearly six times as much FDI in 1990 as did the Philippines.

In interviews with Japanese executives regarding their Asian investment plans, a repeated theme was regret over the Philippine situation and their perceived inability to invest there. These Japanese executives describe the Philippines as an attractive investment site in terms of the high level of education of the labor force, its adaptability, and the attraction (to the Japanese) of the general use of English. The overriding negative

•

factor cited was political instability, underlined by the fact that there have been several widely publicized kidnappings for ransom of Japanese executives.

Regnier speaks of the Philippines as "a peripheral part of South-East Asia." It is neither Buddhist nor Muslim, but Roman Catholic, the one largely Christian nation in all of Asia. It was long a Spanish colony and subsequently a United States colony, and was unique in both respects. Indeed, it might be argued from the examples of Latin America and the Philippines that the combination of Spanish imperialism and U.S. commercialism is peculiarly destructive of native cultures. Such has, in any event, been the case in the Philippines.

In a region where income distribution has been notably egalitarian (in Japan and Taiwan especially, but increasingly in Indonesia and elsewhere in the region as well), the disparities in income between wealthy and poor in the Philippines are enormous. Land reform has been much discussed but never put into effect, as the great haciendalike holdings continue to dominate the agricultural sector. It is hardly surprising that leftist guerrilla groups continue to be a major problem in the Philippines. The Philippines will continue to participate in ASEAN but will for some years remain at its periphery, barring great and unlikely changes in the quality and stability of the government of the nation.

Singapore and the Philippines in many ways present the extremes of the range of economies in Southeast Asia, at opposite ends of the spectrum in per capita output, in sharp contrast in terms of the effectiveness of their respective governments, and in rate of GNP and per capita growth over the past two decades. The two countries that best represent the overall growth and position of the region are Malaysia and Thailand.

INDUSTRIAL NEWCOMERS: MALAYSIA AND THAILAND

Both Malaysia and Thailand are discussed as candidates for the status of NICS and NIEs (newly industrializing countries or economies), joining Korea, Taiwan, Hong Kong, and Singapore in that special status that implies current and continuing economic success. Both economies have grown at an annual average rate of about 7 percent since 1965 and have

•

moved to the $1,500 to $2,500 range in per capita output. Both economies have gross savings and investment rates at or above 30 percent of
GDP, and both have increased their exports and imports at rates of 15 to
25 percent per year in recent years.

Moreover, both countries are planning for continued high growth.
The National Economic and Social Development Board of Thailand announced its seventh five-year plan in late 1991, with projected annual
growth of 8.2 percent, down from the 10.5 percent of the previous five
years, but a rate that would set the pace for most of the world. At about
the same time, the Malaysian government announced its Sixth Malaysian
Plan, which projects a 7.5 percent annual economic growth rate for the
first half of the 1990s, up from the 6.7 percent average of the late 1980s.

These two countries then both represent extraordinary success sto-
ries. Another significant similarity is the contrast between the colonial
experience of Malaysia and Thailand with that of Indonesia and the Philippines. Thailand has never been colonized but was in fact a British pro-
tectorate for a long time, and its government collaborated closely with
the Japanese in World War II. Malaysia was also under British influence
from early in the nineteenth century. It was not until 1946, however,
that the Malay States were combined into the Malayan Union as a crown
colony, with English the national language. And by 1957, the independent Federation of Malaya was established.

This relative freedom from Western colonial rule has provided a degree of social continuity and stability to Thailand and Malaysia that simply was not possible under the Dutch, French, Spanish, or U.S. colonial
governments of the other countries. At a minimum, it has meant that
these nations could move to economic growth as an objective more directly than their neighbors, who had to expend great political and social
energy in establishing themselves as independent entities.

At this point, however, similarities between Malaysia and Thailand
give way to important differences that affect how the region might or
might not come more closely together. A first and basic difference is size.
The population of Malaysia is under 20 million. For Malaysia, like Taiwan, this is a real disadvantage in attracting many kinds of industries or in
building industries that depend on a large-scale domestic market to be
economic. Thailand in contrast has a population of nearly 60 million,
and as incomes continue to rise, Thailand itself becomes a market of
major attractiveness for a great many kinds of goods. Given this differ-

●

ence, it is the more understandable that Malaysia's outspoken Prime Minister Mahathir has been the leader in the movement toward an East Asia Economic Group, broader than ASEAN but excluding the non-Asian Pacific economies.

The economic and social policies of Malaysia are shaped to a considerable extent by the composition of its population. The Malay States were historically sparsely settled and entirely agricultural. As plantations for rubber and other products were established and as resources such as tin deposits were exploited, there was a rush of Chinese and Indian immigration into what is now Malaysia to supply labor to these generally Western-organized businesses. The population of Malaysia is now about two-thirds Malay, one-quarter Chinese, and one-tenth Indian. Shortly after independence, around 1970, the distribution of wealth was about 2 percent in the hands of the Malay, nearly one-quarter owned by "other Malaysians," and about 60 percent owned by foreigners. The Chinese formed the urban population, while the Malays were rural. The Chinese were rich, or were thought to be, while the Malays were seen as poor— in "their own country." the Chinese are Buddhist for the most part, and the Malays are Muslim.

MALAYSIA INCORPORATED

These differences exploded in sustained and widespread riots in 1969, and the economic and social policies of Malaysia since have been addressed to eliminating the economic disadvantage of the *bumiputra* (sons of the soil), the Malays in the Malaysian population. The next year the Malay language was made the language of school instruction, and programs were put in place to change the wealth distribution from 2–25–60 to 30–40–30. The *Bumiputra* Investment Foundation was established to purchase and redistribute share ownership, and its subsidiaries now own 25 percent of the finance sector, 36 percent of agribusinesses, and 23 percent of the manufacturing sector.

This is one mechanism by which the Malaysian government very directly intervenes at the corporate level in the Malaysian economy. In addition, the Heavy Industry Corporation of Malaysia is 100 percent government-owned, active in metals, cement, real estate, and trading,

•

and controlling owner of the Proton automobile manufacturing venture, in which Mitsubishi Motors plays a major part. The current policy has been described as aimed at "the development of capital-intensive, high-tech oriented industries which can produce competitive products . . . for developed countries' markets. A slogan for this purpose, 'Malaysia Incorporated,' has been widely adopted. This slogan calls for efforts at industrial development . . . using the Japanese experience as role model."[6] Under Mahathir, Japan as an economic model has been an explicit and recurring theme in his "Look East" policy of rejecting Western models and turning to Northeast Asian national models instead.

Is the Malaysian effort succeeding? Certainly the programs to redistribute income and wealth to the *bumiputra* are costly, both at the national level in terms of the investment of tax income and at the corporate level, where affirmative action hiring programs to favor (often poorly trained and motivated) *bumiputra* are mandated. Nonetheless, racial tensions have remained under control, so the costs might well be considered worthwhile. Further, the economy does very well for all the seeming inefficiencies of government ownership and interference. It is hard to fault long-continuing success.

The transfer of wealth needed to bring the Malay population to the target 30 percent holdings was not achieved by 1990, but a very significant increase to 20 percent was accomplished. Not all agree however, that the problem is being dealt with. "Have the Malays been successful, under the *Bumiputra* policy, in accumulating capital in the industrial sector? The answer is clearly no. In spite of the government's effort, capable Malay managers have not emerged in significant numbers in most industries. . . . In the industrial sector, in particular, capital accumulation, know-how and experience of technology, and managerial skills are poor on the part of Malays."[7]

Moreover, to an exceptional degree, Malaysia seems to be integrating its economy into the rest of Asia. Three-quarters of the very high level of foreign investment in Malaysia comes from Asian nations, and far from being dominated by Japanese capital— which is considerable—the largest source of investment in the last few years has been Taiwan. Still, the Japanese companies are important. The largest amount of investment by Japan's electrical machinery industry has been in Malaysia—more during the 1980s than has gone to Thailand, Singapore, or other locations. Matsushita Electric alone has 15 affiliates in Malaysia, their sales accounting for about 3 percent of the country's GNP. These foreign investments reinforce the government's plans to move to more sophisticated sectors in manufacturing.

In terms of East Asian position, a Malaysian economist concludes, "Malaysia has benefitted immensely from its strategic geographic location by taking advantage of opportunities arising from the dynamics of the Asia-Pacific region. Malaysia seems well placed to enter export markets being vacated by the NIEs. Malaysia has an edge over other ASEAN countries on account of its excellent infrastructural facilities and technological absorptive capacity. Malaysia's long-term comparative advantage seems to lie in resource-intensive and human capital-intensive activities, which would signify increased complementarily with its immediate neighbors."[8]

As for Thailand, a key difference is the position of the immigrant or Overseas Chinese in Thai society compared with Malay society. The absolute numbers of Overseas Chinese are estimated to be similar in the two countries, between 5 and 6 million. However, this is a much smaller and less visible proportion of the large Thai population, rather less than 10 percent, compared with 30 percent in Malaysia.

Further, there is general agreement that the Chinese in Thailand, like the Philippine case, have been reasonably well integrated into Thai society. "Perhaps because of all-pervasive Buddhist tolerance in their culture, the Thais have never openly discriminated against outsiders. Their religion is not exclusionist like the Islam of Indonesia or Malaysia and instead provides a context for easy assimilation."[9]

This is not to say that the Overseas Chinese position in Thailand is a minor one. Indeed, some estimates have Overseas Chinese ownership as high as 90 percent of manufacturing, although this is undoubtedly lower in recent years. It is the case, however, that nine of the top ten business groups in Thailand are Chinese-owned, and one of these, the Bangkok Bank Group, is the largest private commercial bank in Southeast Asia, which has major industrial holdings as well, with total sales in 1991 of more than U.S.$2.5 billion.

In Thailand, many of the Chinese have Thai names and many are of mixed parentage, given the long history of Chinese presence and the tolerance of intermarriage in Buddhism, a religion shared by most Thais and Chinese. Certainly tensions are possible, in view of the wealth and power of some of the Chinese community, but the issue is not a major one.

●

THAILAND'S NONINTERVENTIONIST GOVERNMENT

Thailand contrasts with Malaysia in another critical respect. It is an open society in many ways, not least in the fact of the minor role the government plays in economic policy. Where Malaysia has looked to the Japanese model of a centrally supported industrial policy—and indeed took the Japanese model to an extreme the Japanese did not—the Thai case does not support the view that a strong government is needed for vigorous economic development. "The Thai state . . . has not played an active developmental role in the country's economy. Instead, the state has refrained from intervention in the economy in terms of regulation and investment, allowing the private sector to take the lead. The low level of state activity in industrial development as well as the initiatives of the private sector in what amounts to a laissez-faire economy suggests that Thailand's growth has been achieved in spite of the state, not because of it.[10]

Indeed, it can be argued that the limited role of government in regulating the economy is giving rise to Thailand's most pressing economic problem. The entire infrastructure of the country, and most especially of the greater Bangkok area, is becoming a bottleneck to further growth. Virtually every aspect of infrastructure is suffering from underinvestment, as even a casual visitor to Bangkok will note. The transport system is choked, the harbor has become a trap for shipped goods, formerly attractive resort areas have been ruined perhaps permanently by uncontrolled growth and rampant pollution, and the air of Bangkok has surpassed that of Tokyo at its 1960s worst.

Even the cautious and diplomatic Asian Development Bank speaks of Thailand's "skill shortages" and need for investment in education, along with other basic needs, such as water supply in agriculture. More ominously, the ADB states, "Serious problems in the health sector also call for attention. Recent information indicates that the rapid rise in the incidence of AIDS could produce major repercussions in the economy."[11]

Laissez-faire has it limits. Thailand needs decentralization to solve the Bangkok bottleneck; it needs regulations to deal with the environmental issues; and it needs investment to deal with infrastructure shortcomings, education needs, and health problems. Some governmental direction and intervention is in order.

•

Perhaps the recent overthrow of the military government of Thailand by student and middle-class demonstrations in 1992, which turned tragically bloody but had as its outcome elections and a civil government, were driven by anger and frustration at the lack of government action. Certainly the level of corruption played a part, but that is hardly new to Thailand. The arrogance of the military also played a part, and that also has a long history in Thailand. It was in any case an upheaval seeking civil government, and more representative and responsible government.

It can only be hoped that the current civilian government, with the support of the much-respected king of Thailand, who serves an important role in uniting the country, can build a tradition of an active, competent, and reasonably honest civil government. Thai history is a long succession of coups, attempted coups, countercoups, and more recently, popular uprisings. The position of the military, and its internal struggles for power, are a curious contrast to the generally stable and peaceful history of the country. As Thailand becomes an economic power, the role of the military and the place of the government in the economy will certainly change in the direction of civilian-led economic planning and regulation.

Thailand has been a major recipient of foreign direct investment and became in the late 1980s the site of first choice for Japanese companies in particular. Japan accounted for more than 40 percent of foreign direct investment in Thailand from 1986 to 1991, a much larger proportion than in its neighbors, and despite a general view that Japanese nationals and companies are rather less welcome in Thailand than in Malaysia and Indonesia. However, with Bangkok's infrastructure problems becoming acute and labor supply and cost less favorable, Japanese investment attention is shifting to Indonesia and China.

Like Malaysia, Thailand is moving toward integration with East Asia through the force of economic events. American policies are reflected in part in the fact that the Untied States provides aid to Thailand totaling only $16 million annually (compared with more than $500 million from Japan). U.S. private investment in Thailand continues, and AT&T, for example, is in the process of building a position both in electronics components and in telecommunications equipment—a critical factor in Thailand's future. But, as with Malaysia, more than 70 percent of foreign investment in Thailand now comes from the economies of East Asia, and that pattern will certainly continue.

•

BREAKING DOWN TRADE BARRIERS

Each of these economies is becoming increasingly integrated with the rest of East Asia, not by political actions and institutional agreements but by the force of investment and trade. If there is a slow drift toward protectionism and the GATT crumbles gradually, the trade, aid, and investment flows within East Asia will transform the region into something akin to the EC, without the need for a vast bureaucracy. "As Noordin Sopiee of Malaysia's Institute of Strategic and International Studies says, the 'process of uninstitutionalized economic cooperation and interdependence is nothing short of remarkable.' Asian governments need only to watch and wait, while economic integration occurs naturally around them."[12]

Not all Asian governments are waiting. Malaysian Prime Minister Mahathir, notably impatient and outspoken, has proposed the expansion of the ASEAN area to include Japan, Korea, Taiwan, and Hong Kong, an East Asian Economic Group (EAEG). The proposed group does not include the United States, Australia, or New Zealand. The United States strongly objected to the Mahathir proposal—causing Mahathir to note that the United States is organizing an exclusive NAFTA while opposing other groups that fail to include the United States. U.S. policy favors a toothless discussion group called Asia Pacific Economic Cooperation (APEC) which includes non-Asian as well as Asian countries.

For its part, Japan has not made, and as yet cannot make, a commitment to an EAEG or other exclusively Asian grouping. Its interests as a leading world economic power are too widespread. Indeed one could say the same for all of East Asia. Reviewing the directions of trade, the *Financial Times* noted, "Adding in Australasia, China and the remaining East Asian countries to the EAEG increases the proportion of intra-regional trade to 44.2 percent, higher than the 41.5 percent of total U.S. Canadian and Mexican exports that were traded within the proposed NAFTA in 1990.

"That both NAFTA and the largest possible East Asian free-trade zone still rely on external trade for more than half their total trade suggests that neither has an interest in undermining the multilateral trading systems."[13] True enough, for now all are better served by a functioning GATT and an open world trading system, the more so as East Asia is still

●

in the early stages of full economic development. However, GATT is tottering, trading zones are being created, and East Asia is rapidly moving to the point where its growth and continued economic success will not depend on outside markets, investments, or technologies to a critical extent. Peter Drysdale uses the term "open regionalism" to describe the current commitment of East Asia in world economic diplomacy—including Mahathir's proposed EAEG.[14] However, if the world is to be divided into exclusive trading zones negotiating access with each other, East Asia will have its zone too and is within a very few years of being a truly powerful zone. U.S. diplomacy might do better to support "open regionalism" rather than insisting that the game be played by U.S.-written rules of membership and access.

7
•

INDONESIA AND VIETNAM

SOUTHEAST ASIA'S FRONTIERS

In an area as vast and dynamic as East Asia, there is a continuing sequence of economies that are frontiers—areas emerging or about to emerge on the world scene as significant and of major importance to global companies. Japan fit this description in the 1950s, and Korea and Taiwan in turn became the business frontiers of the 1960s, as have Thailand, Malaysia, and most lately the South China region in the 1970s and 1980s. In each case, the best global corporate managers have balanced the opportunities offered by these frontier economies with the risks and undertaken investment, generally to their subsequent advantage. Other companies have focused solely on the considerable risks inherent in these developing environments and delayed real commitments, or, more often, were ignorant of or chose to ignore these business frontiers.

Japan, now a mature, massive economic power, dramatically makes the case for frontier ventures. Companies like IBM, Merck, Coca-Cola, Hoechst, DuPont, and Bayer have benefited in every respect—growth, profits, and competitive position—from their efforts at a time when Japan was considered a frontier. Positions were built with difficulty, nurtured with great care, pressed despite Japanese barriers, and embarked

•

upon early, when Japan was a small, obscure, and exotic place in which to do business.

This is not to argue that there are close parallels between the current structure of Japan and the probable future development of Indonesia or Vietnam. Indeed, a central fact of the East Asian economic development is the great differences in the starting points of these nations and the course of their subsequent economic development. It is to say, however, that Indonesia is now, and Vietnam is likely to be in the near future, a business frontier in the sense that Japan was earlier—remote, not yet of great economic importance, offering clear opportunities but with very great obstacles and risks, unfamiliar and uncomfortable as a place in which to operate businesses—but with the clear potential to be a major economic force and competitive setting within a relatively short time.

It is also a fact, and an ominous one, that Western companies in general, and United States companies most especially, are losing position and even failing to try to establish position in these two economies. Make no mistake, Indonesia soon and Vietnam not long after will be among the powerful nations and important markets of the world. Their resource bases, their key positions in the world's fastest-growing economic area, their critical importance to Japan's economic future, and their large populations combine to make them key to world industrial position in the next decades.

This is surely evident even to a casual observer. And it must be no less evident that in Indonesia's economy—leaving aside oil and gas, which are mainly exported to Japan in any case—Japanese companies are making the competitive running in the whole range of businesses from retailing to autos. U.S. firms wring their hands about corrupt practices while Japan's firms, followed now closely by companies from Taiwan and Korea, make the investments. In Vietnam, the vengeful U.S. embargo on relations with that country has kept U.S. companies from any kind of involvement on the economic frontier, while the companies of France, Australia, and Taiwan especially, followed by the Japanese and Koreans, begin to build positions. On both the emerging frontier of Indonesia and the more distant frontier of Vietnam, Western firms in general and U.S. firms in particular are being pushed aside in the rush of development. They will pay over the next decades in forgone world market position.

•

INDONESIA AT THE STARTING GATE

Indonesia is now at the point of takeoff, with a massive population and considerable resources, rapidly increasing industrial output and exports, eased restrictions on investment and private initiatives, and the beginnings of a capital market of substance. Yet per capita incomes, though rising rapidly, remain low, corruption and political favoritism are widespread, issues of succession and stability in political leadership are urgent, and the market for most goods remains fragmented, with distribution difficult.

In its sheer size and social and economic complexity and in its paradox of poverty and potential, Indonesia presents a challenge without parallel to the business strategist. Although now caught up on the great wave of East Asian economic growth, Indonesia is still not classified as a "dynamic Asian economy," in the jargon of the international bureaucrats, but is ranked instead with China and India as one of the region's low-income economies.

Indonesia is an oil-rich member of the Organization of Petroleum Exporting Countries (OPEC), the only East Asian nation in the group. Its annual economic growth rate in the 1980s, 5.5 percent, ranks just behind its East Asian neighbors. An agricultural economy only a generation ago, agriculture now represents only one-fifth of the nation's GNP, and exports of manufactured goods have increased five times in the past six years. Indonesia is in the process of shedding its dependence on its rich supply of resources in favor of a more manufacturing-based economy, which now accounts for 40 percent of GDP. Its participation in the Asian economic revolution will help ensure continued growth: at recent growth rates, in one decade the Indonesian economy will equal the present-day economies of Mexico, Korea, or India.

Not least of Indonesia's accomplishments is a considerable trade surplus with Japan—driven in good part by exports of oil and gas. In important respects, Indonesia and Japan have complementary economies. Japanese trade, aid, and investment are critical to the success Indonesia has achieved. Japan for its part secures stable supplies of energy and key raw materials. The close links between the two will also go far to help ensure continued rapid Indonesian economic growth.

The Japan relationship is key to Indonesia's development. Trade with Japan is 40 percent of the nation's total trade. Nearly two-thirds of

•

all aid received by Indonesia is from Japan, and one-third of all foreign direct investment in Indonesia is made by Japanese companies. There is a very real "special relationship" between Japan as a source of capital and technology and Indonesia as a source of energy, raw materials, and labor. Japan has placed a major bet on Indonesia's future. And Japanese companies also are betting heavily on Indonesia's continued growth into a major world market. The importance of the two countries to each other over the next decades can hardly be overstated.

At the same time, Indonesia is ignored or even rejected by Western companies, with the major exception of oil, gas, and other extractive industries. These, however, being exploitative and generally quite isolated from the society as a whole, create little by way of multiplying the investment effects in subcontracting, worker training, or social infrastructure. In the wider economy, Japanese companies are laying down the foundations for major market positions as Indonesia moves in the early twenty-first century to become one of the world's important markets.

INITIAL SOCIAL AND ECONOMIC SUCCESSES

Indonesia has experienced political stability and steady—even rapid—economic growth for a generation, since the change of government in 1965. It remains a poor country, however, and issues of political succession and continued domestic political stability are very real. It is, for all of the long history of the area, a very young nation with an uncertain identity. Its future, like that of any young and complex nation, is unknown.

The nation sprawls over an immense area. The exact number of islands in the Indonesian archipelago is unknown but is usually estimated at 13,500. They extend over an area wider than the continental United States, or the equivalent of the distance from Ireland to the Urals. The range of peoples is no less great, with an estimated 300 ethnic groups—an estimate that, like the number of islands, varies.

At one time it was thought that Indonesia's population boom would effectively drown any economic gains: in the period from 1965 to 1980, the rate of population increase in Indonesia was terribly high at 2.4 percent per annum. That is rapidly falling now and is projected to be 1.6 percent per annum to end of the century. Indonesia is now fourth in total population, following only China, India, and the United States (depending on current definitions of Russia's boundaries). Earlier projections had Indonesia's population totaling 280 million by the year 2001, but the World Bank projections now put the total for the year 2000 at 209 million.

Declining birth rates reflect economic success. Referring to the "falling demand for children," one study reports what has become a familiar story in developing Asia: "Younger women who had only one or two children said that they did not want to add many more because of the cost of raising children, and their desire that their offspring should have the advantage of good schooling, clothing, and nutrition."[1]

Thus the virtuous cycle of rising living standards and falling birth rates that is an early sign of economic success and social stability exists in Indonesia. Indonesia will always be one of the population centers of the world, but its problematic population growth rate is coming under control.

The changes in Indonesia's economy over the past generation can be captured in two numbers: in 1967, the per capita GNP was only $51; in 1991, it was over $600. Real output has increased 12 times in 25 years. The driving force behind this growth is not hard to find. Gross domestic savings increased from 8 to 36 percent of GNP over the period, as political stability and economic growth encouraged savings to increase to levels at which high sustained growth is possible. Note that over the same period, savings in the United States dropped from 21 to 15 percent of GDP. Proportionately, Indonesia now saves more than twice what the United States saves, and relative growth rates reflect the fact.

These savings drive the investment that drives growth. Indonesian investment rates now match the explosion in savings, with gross domestic investment growing from 8 to 36 percent of GDP from 1967 to 1991. In a very real sense, we can now assume that, barring some natural or political catastrophe, continued growth is assured, with Indonesia now saving and investing at the same quite extra quite extraordinary levels as the rest of East Asia.

THE PRIMARY SECTOR GIVES WAY TO MANUFACTURING

With growth has come structural change. The manufacturing sector, which now accounts for over 40 percent of Indonesia's GDP, has grown

●

at an annual rate of more than 12 percent over the entire 25-year period
from 1965 to 1990, and that growth is continuing. The primary sectors
of agriculture, raw materials, and oil and gas have grown less rapidly, as
Indonesia moves to join the industrializing economies. And with industrialization has come greater equality in distribution of income. "Without doubt, the most impressive achievement of the past decade has been
the remarkable decline in inequality and in the incidence of poverty in
rural Java."[2] As noted by the *Economist,* "In 1970, the first attempt to
estimate how many Indonesians lived in absolute poverty found that 60
percent of the population, 70 million people, lived below the official
poverty line. In 1987, . . . this ratio had fallen to 17 percent, 30 million
people. . . . Although the poor's share is still miserable, it has at least been
growing, which is more than can be said for many countries."[3]

With population growth coming under control and with economic
growth driven by high domestic savings and investment, Indonesia has
also realized a favorable shift in the structure of its trade. Only a decade
ago, oil and gas represented four-fifths of Indonesia's exports, and its
economy was consequently terribly vulnerable to changes in world demand and prices. To escape this vulnerability, and with the support of
such international agencies as the Asian Development Bank and World
Bank, Indonesia has moved to restructure and diversify its economy,
with considerable success. In 1991, oil and gas exports dropped to 40
percent of Indonesia's total exports. In the meantime, the lower value-
added, labor-intensive sectors have become increasingly export-driven,
with the value of footwear exports up from only $23 million as recently
as 1987 to nearly $1 billion in 1991. Textile exports in 1991 were up six
times over 1985 levels. With income and labor rates still very low, and
with adult literacy for the entire country at 77 percent, labor provides
Indonesia's export advantage and the lure to inward foreign manufacturing investment.

Concurrent with these successes, and in fact contributing to them,
has been a steady move toward deregulation and liberalization of the
economy in both the industrial and financial sectors. These moves continue, with foreign investment also benefitting from a relaxation of regulations. Of course, many issues and potential problems still face the
economy. Nonetheless, the long view must conclude that Indonesia has
progressed to the point where it must be given serious and sustained
attention by business strategists.

A NEW NATION, POLITICALLY
VULNERABLE

In considering Indonesia's position and prospects, its relative youth must be a starting point. The various components of what is now Indonesia have long and complex histories whose influences have been carried over to the modern state: the Hindu era, which still flourishes in Bali; the domination of the country by Arab traders, leaving the legacy of Islam as the religion of the majority of the population; the Dutch colonial rule over a congeries of folk societies. All this ended with the Japanese defeat of the Dutch, British, and U.S. colonial structures in Southeast Asia, and in the case of Indonesia with the drawn-out battles for independence to 1949, when the Indonesian Republic was finally recognized.

Not only is the fact of Indonesia as a nation quite recent, but even the idea of Indonesia as a nation is a recent one. "The idea of Indonesia rose suddenly and, within a few quick years, implanted itself forever in the minds of men who now became Indonesians. . . . In October, 1928, a congress of youth organizations brought the idea forth in one echoing phrase, 'one nation—Indonesia, one people—Indonesian, one language—Indonesian.'"[4]

It is then less than two generations, a bit more than 40 years, since this geographically scattered, culturally heterogeneous, resource-rich but desperately poor new nation has emerged from under an oppressive colonial ruler. It is hardly surprising then that it remains in important respects fragile and vulnerable, nor that the weakest point in its structure appears to be political.

In its brief history, Indonesia has had two presidents. The first, Sukarno, a remarkably charismatic personality, focused on the machinations of the political scene to the exclusion of matters of substantive policy and lost power in 1965 after a failed coup, seen to have been instigated by the Indonesian Communist party. The army took power and the Communist party disappeared as a political force. Sukarno's successor and the reigning president, Suharto, then a general in a key division of the armed forces, took control of the nation. At the same time, a bloody massacre of Chinese occurred across Indonesia, in numbers never determined but certainly in the tens of thousands—a ghastly reminder of another source of Indonesian instability.

●

Suharto ushered in what has come to be called the "New Order" in Indonesia. Very roughly, one might think of the period of Sukarno's reign as one in which—however messily—a nation as political entity emerged. In the next stage, the era of Suharto, the fundamentals of an effective economy were put in place. Suharto took control of the nation early in 1966, although he was not officially elected president until 1968. He quickly moved to put an end to a roaring rate of inflation, drawing on the advice of a group of largely U.S.-trained technocrats known as the "Berkeley mafia" from their University of California backgrounds. Throughout his rule, Suharto has focused on economic issues, both domestic and trade-related, taking steady steps to a more open and liberal economy.

There has been essentially no challenge to Suharto's position since he took power, and indeed there is no substantial challenge now—which raises what may well be Indonesia's most critical issue, succession. Like a great many strong leaders, Suharto has been at some pains to ensure that no one close to the center of power has developed a commanding position. When he was reelected in 1993, it was for his sixth five-year term in office, at the end of which he will be 77 years of age. Even before officially committing himself to reelection, he acted like a candidate for office, making a pilgrimage to Mecca, an act of significance for the 90 percent Muslim electorate. As part of Indonesia's national philosophy or *Pancasila,* special emphasis is placed on reaching a peaceful consensus and public opinion polls of political views are not permitted, so it is impossible to verify the extent of his support. Still, Suharto presumably will remain in power as long as he chooses, and there appears to be surprisingly little concern about the absence of an apparent successor.

The nepotism and corruption of the Suharto regime are key issues in Indonesian politics. The president's wife, brother, and half-brother are all seen to have benefited greatly from the leverage provided by Suharto's political power. More recently, attention has focused on what are called in Jakarta "the children," Suharto's six children and their business connections. "Over the past decade, Suharto's six children and their corporate vehicles have enjoyed the fruits of an array of monopolies and preferential trading arrangements. They have been granted billions of U.S. dollars in loans from state banks, privileged treatment in tenders for government contracts, and a variety of agency relationships with foreign firms. Financial information on Suharto family-owned businesses is

●

scarce, but business sources estimate that the combined revenues from operations and investments amount to several billion dollars a year. 'The children have wormed their way into every conceivable corner of the economy,' says one foreign businessman. 'You cannot get involved in an important deal any more if you don't bring in at least one of the children.' "[5]

The issue of corruption and nepotism is tied very closely to what seems to be the most explosive issue in Indonesian affairs—the role and power of Indonesians of Chinese descent in the business community. The issue of the Overseas Chinese is an issue throughout East Asia. As in Malaysia, it becomes a major factor socially and economically in Indonesia.

OVERSEAS CHINESE AND SONS OF THE SOIL

The distinction in Indonesia is between *pribumi* (literally, of the soil)—meaning of Malay descent, the Indonesian equivalent of the Malaysian *bumiputra*—and persons of Chinese descent. In some parts of East Asia the distinction does not matter because Chinese are in the majority—places like Singapore and Taiwan. In others parts, it matters little because of the degree of assimilation of the Chinese into the local population, most notably in Thailand. In Indonesia, however, the distinction is sharp and persists—presumably because of religious differences: to cross Muslim religious beliefs with Chinese Buddhist origins is either inconceivable or impossible and in any case appears to be why Chinese identification persists in Indonesia despite the passage of sufficient generations to make assimilation seem natural.

In fact, Overseas Chinese are estimated to make up a rather small proportion of the total Indonesian population, perhaps 3 percent.[6] In absolute terms this amounts to some 4 or 5 million people concentrated in urban areas that have port facilities and commercial systems in place. They occupy a disproportionate number of places at the very top of the business pyramid, and their importance is further compounded by the high degree of concentration of the economy in a limited number of large companies.

●

The Indonesian term for these combinations of companies under the control of a single holding company is *konglomerat,* and by the mid-1980s, the largest 50 of these were estimated to account for nearly one-fifth of Indonesia's gross domestic product. They are controlled in three-quarters of the cases by Chinese, and these Chinese-controlled groups make up nearly 90 percent of the sales total of 50 largest groups; that is, the very largest of the *konglomerat* are Chinese-owned.[7] "What makes the Indonesian situation unusual in comparison with other countries characterized by a high degree of industrial concentration (such as Pakistan, Mexico, or Brazil) is the fact that so many of the largest groups are either controlled by members of a numerically small ethnic minority (the Chinese), or by the family and close associates of the President. Inevitably this must give rise to a feeling among indigenous Indonesian entrepreneurs that the playing field is far from level."[8]

Great concentrations of economic power and wealth are political issues everywhere. The issues are the more keen in Indonesia because ethnic concerns coexist with economic inequality, political favoritism, and corruption in a highly volatile mix. This combination of factors finds its ultimate expression in the position of the Salim Group, Indonesia's largest private sector company, with sales of more than $8 billion, the equivalent of more than 5 percent of GDP, and about 150,000 employees worldwide. The group is described as including the extraordinary total of 427 companies, a number of them outside Indonesia as the group has diversified geographically in recent years.

This complex mixture of ethnicity, concentrated economic power, and political favoritism comes under constant criticism. Some protection is provided the wealthy Chinese by investing abroad, though there is little indication of the kind of capital flight that has characterized much of Latin America, for example, and local asset accumulation remains very strong. Perhaps greater protection is derived from the close linkages between Chinese and Indonesians at the top levels of the economic and social hierarchies. And at the most level, the Indonesian economy as a whole very much needs the Chinese entrepreneurs. None of this is a guarantee, however, and perhaps ultimately there is none, except for continued political stability and economic progress, which will soften the keener thrusts of jealousy and resentment. Nonetheless, along with the issue of succession to Suharto, the position and prospects of the Chinese businesses must be seen as major questions in Indonesia's future.

●

JAPAN, AN ESSENTIAL PARTNER
IN INDONESIA'S GROWTH

Just as Suharto-led political stability and Chinese-led entrepreneurship have been key factors in Indonesia's industrialization, so the Japanese market, Japanese investment, and Japanese aid have been critical external factors in the process. Until recently, Japan's involvement was driven by its need for sources of energy and raw materials, not by an interest in the Indonesian economy generally or in the Indonesian market. This is now beginning to change with Indonesia's economic success, and Japanese firms are moving rapidly to this investment frontier.

Trade is the starting point of the relationship. Japan accounts for about 40 percent of Indonesia's total trade, and Indonesia maintains a large trade surplus with Japan. Much the largest customer of Indonesia, taking well over 40 percent of its exports, Japan is also the largest supplier to the country, furnishing approximately one-quarter of total imports. Nearly all of Japan's plywood imports are from Indonesia, as is more than half of its natural gas supply and over one-tenth of its petroleum imports. Moreover, Japanese demand has helped drive Indonesia's industrialization because manufactured goods, only one-twentieth of Japan's purchases from Indonesia as recently as 1985, are now nearing one-fifth of the total, a fivefold increase in value in only six years.

By contrast, the United States accounts for a little over one-tenth of Indonesia's total trade, while the EC is nearly twice as important a trading partner for the country—a first indication of what has become increasingly evident over time, namely, the diminishing role of the United States in the economy and polity of Indonesia. Ties with Japan and East Asia, together with a residual of European links, form the core of Indonesia's current international relationships.

With respect to trade, and as further evidence of the strength of the changes in the Indonesian economy, exports have increased from one-twentieth to one-quarter of GDP over the last 25 years. At the same time, the importance of oil and gas has diminished, as has the role of commodities in general. In 1965, nearly all of Indonesia's exports were fuel, minerals, and other primary commodities. Now textiles alone represent more than 10 percent of exports, as the appeal of the Indonesian labor force and rates attract East Asian investors to the industry.

•

Oil and gas remain of critical importance to the economy. Indonesia has been able to maintain its level of crude production at around 1.5 million barrels per day, and there is ample scope for further exploration to maintain reserves, currently at a level that will sustain production for 20 years. However, domestic consumption is rising rapidly, and Indonesia urgently needs to increase its electric power capacity, no doubt drawing down further on petroleum supplies in the process. Although still a member of OPEC, it may well be that by the turn of the century Indonesia will no longer be an exporter of oil. In any case, any decline in oil exports can be balanced by exports of natural gas: Indonesia is the world's largest exporter of liquified natural gas (LNG) and has major gas fields discovered but as yet not developed. Japan buys nearly all of Indonesia's LNG exports, with some product going to Korea and Taiwan.

For all its relative trade success, Indonesia remains heavily dependent on foreign aid, and here again the role of Japan is central. Private and government borrowings abroad have been considerable and the burden of interest payments consequently great. The 14-member Inter-Governmental Group on Indonesia (IGGI), the main source of aid to Indonesia, now supplies nearly $5 billion annually to meet Indonesia's foreign borrowing obligations and to fund development projects.

Somewhat more than half of the IGGI funding comes from the World Bank and the Asian Development Bank. Of the balance, two-thirds comes from Japan—one-third of the entire amount, or about $1.5 billion per annum. The U.S. contribution is less than 3 percent of the total, or one-tenth that of Japan, and the EC member countries supply another 10 percent. According to one report, "In the important category of special assistance—quick-disbursing, non-tied aid—Japan has supplied about three-fifths of the total of the [last three-year] period."[9]

Japanese official development aid is now the largest in total amount of all countries in the world. That aid is focused largely on Asia, and Indonesia is consistently the recipient of the largest share, over 10 percent of the total. By Japanese reckoning, Japan accounts for almost two-thirds of all the aid provided to Indonesia.

Japan's private sector activities track the public sector. Reports by Indonesia's Investment Coordinating Board indicate that Japanese companies accounted for about one-third of total direct investment in Indonesia in the period from 1967 through late 1991, a total of more than $10 billion, some three times the next-largest countries, Hong Kong and Taiwan.

•

Mr. Haryono, the chief representative of the Bank Indonesia in Tokyo, when asked how many of Indonesia's development projects have Japanese involvement, replied, "I can say with almost certainty that the figure would be 10 of 10. If not 10, then 8 or 9. The ones in which the Japanese are not involved would be some of the mining or oil projects that the Americans are running. Even if a consortium is formed, for instance, with Indonesian, American and European companies, it is most common for the Japanese to take the lead with 60 or 70 percent of the capital. Without doubt, Japanese companies are the most involved in our economy. A somewhat distant second would be U.S. companies with Germany and the Netherlands following."[10]

FOREIGN DIRECT INVESTMENT

The reported direct investment data reveal some important trends. First, foreign investment in Indonesia is overwhelmingly by East Asian countries. Japan's recent investment levels have been lower than earlier years, when large raw material–oriented projects such as the Asahan aluminum complex were funded. The shift to labor and market-oriented investments by Japanese firms is only now beginning. Hong Kong, Taiwan, Korea, and Singapore, meanwhile, have moved aggressively, and are now investing more than Japanese firms. In 1991, companies from foreign reserves–rich Taiwan invested more than those from Japan: Asian investment in Asia is driving the system.

Second, American direct investment—apart from oil and gas projects—is becoming minor. Over the entire 1967–91 period, U.S. investment represented about 7 percent of Indonesia's total, less than the totals from Japan, Hong Kong, or Taiwan, approximately equal to that from the Netherlands. In the last three years, it has dropped further, to about 3 percent of all direct investment, or seventh after the NIEs and Holland. U.S. firms as a whole are not taking positions in Indonesia and are allowing Asian firms to preempt market positions there.

There are perhaps 30 companies in Indonesia with substantial Japanese ownership that have more than 1,000 employees. Of these, one-third are in textiles and footwear, and it must be assumed that the export market is the target for their output. However, others with more than 1,000 employees—like Toto, leading producers of ceramic bath and toilet products; Ajinomoto, in foodstuffs and seasonings; Toyota Astra, in autos; and Suzuki, in motorcycles—are major factors in supplying the domestic Indonesian market.

Japanese participants in the Indonesian marketplace are by no means limited to manufacturing. With the liberalization of the banking sector in 1988, 15 of Japan's major banks all made substantial commitments to the Indonesian market. The Sanwa Bank is one of the more active, with a minority position in a merchant bank, a 51 percent position in a leasing operation, and an 85 percent equity holding in a commercial bank. Although the economy is arguably overbanked, and Chase Manhattan sold its retail banking operation to Astra International in early 1992, the commitment of Japanese banks to the economy, bolstered by the growing position of Japanese manufacturers, is likely to be a lasting one.

Note too that the four leading Japanese brokerage firms, led by Nomura Securities, have set up in Jakarta as the city's stock exchange has expanded and capital markets have grown rapidly. Nonlife insurance companies from Japan are also established in Indonesia now, although they still report that their business is almost entirely concerned with insuring Japanese-owned assets and businesses.

Direct investment becomes more significant as the Indonesian government continues to deregulate and liberalize market and investment rules. It is now possible, within certain limits, to establish wholly owned ventures in Indonesia, and Indonesian regulations continue to move in directions favorable to the outside investor who appreciates the value of patience and a long view. Continued political stability and rapid growth, low labor rates, and increased government encouragement mean that Asian, if not Western, investors will move rapidly into Indonesia as their next production base after Thailand. Indonesia now competes with the other economies of Southeast Asia and with the Chinese coastal zones for investment from the northeast.

With all this complex interweaving of the Japanese and Indonesian economies, the question of Indonesian attitudes toward Japan and the Japanese invariably becomes a topic of Western discussion. There is a general view that the Japanese and their companies are disliked, arising out of Japanese behavior during their occupation of the then Netherlands East Indies in World War II, and, more recently, from arrogance and selfishness on the part of Japanese businessmen in Indonesia.

This expectation was reinforced by what is called the Malari, a loose acronym for "Disaster of January 14, 1974," a period of severe riots in

Jakarta that resulted in a number of deaths and injuries. One perceptive observer summarized, "The riot was inspired by the visit to Jakarta of Japanese Prime Minister Kakuei Tanaka, and its ostensible cause was the resentment against Japanese businessmen and their overweening manner of doing business in Indonesia, but it had its deeper roots in complaints that went beyond xenophobia and represented domestic grievances."[11]

The disturbances linked to the 1974 Tanaka visit have not been repeated. Nearly 20 years have passed and substantial Japanese aid and investment in Indonesia, an absence of critical issues, and better understanding on both sides appear to have largely overcome earlier tensions. Certainly Japanese businesspeople resident in Jakarta and environs now report no problems from prejudice for themselves or their families. With no public opinion polls, however, a direct assessment of public attitudes is not possible. There is now no evidence of special hostility or dislike, however—nor yet evidence of any great fondness—but rather a reserved neutrality on both sides.

WESTERN APATHY IGNORES OPPORTUNITIES

A more important question is raised by the seeming failure of major Western companies to take positions in Indonesia commensurate with the country's position and potential. Only a few Western companies list their local subsidiaries of the Jakarta Stock Exchange, including Unilever, INCO, Goodyear, Bayer, and BAT, with all but INCO reporting good growth in sales and profits. Japanese and more recently Korean and Taiwanese investment is dominating the Indonesian manufacturing sector, however. Where are the Western multinationals?

No doubt some of the Western indifference to Indonesia results from sheer ignorance. The country remains very poor, on average. But statistics can be deceptive, and the market is more significant than national averages would indicate. The World Bank's International Comparisons Program, adjusting GDP figures for purchasing power, places 1990 per capita Indonesian output at $2,350 in current international dollars, which places the country in the lower middle-income group, as compared with the low-income level of $570 recorded by more usual calculations. The Indonesian GDP per capita averages a West Irian native, whose most valuable possession is his penis sheath and who lives outside a monetary economy, with the head of the Salim Group, arguably one of the world's wealthiest individuals. Geographically, of the thousands of islands in the Indonesian archipelago, only Java is critical as a market. "What might be termed 'Greater Jakarta'—the city itself plus the surrounding *kabupaten,* the city of Bogor and the Cilegon complex to the west—produced about 36 percent of the nation's non–oil industrial output in 1985. These two provinces and the other major industrial region, East Java, account for two-thirds of the total; Java's three big cities, Jakarta, Surabaya, and Bandung, and their surrounds generate some 54 percent of the total. No other province is of much significance."[12]

The three cities have a combined population of more than 12 million, not including surrounding built-up areas, while Java as a whole, one of the world's most densely populated areas, has a population of more than 110 million, some 60 percent of the total population. It is important to bear in mind the extent to which population and wealth are focused on Java and more particularly, Jakarta. These are the markets for modern goods that foreign businesses should target and that have the transportation and communications systems that would allow effective market penetration. Income levels in Jakarta are clearly far above national averages (Matsushita Electric executives suggest an average well over $2,000) and are growing more rapidly than in the nation as a whole.

DESTABILIZING FACTORS

If the market is quite adequate to justify consideration, what then are the obstacles? Concerns about political stability might well be a factor, and internal, potentially destabilizing factors are many. The most obvious is the succession question. A successor to Suharto—who by general agreement will be from the military, from Java, and a Muslim—and a mechanism to ensure succession is not in place. Another factor could be religious. Indonesia has the largest number of Muslims of any country in the world, and there are periodic bursts of Muslim fundamentalism in Indonesia as elsewhere. Although this kind of religious fanaticism runs against Javanese culture, the future pattern of Islam remains unclear and unstable.

A more predictable crisis, and yet one whose outcome is less predict-

•

able, is the move of the new middle class of Indonesia toward greater political involvement and the establishment of a broader, more popular base for political power in the nation. As incomes and education levels rise, paternalistic and military regimes come under attack—witness Korea, Taiwan, and Thailand. No doubt Indonesia will have a middle-class uprising in its turn if the current leadership fails—as it certainly has so far—to broaden its political power base.

Still another possible issue is the sheer geographic spread and cultural diversity of Indonesia. Indonesia may not be immune to the worldwide tendency of multigroup nations to separate into their component parts. There has long been an active separatist movement in Aceh, the north-ernmost part of Sumatra, where frequent violent anticentral government outbursts occur, and leaders are jailed or in exile. Although the Javanese are generally well regarded throughout the complex archipelago, Java alone is quite sufficient in size and resources to be a major nation or to continue to be a cohesive force for the otherwise scattered and frag-mented parts of the nation.

Many of these potential causes of instability exist throughout East Asia—issues of succession, of a politically stirring middle class, and of ethnic differences—in the context of youthful and in many ways still fragile national identities. Yet the area has remained exceptionally stable, despite upheavals elsewhere in the world, no doubt owing in large part to continued economic growth and rising living standards, and a resul-tant highly pragmatic, nonideological approach to dealing with prob-lems. A bet on Indonesia's managing to deal with its particular divisive issues seems still a good bet.

Perhaps Indonesia is another Brazil, whose future seems very bright but always in the future, but probably not. The sheer momentum of the surge of economic growth throughout East Asia has now passed to Indo-nesia as well, and its synergistic links to the extraordinary power of the Japanese economy nearly guarantee continued rapid progress.

REBUILDING VIETNAM

Indonesia is the current frontier for international business, a frontier where Japan's companies are moving quickly and Western firms are being left behind. Vietnam is the next frontier in East Asia. Indonesia, with per capita output now well over $500, is moving to economic take-off. Vietnam, with per capita output still in the $200 range, is only now emerging as an economy relevant to corporate strategies. Western companies need to begin activity on the Vietnam frontier.

Vietnam will be a major player in Asia and the world in the early twenty-first century. It has the requisite population base—60 million people, with a high level of literacy, aggressive and competent, sharing many of the Chinese cultural elements that distinguish Japan, Korea, and Taiwan. Wage levels are very low, competitive with those of China and well below those of Indonesia. The resource potential is substantial and has hardly been touched as yet by modern development. Oil and gas promise foreign-exchange earnings. And the nation sits squarely in the center of Asia's dynamic economies, directly athwart the main transportation routes crossing the area. Vietnam's potential is simply enormous.

Yet Vietnam is the least developed of the major nations of East Asia. Closed for a long time to the West because of its alliance with the now defunct Soviet empire, Vietnam has recently, with its *Doi Moi* policy of national reformation, increased its accessibility to Western businesses and begun the internal moves to create a market economy that are a necessary preliminary to economic growth. To a visitor, Vietnam today is reminiscent of Japan shortly after the end of World War II, a very poor country with all the terrible problems from a long war, but proud and determined to achieve prosperity, its able people straining every muscle and nerve to rebuild and move ahead.

They will succeed. The internal changes in government and economy that began in the late 1980s are having their effect, while the external environment steadily improves. In 1992, Japan reinitiated aid programs, Korea entered into diplomatic relations with Vietnam, the premier of China visited the country for the first time in two decades, and even the costly and brutal U.S. embargo eased somewhat, with continuing easing highly likely. "While we appreciate and sympathize with those Americans who still suffer from the unresolved MIA/POW issue, we must not forget the plight of the Vietnamese people who have been suffering for years from a series of wars and violence . . . If the MIA/POW situation is a humanitarian issue, the cause to free Vietnam from chronic economic poverty through economic development is also a great humanitarian issue."[13]

However, as with Indonesia, Western companies have been slow to move into the Vietnamese frontier. American firms have done little or

●

nothing to change the embargo terms and as a result have been entirely excluded from the current phase of Vietnamese developments—including oil exploration contracts. Foreign investment has been largely from Taiwan and Hong Kong, with the Japanese trading companies all very active in trade and supporting other Japanese corporate interests in the economy.

Specifically, when Japanese aid programs were renewed in late 1992, the Vietnamese government provided a list of 548 projects in 18 sectors from agriculture to chemicals to textiles for which Japanese investment has been invited. At the same time, the government of Japan is focusing aid programs on infrastructure support to Vietnamese development, with special attention to telecommunications and electric power generation. Vietnam currently enjoys a trade surplus, despite its many economic problems, mainly from the fact that Japan has taken up the slack left by the Russians and is the main buyer of Vietnam's increasing petroleum output. Vietnam's growth will happen. The issue is whether Western companies will profit from it or not.

LESSONS FROM HISTORY

An appreciation both of the problems and potential of Vietnam must be made against the background of the nation's long and often difficult history. It would have made a great historical difference if United States policy had taken account of the long history of confrontation between China and Vietnam, rather than assuming Vietnam to be a willing instrument of Chinese policy. It would benefit both the American nation and its corporations to take the trouble to learn more of the history of Asia's peoples—and avoid the costly mistakes that arise from ignorance.

Vietnam freed itself from Chinese domination in the tenth century, but subsequent dynasties and the political and social system were deeply influenced by Confucianism and Chinese-style bureaucratic structures. A millennium of independence ended when the nation fell again to imperial power in the nineteenth century, as the Europeans divided much of East Asia into imperial territories.

Vietnam fell to the French, who began their imperial rule of Vietnam in the 1860s. Generally highly exploitative of their colonies, the French did little for Vietnam during their period of rule by way of edu-

•

cation or training, or in the construction of an infrastructure and industrial base that might have served, as Japanese investment in Taiwan effectively did, as a basis for modern industrial development.

The long French dominance ended with defeat in the 1950s, only to be succeeded by U.S. intrusion in support of a separatist South Vietnam. U.S. support of the South in the civil war ended with the U.S. retreat from the country in 1975. Still there was not peace but more war, with the Cambodian invasion and Chinese attacks on Vietnam in 1978 and 1979 and a general severance of Vietnam from much of the world, aimed at ending Cambodian occupation. As this crisis began to ease, Vietnam's superpower ally and main source of trade and aid, the Soviet Union, went into political disintegration and economic collapse.

That the nation has survived at all as an independent and functioning political and economic entity through this appalling history of the last 130 years must be reckoned a near miracle. That it has survived in reasonable health, with continuing central government control, a growing albeit impoverished economy, and fast-improving international relations is a powerful testimonial to the abilities and determination of the Vietnamese people.

In gauging the attitudes of the Vietnamese people and the policies of the government, it is very important to keep in mind their view that they have defeated in turn the great powers—France, the United States, and China—and done so on their own with only marginal aid from the USSR. The price in human suffering has been very great, but the sense of pride in victory and the sense of national independence and capability is very strong indeed. The contrast to much of eastern Europe is striking. It is remarkable too to see the rather high level of interest by U.S. and other Western companies in the small, struggling, and relatively insignificant countries of eastern Europe and the lower level of interest in a large, potentially very powerful, and on the whole relatively well-managed Vietnam.

What if the French had acted in Vietnam as the British did in Malaysia, working to create and leave behind a strong and independent nation? What if the Americans had understood and built upon the centuries of Vietnamese battles for independence against the Chinese rather than seeing Vietnam as a passive instrument of Chinese Communist expansion? What if Vietnam had been able to follow the kind of course from, say, 1965 that South Korea with Park and Indonesia with Suharto were able

•

to pursue? Would we be talking of a fifth Asian economic dragon rather than a war-torn, poverty-stricken, struggling economy?

VIETNAM'S ASSETS

The advantages for Vietnamese economic development are considerable and even now are working to increase the great potential of the economy. Vietnam's population of some 66 million, estimated by the World Bank to grow to 82 million by the year 2000, is about equal to Germany's. The population is highly literate, with 88 percent adult literacy, and life expectancy is 67 years. The education and health levels—leaving to one side a large population of war-wounded—are exceptionally high for a developing nation.

There are in addition some 1.5 to 2 million Vietnamese abroad, perhaps two-thirds in Europe and the United States. Even now returnees are becoming more numerous, and with an improved economy and increased political liberalization, potential returnees trained in market economies and industrial skills will be an asset to the nation and to those Western companies that draw employees from this pool to manage their Vietnam operations.

Vietnam's largely unexploited mineral wealth—oil, coal, bauxite, rare earths—is a further asset for its economic future, as is its location on major sea lanes, with a long coastline and several world-class harbors, squarely in the middle of the fastest-growing economic region in the world.

A measure of the economy's potential has been the response to the *Doi Moi* policy introduced in late 1986, aimed at freeing the economy to respond to market forces, and the weathering of the crises brought on by the political and economic collapse of eastern Europe and the Soviet Union. *Doi Moi* was a systematic recognition of the need to reform the economic system, by privatizating agricultural production, increasing the role of the private sector in business and industry, rationalizing state-run enterprises and adopting an export-oriented trade policy.

Some of the results of the *Doi Moi* reforms have been spectacular. Vietnam is already the world's third-largest rice exporter, inflation is down from 1988's hyper-level of 600 percent to 25 percent in 1992 and

•

still dropping rapidly, and 350,000 private businesses have been established in a short five-year period. Monthly wage rates average some $40, making the Vietnamese labor force, given its relatively high quality, arguably the most cost-effective in the world. Annual GDP growth has been in the 4 to 5 percent range, less than Vietnam's Southeast Asian neighbors but high by world standards and tremendous, given Vietnam's circumstances.

Not the least of the nation's problems, one that might well have been economically disastrous, has been the economic failure of the Soviet Union. Cut off entirely from Western aid by the U.S. embargo, Vietnam depended substantially on aid from the former USSR, estimated to have reached more than $1.5 billion in 1987. "Total Council for Mutual Economic Assistance or Comecon (CMEA) assistance before 1989 was about $1 billion per annum. By 1991, all financial assistance had ceased and other sources of imports had to be found."[14] Trade with the former Soviet Union dominated Vietnam's exports and imports until 1990 and then collapsed, but the economy compensated by balancing the losses with entirely new markets and sources through Singapore and Hong Kong and in Japan (see Table 7–1). Management of the economy has shown considerable resilience and competence in a period of extraordinary difficulty.

One additional advantage must be noted, for further reference in discussion of foreign investment patterns. Vietnam's population includes an estimated 700,000 to 800,000 Overseas Chinese, the majority in the

Table 7–1   Vietnam's Main Trading Partners, 1989–91 ($ million)

	1989	1990	1991	Change, 1989–91
CIS (former USSR)*	2,118	2,123	524	−1,594
Singapore	111	692	886	+775
Japan	366	513	709	+343
Hong Kong	182	440	502	+320

*Rubles until 1991; dollars with some rubles in 1991.
Note: These are from Vietnam statistics, with individual countries, (e.g., Japan) reporting rather different totals.
Source: Data from "Kakudaisuru Vietnamu Toshi," *JETRO Sensa* (Tokyo: JETRO), July 1992, p. 26.

•

Cholon district of Ho Chi Minh City. Speculation exists that a good deal of the some $500 million in annual remittances from abroad that Vietnam receives may include informal flows of investment funds from Overseas Chinese to their counterparts in Vietnam.[15] In any case, these links to the Chinese communities elsewhere in Southeast Asia and China will no doubt serve Vietnam well in the coming years of building relations in the ASEAN area.

Vietnam's assets are substantial but are balanced by problems, many of which are deep-seated and not likely to be resolved quickly. The first is poverty. Per capita GDP is only about $200, compared with neighboring Malaysia's $2,500 or Indonesia's $600. The reality for Vietnam is a level of output and income well below that necessary to make sustained economic growth possible; Indonesia generates a level of savings and investment that makes the beginnings of industrialization possible.

INFRASTRUCTURE AND GOVERNMENT BOTTLENECKS

A consequence of the very low level of investment and income are a low level of infrastructure facilities, most notably electric power supply, but also including air, ocean, rail, and highway transport facilities. Not surprisingly, telecommunications are in short supply, as is office space and housing. The problem of electric power supply in the Ho Chi Minh City area is so acute that in early 1992 industrial production actually fell as a result of no power for four days a week. The remedy in the short term is standby generating facilities until a national grid allows the power surplus in the north to supply the south as well.

Surmounting all this is a socialist government, inexperienced and uncomfortable in the management of a market economy. Its lack of experience shows in frequent changes of regulations and a failure or inability to deal with some serious problems. As an example, a major barrier to foreign investment is the extreme difficulty of funding with local borrowings—by law, all funds must be supplied in foreign currency, a rule that most investors are not prepared to accept. In addition, land in Vietnam belongs to the people as a whole and is administered on their behalf by the state. Therefore, rather than legal title to real estate, a right to use is granted, another hazard for the foreign investor.

●

With Vietnam's socialist history and current management, the inevitable problems of state-owned enterprises arise. The *Financial Times* quotes a Vietnamese government adviser: "State-owned enterprises produce 26 percent of GDP, using 75 percent of fixed capital and 13 percent of the labour force, but using entirely the educated intelligentsia, and 86 percent of credit volume."[16] With obsolete equipment and uncompetitive products, the state-owned enterprises require subsidies and price supports, further distorting the economy. Correcting many of their problems will increase the costs and political hazards of increased unemployment, already estimated at 20 percent of the labor force. At least in the former East Germany there were potential West Germany buyers of these socialist industrial disasters; Vietnam has to live with them.

An elaborate and inefficient state apparatus in a poor country brings with it corruption, and at the lower levels of government this is a problem, though probably exaggerated. More common is the lack of clarity in governmental decision-making processes, with competing agencies of overlapping jurisdiction resulting in ambiguity about who in fact is in charge—a problem that veterans of negotiations with China will find familiar.

NORTH VERSUS SOUTH

Still, for all this formidable list, the most serious problem for Vietnam and for companies interested in marketing and investing there may well prove to be Vietnam's internal north-south problem. One Vietnamese spoke of "one culture, one society and two nations" when describing the differences between the two areas. Introductions from senior government officials that swing doors open wide in Hanoi are barely powerful enough to arrange a rather stiff interview in Ho Chi Minh City. It is in some ways like the Milan-Rome difference, with the bureaucratic structure in Hanoi and the commercial focus in Ho Chi Minh City. The gap is deeper than that, however, and again history is the key.

For a long time, the south was Vietnam's frontier in the fashion that the West was for the United States, a raw and largely unsettled area. "Of the 1,024,338 officially recorded male taxpayers in all of Vietnam in 1847, only 165,598 of them lived in the six southern provinces."[17] The separation of north and south became official under the French as southern Vietnam became Cochin China, distinct from Annam and Tonkin in the north. There were differences in the structure of government between the areas as well, with French control in the south more direct.

The divide between north and south Vietnam is in part a geographical fact resulting from the dumbbell shape of the country, with two great river basins and rice-growing areas at either end of the elongated national boundaries. The historic and geographic separation was made much more marked following World War II and the division of the country, with French and U.S. efforts to support the south and extended warfare between the two parts of the country. "From the perspective of 1990, it is clear that it is now the southern economy that is the 'engine of growth' for the nation as a whole. . . . Ho Chi Minh City now produces nearly one-third of the nation's industrial output and receives 80 percent of its foreign investment. Its share of national industrial output was 28 percent and the city produced about twice the industrial output of Hanoi and Haiphong together. Industrial labor productivity is clearly higher in the South too: 60 percent of total industrial output is produced by 42 percent of the industrial workforce."[18]

The north is the center of government and the site of heavier industries such as coal, cement, fertilizer, and electric power production. No doubt a number of factors make the South more market-oriented and able to shift to *Doi Moi*-encouraged, private sector, market-defined economic activities. The Chinese presence has some influence, as does prior American investment in transport systems, badly damaged in the north by U.S. bombings. In addition, the notably inefficient state-owned industries are largely in the north, and virtually all visitors to Vietnam remark on the difference in mood, pace, and apparent energy level between Hanoi and Ho Chi Minh City, to the south's advantage.

The northern handicap can be overstated, however. A perceptive and experienced Japanese observer noted, "Arriving in Hanoi, I was amazed by the city's tremendous economic vitality. . . . There was a vast gulf between the stereotypical description of [northern] Vietnam and the reality I encountered. Hanoi's markets and streets were jammed with shoppers and merchants. The roads were heavy with traffic. . . . The pace of housing construction was also remarkable."[19]

There are clear hazards to a widening of the differences between the two geographic areas of the nation. Some preferences in land availability and tax treatment are already being offered to investors in the north, and it can be assumed that as international aid begins to flow into Vietnam,

•

the north will receive a disproportionate share, with light industry focused on the south and heavier industry on the north. In the meantime,
the deep division in the nation will continue to be a major political and
economic problem.

FOREIGN INVESTMENT ON
THE INCREASE

As it adopted the *Doi Moi* policy, the government of Vietnam, appreciating the developments in the rest of East Asia and not least in the South
China region, made attracting foreign investment a major part of its efforts at renovation. A new foreign investment law went into effect in
1988, with substantially liberal provisions for treatment of foreign investors. One hundred percent ownership is now possible, with generous tax
treatment for investors in priority sectors. The State Committee for Cooperation and Investment (SCCI) screens foreign investment applications, carries out feasibility and evaluation studies, and offers assistance in
finding and dealing with local partners. With main offices in both Ho
Chi Minh City and Hanoi, the final decisions for all investment projects
is taken in Hanoi—with tensions and jockeying for position evident between the two office locations, to the occasional detriment of the foreign
applicant who needs to deal with both offices with some care.

The amendments to the investment rules have had effect, as the
number of investments approved annually quadrupled from 1988 to
1992, with a similar increase in the amounts approved, the average investment totaling about $10 million. Cumulative totals of the number of
investments and amounts approved are shown in Table 7–2. Taiwan and
Hong Kong together account for about two-fifths of the total over the
five-year period and more than half of the most recent approvals, with
Taiwanese companies the largest investors in Vietnam, as they have been
in Malaysia and Indonesia since the early 1990s.

A major sector of foreign investment interest has inevitably been petroleum, as Vietnam is believed to have substantial offshore oil and gas
reserves. The one operating field was a Mobil find, its exploitation in the
hands of a Soviet-Vietnamese joint venture after the U.S. development
was halted in 1975. Nearly two dozen licenses have been issued for petroleum development with the majors—Shell, Total, BP—represented

●

Table 7–2   **Foreign Investment Approvals Cumulative to Dec. 25, 1992**

Country	Total Investment ($ million)	Number of Cases
Taiwan	1,095	70
Hong Kong	476	98
France	322	29
Netherlands	310	29
Japan	304	12
United Kingdom	280	22
Australia	272	7
CIS	221	43
Korea	150	17
Canada	112	10
ROW	1,084	219
TOTALS	4,626	556

Source: Reprinted from *Vietnam Investment Review* (Hanoi: The [Vietnamese] State Committee of Cooperation and Investment), May 1993, p. 21.

along with three Japanese firms, the Belgians, Swiss, Indians, and a mix of others; American firms alone are not yet represented. Oil exists, and its exploration could be the platform for the launch of the economic development of the nation.

Telecommunications have drawn considerable foreign interest as Vietnam's needs for improved systems are massive. Overseas Telecommunications Corporation (OTC) of Australia was an early and very successful investor, in a satellite station, and has followed up on its early success with additional telecommunications investments, while Alcatel and Siemens, using in part loan funds from their governments, are competing with Japan's NEC in the telephone field. The Italians and Japanese are working on fiber-optic cable systems as well. Clearly, when World Bank and Asian Development funds are available for projects in Vietnam, telecommunications will be a competitive battleground for the world's major firms—just as power systems will provide another competitive, large-scale sector for sales and investment.

In the much-needed banking sector, the first foreign banks set up branches in 1992, and a number of banks from around the world are ready to follow, with a dozen licenses already granted. These banks

•

should facilitate the financing of foreign investments and help break the financial barrier to entry.

For while foreign investment is increasing, the amounts are still small, and the number of SCCI approvals are misleading. About 15 percent of the approved investment licenses have been withdrawn, most having been issued to foreigners lacking the resources to execute the projects. Moreover, problems of obtaining funding have meant that most of the approved projects have not yet been activated, and SCCI estimates that perhaps one-quarter of approved investments have actually been made.

Three types of investments can be made—100 percent foreign-owned companies, joint ventures with local partners in which the foreign party has at least a 30 percent equity holding, and business cooperation contracts related to specified products in a fixed volume for a defined period, without the need to create a new company.

Three-quarters of the foreign investments are joint ventures. A venture announced in late 1992 by Japan's leading food company, Ajinomoto, already well established elsewhere in Southeast Asia, is a representative example. Ajinomoto is setting up B & W Vietnam, a Ho Chi Minh City–based company, in which it will have 60 percent equity and Vietnam Food Industries will hold 40 percent. Ajinomoto's international sales manager will be president of the 200-person operation, to which Ajinomoto will dispatch four staff members. The business will import, manufacture, and sell condiments and flavorings, and expects a French and two Taiwan competitors in the monosodium glutamate market, of which Ajinomoto now has the leading share.

The limited foreign investment to date is caused by financing problems but also by issues of recruitment of labor. Labor for wholly owned foreign firms can be obtained only through government-owned recruiting companies, which at least doubles the wage rate. Because the low labor rates in Vietnam are often the major attraction for an investor, this rule effectively makes Vietnam uncompetitive as an investment site when compared with other locations in Southeast Asia. The joint venture avoids this kind of problem, while it raises other issues of partner relations and management control.

Relief from some of the investment hazards will come as the Vietnamese government is able to get its proposed Export Processing Zones in operation. These will speed up approvals as there is no requirement to deal directly with the SCCI, tax holidays and reduced rates will

•

be available, intrazone transactions will be freely convertible, there will be duty exemption for raw material imports and product exports, direct hiring will be possible, and each of the SEPZONES is to have its own minipowerstation. Altogether, these are likely to be very attractive, with two already under construction in the Ho Chi Minh City area and two more planned for the north.

Perhaps these initiatives will speed up much-needed investment from abroad. By the end of 1992, foreign-invested companies employed fewer than 10,000 workers, even though the average monthly wage was only $40, with skilled workers earning $60 and management salaries from about $170. Still, for most companies attracted by the Vietnamese labor supply, the preferred approach is likely to be the business cooperation contract route, with no equity at risk and the ability to withdraw should the venture prove unsatisfactory.

Leaving aside petroleum and other raw material exploitation, which is always a special case, we note that the market opportunities will be mainly in infrastructure projects as international funding becomes available. Investment opportunities for most companies will be found in taking advantage of the labor resource—and that can be accomplished without equity investments.

Care must be taken to keep Vietnam in perspective. Caught up in the general enthusiasm about East Asian growth, investors have made more of Vietnam possibilities than is generally warranted. It is suggested that the positions that U.S. companies might achieve are being pre-empted by others while the U.S. government embargo continues in effect. That seems not to be the case. It is very early still in Vietnam, and there is ample time to establish positions as the course of development becomes clearer. In the meantime, Japanese firms might have the best of it because, as so often before, the great Japanese trading companies—Itohchu, Mitsui Bussan, Mitsubishi Shoji, Nissho Iwai, Tomen, and others—have experienced staff in well-equipped offices in Hanoi and Ho Chi Minh City fully conversant with the local situations and ready to help their client Japanese firms as the opportunities arise. This kind of watching brief is most appropriate for most foreign companies at this time, and the trading companies and their obsession with information give Japanese competitors a valuable advantage.

While being cautious about premature commitments, real optimism about the larger prospects for Vietnam seem well justified. As the Cambodian issue is dealt with, full Vietnam participation in world affairs will

•

take place. Having acceded to the ASEAN treaty, Vietnam will be drawn into that grouping. Relations with China will remain tricky, with territorial disputes a problem, but both sides need stability first of all to deal with their internal concerns. Vietnam is a member of the UN, the IMF, the World Bank, and the Asian Development Bank, although the benefits of these memberships have been limited by U.S. vetoes. The prosperity of East Asia will boost the economy of Vietnam, and impending international fund flows will reinforce the process.

While serving as Australian ambassador, Graham Allibrand wrote, "I foresee little substantial change in the internal political landscape in Vietnam, particularly if there are no serious setbacks in the gradual improvements in the economy. For the vast majority of the Vietnamese people, I believe, their overwhelming concern is for improvements in their material well-being. . . . It is unlikely that in Vietnam there will be political upheaval and transformation on the East European model, or disturbances and bloody repression along the lines of Tiananmen Square. The energy of the leadership will be primarily geared to meeting the economic and social aspirations of the Vietnamese people. This is what *Doi Moi* is really all about."[20]

Vietnam, after 130 years of colonial rule and warfare, is entering the world community at last. It will not be isolated from the dramatic economic progress sweeping through East Asia. Its well-educated and inexpensive labor force, store of resources, hard-earned independence and pride, and proven competence in coping with economic disasters ensure that it will take its proper place as one of the most powerful nations of East Asia. It is, for world business, the future frontier, an economy that can and should be shared by Western companies as well as those from Japan and elsewhere in East Asia.

8

•

NETWORKS, GROUPS, AND GROWTH

The technology and systems of organization that shifted the world economy to industrialization and sustained economic growth were Western developments, and for a long time were found only in the West. Western imperial dominance of Asia was one result of the power that arose from this industrial system. Japan was the first non-Western nation to industrialize, and its success is a main cause of the historic move of all East Asia to rapid economic growth and industrial power.

Despite recent Asian successes, there is still a widespread view that the Western approach to industrialization is somehow the correct and proper approach. The cultures of Asian nations are in many important respects quite different from those of the West, however, and it should come as no surprise to find differences in industrial and economic organization. Technology can be culturally neutral; organizations and their values cannot.

Differences are seen most often in comparisons of opposites such as Western individualism and Asian group identity, Western rationality and Asian paternalism, Western independence and Asian dependency. Much of the vocabulary contains references to family, and there is a view that differences in family systems drive many of the differences in approach to

•

industrial and political organizations. "The Asian family was probably stronger historically than the Western family, and certainly it has remained a strong refuge in an otherwise rapidly changing social scene. . . . There are of course strains on the family in Asia . . . In general, however, the authority of the family, and of lineage, remains strong, and Asians continue to be socialized into accepting the obligations of deference toward paternal authority and sacrificing individual interests for the collectivity.

"Thus the cornerstone of power-building in the Asian cultures is loyalty to a collectivity. Out of the need to belong, to submerge one's self in a group identity, is power formed in Asian political cultures. The sense of security that the family can provide becomes the ideal to be recaptured in new bonding relationships. Loyalty to a collectivity can offer the exhilaration or thrill of being on a 'team.' "[1]

Asia is of course culturally and socially diverse—just as the West is. For both areas, generalizations are hazardous. Yet there is a persistent differentiation along the lines of group values, in contrast to Western emphasis on individual values, a difference ascribed to differences in family organization and strength. These carry forward into economic and business behaviors and values.

Antitrust laws and their enforcement might serve as a good example. In the United States in particular, antitrust laws are treated as a kind of moral imperative, a set of absolutes that admit of exception or relaxation only under the most urgent conditions. Thus, formal legislation is required to allow cooperative research, even of the most basic sort, by companies in the same industry. Moreover, the United States government presumes to seek to impose its definitions of and approach to enforcement of antitrust laws throughout the world and especially in Asia.

Asians, in contrast, are quite prepared to recognize that antitrust laws can be economically useful and that, for example, unregulated monopolies are intolerable, price competition is beneficial, and collusion on contract bidding is costly—to take a few accepted examples of bad practices. This does not mean, however, that cooperation between firms is necessarily bad, at all times, in all fashions, and to any ends. Interfirm relations can in fact, in the Asian view, be of very real economic benefit. And out of such differences arise trade frictions.

It is in this area of relations between firms, as well as the kind and degree of linkage of the individual to the firm, that the differences between business practices in the West and in Asia often appear to be con-

•

siderable and to create problems in relations. Groupings of businesses, or networks of businesses, appear to be a special feature of the business structures of the economies of East Asia. The Overseas Chinese family firms and their linkages to other companies, the role of the *chaebol* in the Korean economy and the phenomenon of *keiretsu* in Japan can all be seen as networks. "The Chinese business networks are largely personal networks and are organized primarily through kinship circles and ties of common origins. Japanese business networks are predominately intercorporate ties that cement together a vast network of firms. The South Korean business networks are dominated by elite business families that have been privileged by a strong state.

"In every country of the region the business networks are more significant—that is, stronger—than the individual firms that make up the networks. Networks are the main units of analysis for all of the economies. Therefore, if one would understand Asian business development, one must first understand Asian business networks."[2]

Even if networks are not so critical to Asian development as these authors suggest, it is clear that the successful positioning of Western companies in the area depends on understanding, dealing with, and relating to them effectively. What makes the issue of special importance is the rise to central position throughout East Asia of the Overseas Chinese.

THE ECONOMIC STRENGTH OF THE OVERSEAS CHINESE

As the tide of growth has moved across the nations of Southeast Asia, a new economic force has come into play, the Overseas Chinese. Over the centuries, emigration from China, especially into the nearby areas of Southeast Asia, has been substantial, as Chinese emigrants played a major role in trade in what was then the East Indies, even before the Europeans. Seen as hardworking and generally undemanding, Chinese labor was imported by Western mines and plantations, established in the nineteenth century, into Southeast Asia. Wars, famine, and other pressures also spurred emigration, even though officially banned by the Chinese authorities.

The results of the emigration are a population of perhaps 26 million that can be classed as Overseas Chinese, two-thirds of these in the

•

ASEAN nations (see Table 8–1). Another 26 million Chinese live in
Taiwan, Hong Kong, and Macao, and these too are often considered as
Overseas Chinese. Most of these statistics are approximate, because intermarriage and adoption of local citizenship make precise definition difficult. We can assume, however, that the "Sojourners to the South Seas,"
the Chinese expression for this group, total about 50 million.

Their economic influence is considerable, whatever the actual number. Two comments illustrate this: "The GNP of China is somewhere in
the order of $300 billion, with 1,008 million people. An estimate of the
equivalent for the Overseas Chinese, taking account of their officially
unacknowledged power in the ASEAN economies, would be somewhere in the region of $200 billion GNP, with around 40 million peo-
ple. With only one-twentieth of the manpower, the Overseas Chinese
are playing in the same league-table economically as the whole of
China."[3]

More recently, the *Economist* said, "Overall, one conservative estimate puts the 1990 'GNP' of Asia's 51 million overseas Chinese, Taiwan
and Hong Kong included, at $450 billion—a quarter bigger than China's
then GNP, and, per head, at about 80 percent of the level of Spain or
Israel."[4]

However calculated, it is a fact that the position of the Overseas Chi-

Table 8–1   Overseas Chinese by Country of Residence

Country	Overseas Chinese Population (approximate, thousands)	Percent of Total Population
Indonesia	6,000	3–4
Thailand	5,000	10
Malaysia	4,700	30
Singapore	2,000	0.5
United States	1,200	75
Philippines	1,000	1–2
Vietnam	1,000	1–2
Myanmar	800	2
Canada	500	2
All other countries	3,800	
Total	26,000	

Source: Reprinted from Yu Chukun, "Kakyo/Kajin no Sekaiteki Bocho," in Yu Chu Kun, Ed.,
Sekai no Chiyanisu (Tokyo: Simal Press, 1991), pp. 28–29.

nese in Southeast Asia represents, if measured collectively, exceptional economic power. They do not form an integrated single community, however; rather, they belong to several different language groups and often identify fairly strongly with their respective communities. Further, the level of economic power held by each group and the tensions and problems arising from that power—often augmented by a tendency to hold themselves separate from the larger community—differs considerably from country to country in Southeast Asia.

The position of the Overseas Chinese appears to be especially strong in Indonesia, where they make up only 3 or 4 percent of the total population but account for as much as three-quarters of all privately held domestic business assets. All of the largest business organizations in Indonesia are controlled by Overseas Chinese, led by the largest, the Salim Group and its 350 to 400 subsidiary companies, with more than 150,000 employees and assets estimated several years ago at more than $3.5 billion.

In Thailand, "almost all the owners and controllers of Thai big business are descendants of Overseas Chinese. Probably there is only one distinguished 'indigenous' capitalist group, the Siam Cement group, which is financially supported by the Crown Property Bureau. However, although the dominant domestic capitalist groups of Thailand have always been ethnic Chinese, they have most been locally born, hold Thai nationality and use the Thai language."[5]

In Malaysia, where the Overseas Chinese make up about one-third of the population, there has been in force since 1970 a policy to shift economic power away from foreign holders and Chinese toward the Malay population, the *bumiputra,* through direct government intervention and share acquisition. Malay holdings of domestic assets have increased from under 40 percent in 1970 to 75 percent in 1990. Ironically, however, much of that change is at the expense of other than Chinese foreign holders, down from 60 percent to 25 percent over the period. Shareholdings of the Overseas Chinese in Malaysia actually increased substantially over the period, in spite of official policy, from 22 percent in 1970 to about 33 percent in 1990.[6]

Or as one commentator put it, "In examining the resilience and success of some leading members of the Chinese business community in Malaysia, we find an apparent paradox: while the Chinese family-oriented closed corporation, based on an individual tycoon and his family, has heretofore often been thought to limit Chinese capacity for capital mobilization and organizational expansion, it is precisely such firms which, in alliance with powerful Malay patrons, have prospered the most. . . . Chinese business activities in Malaysia have in many respects held their own, and some businessmen have vastly expanded their fortunes."[7]

The economic strength of the Overseas Chinese in the Philippines is less than in Thailand, Indonesia, and Malaysia (this might help explain the relative lack of economic success of the Philippines). Still, former president of the Philippines Corazon Aquino is of Chinese descent, and her family is one of the major landholding and industrial groups in the country. Assimilation of the Chinese has progressed rapidly in the Philippines, owing in part to easy access to citizenship.

Overall, the position of the Overseas Chinese in the economies of Southeast Asia is quite clear. Yoshihara concludes, "The post-war period has been one of decline for Western capital, but for Chinese capital, it has been one of expansion. Being an element of domestic capital, it benefited from the nationalization of Western capital, restrictions on the entry and operation of foreign capital, and protection and promotion of domestic capital—the measures the South-East Asian governments launched after independence to put the economy on a new development path. . . . The combination of Chinese business acumen and the governments' nationalistic policy seems to have made Chinese capital the most important element of capital in South-East Asia. . . . In no major area is private indigenous capital more important than Chinese capital."[8] From another perspective, Ruth McVey concludes, "All these studies of individual countries show Southeast Asian domestic private enterprise to be overwhelmingly in the hands of local Chinese."[9]

This wealth and economic power, together with a continuing identity with Chinese culture and pride in Chinese heritage, make for resentments among the indigenous locals that are reflected in political tensions and, on occasion, violence. Assimilation of the Chinese immigrants has been extensive in Buddhist Thailand and in the largely Christian Philippines, both countries where there are no religious barriers to intermarriage and where local citizenship by Chinese immigrants is the rule.

It is in Malaysia and Indonesia, however, where the Chinese are a very real issue. In both countries, there have been savage riots directed against the Chinese, with large-scale incidents in Indonesia in 1965 with the fall of Sukarno, and in Malaysia in 1969 following a controversial election. Both countries are predominately Muslim, Indonesia being the largest Islamic country in the world, and marriage outside of the Islamic faith is discouraged.

Even in the Philippines, local Chinese have become targets, suffering the kidnapping of their children, because Overseas Chinese are seen as wealthy and vulnerable. Throughout the Southeast Asian area, including Singapore, whose political leadership is Overseas Chinese, policies have been promulgated to eliminate Chinese languages, Chinese customs, and even Chinese names. No doubt while mainland China is seen as a potential threat to national integrity, and while the upper echelons of economic power are held by Overseas Chinese businesspeople, anti-Chinese policies will continue to be the general rule, gradually alleviated by assimilation and lessened security concerns.

The use of the blanket term "Overseas Chinese" and the tendency to view the group as monolithic are both inaccurate. The migrations to the south took place from several areas along the Chinese coast. There are five main language and social groupings involved in the Chinese diaspora—the Hokkien, the Chiu Chow, the Hakka, the Cantonese, and the Hainanese. Most of these emigrants came from the two provinces of Fujian and Guangdong, and these two provinces now are special economic zones and the focus of foreign capital flows into China.

Each group has its own language, and identity by clan and lineage is strong, which makes for strong group differences and distinct group identities. Furthermore, the notion of family group is a strong one, especially in the south of China, and this too makes for separateness within the larger Overseas Chinese grouping. Indeed, the sense is of a pattern of loyalties rather like that attributed to the Italians—family first, always; lineage, second; village, third—and some distance back, company and nation.

THE TRAVELING FAMILIES: WHY ARE THEY SUCCESSFUL?

Among the language/regional groups of the great emigrations of Chinese, a seeming disproportionate number of Hakkas hold prominent positions. The Hakka name is an interesting one, made up of the character for traveler or guest and the character for household or family—the "traveling family." And indeed the Hakka have traveled, first to the

•

south of China from their original, more northern home, and then in great numbers abroad, estimated at 5 million, or about 20 percent of all Overseas Chinese.

A recent Japanese discussion of the Hakka cited their characteristics: "Strong unity, diligence, patience, enthusiasm for education and martial spirit." The Japanese report notes further, "Many of China's political leaders are said to be descendants of the Hakka. Among them are Deng Xiaoping, Prime Minister Li Peng, Deputy Prime Minister Zou Jiahua and Ye Xuanping, governor of Guangdong province, who holds the key to development in the South China Economic Zone.

"Lee Kuan Yew, former prime minister of Singapore, Goh Chok Tong, present prime minister of Singapore, and Lee Teng-hui, President of Taiwan, are also descendents of the Hakka. Philippines President Corazon Aquino is said to be related to the Hakka. . . . In business, Soedono Salim, head of the Salim Group in Indonesia, and Chatri Sophonpanich, chairman of the Bangkok Bank Group, are Hakka. Both groups are among the largest conglomerates in Southeast Asia. They are at the center of the human and financial networks of Overseas Chinese and exercise great influence over the overseas Chinese economy as a whole."[10]

"Networks" is a recurring and central theme in discussions of the Overseas Chinese. The close ties forged by language, family/clan, and village identities persist very strongly even after a long period as émigré, and they continue over generations. But the networking has no doubt other strong reasons for persisting. These émigrés are survivors of whatever crisis caused them to emigrate and often conditions of near slavery after emigration. Networks of those who could be trusted by reason of common descent become valuable properties to survivors, to be maintained and nurtured. They are in fact safety nets.

The contrast can be made with Japan. Lin Yu-tang in a much-quoted phrase described Japanese society as monolithic and cohesive, like a block of granite, while China remains a tray of loose sand, each grain a separate family. The metaphor overstates each case but in a useful fashion. It implies a further characteristic of the Chinese networks—the limited amount of cooperation between Chinese clans and groups.

This networking phenomenon helps make foreign investment statistics unreliable. The Taiwanese business traveler of Xiamen makes an informal arrangement to fund a schoolmate in exchange for supply of output through Hong Kong. No one is troubled with obtaining approval for the investment or filing documents. The Hong Kong trader visits a cousin living in the Cholon district of Ho Chi Minh City, bringing funds to start some apparel manufacture. And so on to much more grand and sophisticated arrangements. The sprawl of the nations of East Asia is much diminished by these networks of relations and helps make national boundaries in these newly established nations porous. "Traditionally, merchants who set up businesses away from their hometowns formed native-place associations to lend each other support and to provide networking for newcomers. The same merchants could then form associations with others with whom they shared a common line of trade, common surname, even with some other combination of native-place origin, and so forth.

"Many scholars have been critical of these forms of networking because their reliance on particularistic values breeds nepotism, parochialism, inequities, and malevolent authoritarianism. What is often left out of these critiques, however, is that the same value system also emphasizes trustworthiness, reliability and sterling reputation, all of which may be subsumed under the Chinese term *xinyong*.

"Good entrepreneurs are influenced by sentimental factors to begin a networking . . . On the other hand, when such a relationship is exploited, the successful entrepreneur would probably cut them off."[11]

Another feature suggested as helping to explain current business successes is that the early Chinese immigrants to Southeast Asia tended to be active in trading and commerce, over a broad range of activities, from tiny retail shops to representing officials and nobility in commercial transactions. The proposition is offered that, in contrast to the native cultures, the values of the Chinese immigrants were much more focused on money, or what is termed money-mindedness. It is even suggested that the southern Chinese—those in the provinces from which most emigration occurs—place special value on money.

Inevitably, parallels are drawn between the Overseas Chinese and the emigrant Jew, the Overseas Chinese as "the Jews of the Orient," an analogue that seems to have been drawn quite early in Western comments on Chinese emigrants. The parallels are real. Discrimination against the Chinese immigrant, forced residence in ghettolike separate settlements, a shift into occupations such as trading not well regarded by or even closed to the native populace, drawing together in special associations—these are in common with the emigrant Jew, but with a great many other emigrant groups as well. One thinks immediately of Indians in East Africa as another Asian case. Like the attribute of working hard, also attributed to the Overseas Chinese, much of this can be explained as simply the hard lot of the impoverished stranger in a new land.

Still another explanation for Chinese success is the tradition of Confucianism and the values associated with it: respect for authority, filial piety, harmony within the group, and stress on education. Because the rapidly growing economies of East Asia—Japan, Taiwan, Korea, Hong Kong, and Singapore—share a Confucian tradition, Confucianism was taken to be a causal factor in these successes and by extension to the success of the Overseas Chinese. However, "The 'Confucian Culture' argument has had a curious career, for it began not in its present role of explaining why capitalist development in East Asia had been such a success but rather of suggesting why the Chinese were unlikely to make good capitalists."[12] Indeed, Confucianist Vietnam has yet to begin its move to prosperity, and the birthplace of Confucianism, China, serves still to illustrate better the notion that Confucianism is a hindrance rather than a help to economic growth.

The success of the Chinese immigrants in Southeast Asia, if indeed they have been successful (and most have not been), is no doubt a coming together of a great many factors, including chance. Some of the factors are summarized by Yoshihara: "The Chinese have tremendous advantages over the indigenous because they had networks which helped them to get training, a start in business, and credit, supplies amd information. However, they do not seem to be the only reason for Chinese strength in business. The built-in bias of indigenous society against plain money-making and toward nonmaterialistic aspects of life; the fact that the Chinese communities were, until recently, constantly being replenished with immigrants who were willing to work hard to make money; and the social pressure which forced the Chinese from the second generation onwards to adopt the value system of their immigrant ancestors as a matter of survival where the Chinese were discriminated against . . . these seem to have conjoined to make the Chinese a more dynamic element of the South-East Asia economy."[13]

EVOLUTION FROM
FAMILY-HELD BUSINESSES

The kinds of organizations developed in Southeast Asia by the Overseas Chinese vary with the background of the entrepreneurs and the country in which they found themselves. The prototype is the family-owned or

•

-dominated closed corporation, with the founder/tycoon and his family as the decision makers, and the sons taking control on the death of the founding father.

Much the greatest part of the largest businesses in Southeast Asia is Overseas Chinese–founded and shares this pattern of close family ownership and control. The Cheung Kong group of Li Ka-shing in Hong Kong recently had an outside Westerner as managing director of its key holding, Hutchinson Whampoa, but the two sons of Li are clearly being prepared for the succession. The late Y. K. Pao of shipowning wealth in Hong Kong had no son as successor and took the extraordinary step of dividing his empire among his four sons-in-law, one Austrian and one Japanese as it happened. His example has not been followed by others, such as the great Thai groups of the Bangkok Bank and CP Pokphand, where the sons of the founders now are the heads of these groups.

It is some interest to note, though, that in the founder-to-son succession in several of these groups, the Confucian dictate of the oldest son as heir has given way to business needs for ability. For example, the successor to Liem Sioe Liong, founder of the Salim Group, will be his youngest son, Anthony, who is already designated heir.

Still, all these patterns are familiar in businesses that are quite remote from China and its traditions. The notion of a powerful founder, holding his empire close in terms of ownership and control and conveying his fortune and power to his heirs, is an old one, chronicled in the histories and novels of the West. And just as in the West, these Overseas Chinese companies and groups of companies are yielding to both internal and external pressures for change. "We must bear in mind that the very newness of most big Southeast Asian businesses means that we are talking about change within one generation, and it is very hard to expect men who rose from nothing to head great corporations to relinquish the methods that were their key to success and remain the basis for their current power."[14]

Several trends are evident and foreseeable. First, not all the transitions to the next generation are smooth or even successful. Even the Astra group of Indonesia, generally considered the most professionally managed group of its type, came on hard times as one of its main holdings, run by the son and heir of the group founder, got into deep financial trouble. The Astra group founder, William Soeryadjaya, stepped down from his position as group head to take over the troubled business from his son, while an outsider took over chairmanship of the Astra

•

group itself as the result of heavy pressure from investors and the Indonesia government.

Of more general significance is the issue of ownership. Over time these groups will pass out of family control, and for several compelling reasons. One is the need for additional capital. Throughout Southeast Asia local stock markets are now attracting considerable interest and large amounts of money. As these groups continue to grow, additional capital is required beyond the interest or ability of the family owners to provide. Taking some part or all of the family business public can provide the required capital and can be attractive for family members looking to diversify holdings or to cash out.

Taking some or all of the business public also provides a way of dealing with the continuing political pressures that these groups face. Even with strong political backing from well-placed patrons—a consistent characteristic of the rise of these entrepreneurs—there is always a danger of political upheaval and reversals that can threaten the existence of the family business. Sharing ownership with the local public provides a shield against this threat. Moreover, there is often pressure from local politicians to take the enterprise public. President Suharto of Indonesia has pressed hard for increased public participation in the ownership of the Great Indonesia corporate groups.

With these changes in ownership there are consequent increased disclosure requirements and a need to take a somewhat longer-term view of return on investment, countering the well-known secretive tendencies of emigrant Chinese and desires for a quick turn and return on their invested funds. In turn, these changes help convert developing economies into more sophisticated and developed capital markets and business centers. Over time the enterprises of the Overseas Chinese are likely to be managed in the style of big businesses in most developed economies, run by professional managers and owned by a wide range of investing shareholders.

All of this said, it is still very much the case, however, that the businesses of Southeast Asia are Overseas Chinese businesses, closely held and family-dominated. The extent to which the Chinese connection is critical to these economies can be gauged on the basis of the capital flows shown in Table 8–2. As the economies of Southeast Asia have taken off, especially since 1985, the flows of direct foreign investment have increasingly come from the Chinese-dominated economies in the area. While direct investment into ASEAN from the United States increased more

•

Table 8–2   **Foreign Direct Investment in ASEAN, 1986–90 ($ million)**

	1990 Total	1986 Total	Change 1986–90
Chinese-descent countries	$7,479	$447	16.8 ×
Taiwan	$3,868	92	42.1 ×
Hong Kong	2,411	86	28.4 ×
Singapore	1,200	269	4.5 ×
Japan	6,810	928	7.3 ×
United States	1,513	347	4.4 ×

Source: Reprinted from Yozo Tanaka, Minako Mori, and Yoko Mori, *RIM Pacific Business and Industries* (Tokyo: Sakuin Institute of Research), June 1992, p. 18.

than fourfold in four years, the flow from Taiwan, Hong Kong, and Singapore increased by more than 16 times in the four-year period.

It seems safe to assume that the United States numbers are reasonably accurate owing to official reporting requirements. It also is safe to assume that the numbers for the Chinese-descent countries are considerably understated, as unofficial investments tend to predominate. The actual totals then may well be, and in fact almost certainly are, even more stunning. No doubt these data reflect information and investing networks within the Chinese community as a whole, with capital able to move relatively freely across political boundaries.

Some special note might be taken here of the effect of this on Japanese investors. It seems quite clear that less tension now surrounds Japanese investment in Southeast Asia than was the case some years ago when the Japanese were perceived as "economic animals" and were targets of real animosity. The reduction of tension undoubtedly owes something to improved Japanese management of their position and to a better appreciation of the advantages of Japanese investment by each recipient country. It is also surely due to the fact that as Chinese investment comes to dominate incoming investment, Japanese investment is less conspicuous, and thus a less visible target for critics.

As their success has continued, the Overseas Chinese groups have begun to move out of their local bases into the international business arena. Thailand's agrobusiness CP group has set up a Hong Kong holding company for its considerable interests in China, Indonesia, and else-

●

where in the region, providing access to the Hong Kong capital market, among other advantages. This follows the move of the Salim group of Indonesia, whose Hong Kong company, First Pacific, manages the increasingly diversified interests of the group, including substantial positions in chemical production not only in Indonesia but also in Vietnam, Australia, and the Philippines.

As the Overseas Chinese–owned businesses of Southeast Asia reach the point at which their resources make international moves possible, China becomes—as it has for Overseas Chinese investors from Taiwan, Hong Kong, and Singapore—another site for investment, drawn by Chinese government programs to attract their investment and by their strong personal linkages with the country. CITIC Pacific is a listed company on the Hong Kong exchange, the investment vehicle of the China International Trust and Investment Corporation, a major corporation of the Chinese government. In turn, CITIC Pacific has acquired a Hong Kong trading company in association with Li Ka-Shing and Malaysia's Robert Kuok. CP of Thailand is another investor in China as the Chinese government encourages the Overseas Chinese business community to support China's development efforts.

The personal links lead to investment as well. Liem Sioe Liong, believed to be the richest man in Indonesia, left the Fujian village of Fuqing as a young man and has now returned as its benefactor, investing more than $100 million in hotel, factory, and port facilities in his impoverished birthplace.[15] These kinds of involvements are the network phenomenon operating again, and the result will surely be the furthering of the growth of the South China regional economies as well as the building of effective, although unofficial, ties to the economies of ASEAN.

With these somewhat nostalgic investments, the pattern of Overseas Chinese influence comes full circle to the nation and even village from which they began their emigration. Their power and influence must be kept in perspective, however. First, as with any businesspeople, these individuals are vulnerable to business errors. One of the wealthiest, Hong Kong's Li Ka-Shing, has been a major investor in North America, acquiring the Vancouver site of Canada's Expo and buying into Canada's Husky Oil, hoping to diversify his interests (and perhaps also to find a safe haven in North America). The Husky venture is proving to be an extremely costly error, however, bought at the top and requiring heavy additional funds to stay solvent.

•

POLITICAL VULNERABILITY
AND ASSIMILATION

The most important aspect of their vulnerability remains their position as a highly visible, wealthy minority in largely poverty-stricken environments. Throughout Southeast Asia, the Overseas Chinese tycoons depend on local politicians, bureaucrats, and the military for support and favors, and there is the constant risk that a political upheaval will bring down supporters—even when the upheaval falls short of the kind of racial disturbances that occurred, and still threaten on occasion, in Malaysia and Indonesia.

Throughout Southeast Asia, the fortunes of the Overseas Chinese have been tightly intertwined with indigenous political power. Indeed, it was the overthrow of the Western colonial regimes and the consequent loss of power of Western businesses that have been an important factor in the rise of the Overseas Chinese. As British banks and businesses were displaced in Thailand and Malaysia, and the Dutch in Indonesia, the Chinese, who already worked as intermediaries between the Western interests and local society, found their way to open in business. Their role as intermediaries—as *compador* and *kapitan*—provided them with business knowledge and experience not generally available to the local population, who in any case tended to shun business. A kind of symbiotic relationship arose, often facilitated by corruption on a grand scale, between local political leaders intent on building the structures to replace imperial regimes and the Overseas Chinese, who were the businesspeople providing the capital and business acumen. "In much of Southeast Asia, it is well known that it takes two to get an 'Ali Baba' business off the ground—Ali the Indonesian or Malay who qualifies for government handouts, Baba the Chinese with the capital and the skill."[16] In Indonesia, where the army's role was critical in the early years of independence, the term *cukong* became popular. "*Cukong* is a Hokkien Chinese word meaning 'master,' but in Indonesia the term is used of an arrangement whereby Chinese businessmen act as financiers and corporate managers to powerful political figures, in particular the military, in return for access to government contracts, funds, favours and protection."[17] The most conspicuous of such relationships in Indonesia is the close relationship between President Suharto and his family with Liem of the Salim group.

Memories of the terrible disturbances in Indonesia and Malaysia and

•

the violence wreaked on the Chinese communities remain vivid, and the issue of discrimination is always near at hand, especially in these two Muslim nations. Less dramatic but even more possible is the fall from power of a key supporter and change in the power structure—many local and foreign interests in Indonesia have never regained the positions they enjoyed before the fall of Sukarno.

No doubt the fragility of these Overseas Chinese businesses is gradually being overcome. One reason is that the sheer importance of these companies and groups in the economies of ASEAN now helps to ensure their survival, though this is obviously no guarantee against measures such as expropriation. Other safeguards are developing, however. As noted, some of these companies are being listed on stock exchanges, with a wider spread of ownership as a result. Further, it is estimated that 90 percent of the Overseas Chinese now have local citizenship. Assimilation into Muslim-dominated communities is very slow and difficult, but in Thailand and the Philippines the process is well advanced. Vulnerability in Indonesia in particular, however, seems still a real problem and a real risk to the economy.

In the meantime, in both Malaysia and Indonesia, anti-Chinese measures and affirmative action programs to bolster the position of indigenous businesspeople and laborers exact a considerable economic price, not least in terms of Chinese business leaders seeking investment havens abroad. It is not clear what impact a resurgent China will have on this problem. The Overseas Chinese are seen, generally with good reason, as being closely tied to their homeland. Indeed, during the era of confrontation with China, the Overseas Chinese were often seen as a kind of fifth column, and in the period of the Malaysian Emergency as well as the Sukarno-period coup, with some cause. A resurgent and expansionist Communist China could make for a revival of the worst of discrimination and reaction against Overseas Chinese economic power. Assimilation and integration is of course the solution, but it will be a long time before it is achieved throughout the area.

THE OVERSEAS CHINESE AS PARTNERS

These large Chinese groups in the fast-growing economies of Southeast Asia raise some interesting issues of international business strategy, first as potential channels to business in Southeast Asia through joint ventures

•

and alliances, second as competitors, first in the region and ultimately perhaps on a wider basis. After all, it was only a few years ago that Samsung and Hyundai were only local firms, competing with each other in the Korean market, as little known in the West as Salim, Kuok Bros., Cheung Kong, and CP are today.

Not surprisingly, the Japanese have asked themselves about the competitive strengths of these groups and how best to work with them. A JETRO researcher notes the very substantial advantage the Japanese enjoy in engineering and R&D over these groups, and their relatively weak position in manufacturing. At the same time, the Overseas Chinese groups are seen as having competitive advantages as well, relative to Japanese firms. One is their internationalization, based on a tradition as émigrés requiring them to build strategies to suit whatever environment in which they found themselves, as well as their more international education and language skills.

A further advantage from the Japanese point of view is the ability of the Overseas Chinese group to make rapid decisions, unencumbered by the organizational structures of Japanese firms, able to move in a "one-man" decision-making style, in contrast to Japanese companies' committees and consensus seeking. Finally, the networks of relations that are characteristic of the Overseas Chinese are felt to provide channels for obtaining information and cooperation, not only in China but much more widely.[18]

There does seem to be a general view on the part of Japanese businesspeople that cooperation with the Overseas Chinese is both possible and advisable. As an example, the research facility of the Sakura Bank (formerly Mitsui Bank), which has long been the leader among Japanese banks in terms of expansion in East Asia, urges cooperation, arguing, "There are a number of things Japanese companies must keep in mind when investing in Southeast Asia. . . . Chinese in Southeast Asian countries have enormous economic power. Consequently, liaison with Overseas Chinese there is essential to Japanese investment in Southeast Asian countries. In order to promote economic exchanges between Japan and Southeast Asia, it is necessary to establish and maintain a relationship of coexistence and cooperation with Overseas Chinese in the region."[19]

A good deal of Japanese investment in Southeast Asia has occurred through joint ventures with local Chinese interests. This has been particularly true in Indonesia, where Toyota's involvement with the Astra group is an example. When General Motors refused to commit to local

manufacture in 1971, Astra took over its facilities that had been nation-
alized by the Indonesian government and linked up with Toyota in a
joint venture that in 1991 held a 29 percent market share. Toyota's related producer of smaller cars, Daihatsu, is also in a venture with Astra
that had 17 percent of the market in 1991. (General Motors's market
share of the 250,000 to 300,000 Indonesian market was 0.6 percent in
1991.)

    When the Soeryadjaya family, then owners of three-quarters of
Astra's shares, encountered major financial problems in another of their
businesses in 1992, Toyota was reported to be active in naming a re-
placement for William Soeryadjaya as Astra chair. Toyota was also reported to be buying shares in Astra as the Soeryadjaya interests sought
funds. Toyota clearly is more than a junior partner in this large and pros-
pering operation. In Thailand, Toyota held a 28 percent market share of
the automobile market in 1991, where it holds a majority share in a joint
venture that includes the Sophonphanich colossus, the Bangkok Bank
group.

    If the Overseas Chinese firms continue to grow at anything like their
recent rates and the growth rates of the economies in which they operate, they will arrive at world scale within a decade. For example, take the
current estimated revenues of the companies in the Salim group of $4
billion; assume growth at a 15 percent rate, not an outlandish assumption
given current East Asian economic performance; in ten years the Salim
group will have estimated revenues of some $24 billion. Nor would it be
lonely at this size, for a number of other Southeast Asian groups would
be of similar or even greater size. They will be players not only in regional but also in global business. They will have major positions along
the North American West Coast, where they have already begun operations. They will be major operators in China as that nation moves rapidly
to economic power. And they will be among the major drivers of the
growth of East Asia, the center of world industry.

    To review briefly some of the common features of the Overseas
Chinese companies and groups:

- They have achieved success in a period of great political and social
  change.
- A strong individual founder/entrepreneur has brought the group
  into prominence.
- The company or group has been family-owned with public

●

shareholding of some parts occurring because of political pressure and internal demands for capital.

- The company or group has been founder- and family-managed until the second or third generation of family operations, when professional managers begin to take charge.

- The founder has been deeply involved in and has drawn support from an extensive network based on family, hometown, and language connections.

- A patron/sponsor from government has been a critical factor in the founder's success.

- A multisubsidiary organization of as many as several hundred companies in a holding company serves to maintain family and central control.

GROUPS IN JAPAN AND KOREA

What is of interest about this pattern is that it also describes the enterprises that have been critical to the development of the economy of Japan in the first instance, and later of the Korean economy. In Japan, business groupings are still the general pattern, now under the umbrella term *keiretsu,* whereas the Korean groups are so recent that they retain a form quite similar in important respects to that of the Overseas Chinese groups.

Of course, the histories and cultures of Japan, Korea, and China differ greatly, and there are resultingly important differences in business organization. Yet the similarities are striking and greater than can easily be explained by chance or coincidence. The question needs to be addressed as to whether there is in fact an Asian pattern different from that of the West in business organization, and what that difference might imply for global business strategies.

Japan's *zaibatsu,* the centers of finance and industry as Japan's move to industrial power began, were, for the most part, products of a period of very great economic and social change following the opening of Japan to the West and the Meiji Restoration period. The Sumitomo and Mitsui interests had much longer histories, but they took on their modern configuration in the late nineteenth century. Family-owned and managed in the first generation at least, "the *zaibatsu* founders got their start as so-called Meiji political merchants . . . who used their ties to powerful political figures to obtain government favors enabling them to earn substantial profits in return for providing goods or services to the state. . . . Political merchant activities or mining or some combination of the two yielded the enormous fortunes that made possible the founding of the *zaibatsu*."[20]

As in the case of the Overseas Chinese groups, ownership of the *zaibatsu* holding company remained in the family, with public ownership of parts of the group arising only reluctantly under pressure, and professional management was introduced as generational transitions required. When the *zaibatsu* holding companies were abolished by Occupation dictate, the separate component companies tended to rapidly regroup with interlocking shareholdings and shared investments, a networking like the Overseas Chinese formed but one that was confined to national boundaries.[21]

Indeed, the principal difference between the Japanese *zaibatsu* groups and the Overseas Chinese groups is the nature of Chinese networking by family and language links across national boundaries, as a consequence of emigration. If the emigration factor is left to one side, the pattern of business groupings seems quite similar.

Korea's groups, the *chaebol,* are products of Korea's special history. Again, however, the similarities to the earlier *zaibatsu* and the Overseas Chinese groups are striking—family control and management, government officials as patrons/sponsors/protectors, family ownership yielded reluctantly under government pressure, a strong founder/entrepreneur who with government favors drives the system with an iron hand, and the multisubsidiary form of structure to help perpetuate family control.[22]

A STAGE IN ECONOMIC DEVELOPMENT

Are these patterns of networking and family-based group approaches to business organization special features of East Asian business and industry? Or are they simply a typical pattern as an economy and society moves from preindustrial to industrial status? The question becomes immediate as the position of the economies of East Asia becomes ever more central in world trade. The networks and groups of East Asia are by definition exclusive, favoring group members over outsiders and thus trading, sourcing, and investing to group member advantage.

This exclusive aspect has caused the issue of Japan's groupings, or *keiretsu,* to take prominent position in the trade discussions between Japan and the United States, called the Structural Impediments Initiative. For groups and networks, to the extent that they are exclusive—and by definition, they must be in some degree—are structural impediments to free and open trade.

Moreover, it can be argued that there are competitive advantages from organizing as networks and groups. Long-term commitments between supplier and customer allow shared investment in new projects, with each party supporting the other in times of business difficulty. Product development risks can be shared with suppliers, with the understanding that profits in the system will be shared reasonably equitably among the parties to the system. Companies in the group facing competitive threats or special investment opportunities can draw funds, management, and even technology from group associates. Contrast this to the presumed arms-length supply from the lowest bidder and impersonal relations presumed to occur in the more "rational" Western system.

The presumption that these patterns of networking and of family-based group organizations are a special feature of business structures in East Asia seems to rest on the general observation that social systems in East Asia are more group-centered than in Europe or North America, where the emphasis is on the individual and his or her needs and motives. Asia is seen, at least from the distance of the West, as more often demanding group identification at the expense of the interests of the individual, requiring more conformity in behavior and putting high priority on the attainment of group goals.

Like most very broad generalizations, this group versus individual characterization of East and West demands a good deal of qualification if it is to fit specific realities. But it does serve to identify what seems generally agreed to be a difference in fact, if in degree rather more than in kind.

Is East Asia really different in some fundamental fashion in its approach to business organization, or is this networking and group approach a function of the stage of economic progress of the region? Family firms, founded by an aggressive entrepreneur who holds ownership tightly within the family, are hardly peculiar to East Asia. Nor is political

•

patronage or sponsorship unknown in the West; during the glory days of fast growth and no antitrust laws, the U.S. Senate was well known for accommodating the needs of the railroad barons and emerging U.S. industries.

In fact, groupings of companies in a manner not greatly different from the approach of East Asian entrepreneurs is rather common in much of the West. The Wallenberg interests in Sweden, for example, still hold controlling interests in a good share of that nation's industrial output, their empire including such major international firms as ABB, Ericsson, and Alfa Laval. The Rothschild family has worked for several centuries as a financial power in Germany, France, and Britain in a cooperative fashion across national boundaries. As financial *keiretsu,* or groupings, the Banques d'Affaires of France are centers of industrial holdings, and Germany's Deutsche Bank holds a controlling interest in that country's largest industrial complex, Daimler Benz, along with many other major players in the German economy.

One conclusion seems warranted. The family-dominated group pattern of business organization is by no means peculiar to East Asia but seems to be common in the West as well, particularly in the earlier phases of industrialization when corporate scale is limited and family resources of finance and management can hold their own in competition. Moreover, in many parts of the West, continued financial groupings of the kind that in Japan are called financial *keiretsu* are also common, and in some cases even more tightly knit than the financial groups of Japan.

Indeed the Anglo-Saxon countries, if Britain and the United States can still be so designated, might well be the exception, in that in both, by practice and by law, interconnected financial groupings are less common and are seen to be in restraint of free trade. It appears that the Americans rather than the Asians are out of step with the world in this regard. And it might follow from this that the Americans need to reexamine their practices and laws to improve competitiveness.

In fact something like that seems to be happening as joint research efforts and organizations are exempted from U.S. antitrust, and as U.S. companies like General Motors make a concerted effort to reorganize supplier relations to reduce their numbers and increase the effectiveness and cooperative efforts of the survivors of the rationalization.

The persistence and pervasiveness of the *keiretsu* groupings in Japan suggests that a reasonable conclusion might be that the networking and group patterns of East Asian business will remain strong even after eco-

●

nomic maturity is reached, as it has been in Japan. This may well reflect underlying sociological differences, with an Asian preference for group focus over focus on the individual. In any case, at the current state of economic development in most of East Asia, Western firms seeking position in these flourishing markets must accommodate themselves to the reality of the exclusive tendencies of these approaches to organization.

The solution would appear to be the general approach of the Japanese, to join with these groups in some form of joint effort—perhaps in a formally structured joint venture company, perhaps in a less structured alliance for marketing or manufacturing capacity. These can, and probably should be, country-specific, for as the Sakura Institute noted in advising its Japanese clients, "One should not generalize about Overseas Chinese in Southeast Asia since they have different characteristics depending on where they live. Thus, in order to promote co-existence with Southeast Asian countries, Japanese companies should make an effort to interact with Overseas Chinese with better understanding not only of the local situation of each country, but also the specific situations and characteristics of the Chinese in each of the countries."[23] The advice is sound and can be applied to East Asian countries and groups generally. It applies to Western no less than to Japanese companies.

9
●

JAPAN'S *KAISHA* IN
EAST ASIA

"Japan's economic influence in Southeast Asia has increased so much in recent years that the region could no longer survive without Japanese capital and economic cooperation. The numbers of employees directly hired by Japanese companies in the five Southeast Asian countries amounted to 520,000 at the end of last year. . . . Including the number of workers employed by subcontractors of Japanese companies, millions more are estimated to be dependent on Japanese companies.

"The stepped up presence of Japanese business was the result of Japan's global economic strategy—relocating production bases to areas where wages are cheaper and raw materials are available. The perception is that Japan is close to dominating the economies of Southeast Asia, beyond just having a greater influence," according to the Korea Trade Promotion Corporation. The state-run company warned that "Japan's enhanced economic power in the region will likely result in the resurrection of the 'New Great Asia Co-Prosperity Zone.' "[1]

That a Korean government agency would take this view of Japanese investment in East Asia might be dismissed as another example of Korean-Japanese mutual antipathy. But it might also be seen as an effort to dampen Japanese investment thrusts into East Asia, because it is Korea,

●

with Taiwan, that is now becoming a major investor there—with no great relish for having larger Japanese companies as competitors.

How great an issue is the investment by Japan's *kaisha* in East Asia? Whatever the realities, and they will be looked at in detail here, reference to an East Asia Co-prosperity Sphere, conjuring up the tragedies of World War II, is hardly appropriate. One objective observer has remarked, "If I were dictator for a day and could zap words out of the language, 'Greater East Asia Co-prosperity Sphere' would be among the first to go. I find the term singularly unhelpful in describing today's Asian reality."[2]

Investment by Japanese companies in the economies of East Asia is indeed substantial, although arguably less than the requirements or opportunities might suggest. Japanese investment decisions are not driven by a global economic strategy, however, but rather by the general economic environment, by the specific and changing economics of different industries, and by the interests of the management of individual companies. In Japan, as in all the other market economies, the management of individual companies takes these decisions, not governmental agencies.

As Japan's economy becomes more sophisticated, labor- and land-intensive industries must be transferred to offshore locations to retain company competitiveness through lower cost inputs and to allow the shift of labor, capital, and technology in Japan to higher value-added sectors. Investment abroad provides capital and technology, as well as markets, to the host country, allowing that economy in turn to move to higher levels of output and income. The result is certainly "coprosperity," but not in the pejorative sense that the Korean Trade Corporation chose to use it.

It is precisely this virtuous cycle of investment and growth that is propelling all of East Asia to higher income levels—Japan included. It is in the interests of all for the process to continue, the more so because the companies of the United States and western Europe, preoccupied with their own internal issues, are failing to take advantage of the production and market opportunities presented by the economic revolution taking place in East Asia.

THE EFFECTS OF YEN REVALUATION

After small beginnings, foreign direct investment by Japanese companies got its real boost from the dramatic and drastic revaluation of the yen in 1985 and 1986, marked by the Plaza Agreement of the G-7 aimed at devaluing the dollar, particularly against the yen. No doubt there were hopes that a revaluation of the yen—nearly doubling its value against the dollar from about ¥260 to about ¥140—would slash Japanese exports: a much more valuable yen would be expressed in much higher export prices.

In the event, this expectation was naive: when did a strong currency ever become a handicap to development? Manufacturing costs in Japan dropped as raw material inputs, denominated in dollars, plunged in yen terms, which had the effect, for example, of halving Japan's import oil bill. This expectation also underestimated the ability of Japan's *kaisha* to reduce costs and to increase export prices on goods like VTRs, that were produced only in Japan.

In retrospect, it appears that the real impact of the sharp increase in the exchange value of the yen was the resulting requirement and commensurate capability of Japanese companies to invest in businesses abroad. Foreign assets suddenly became very much less expensive, their price from a Japanese point of view having been halved by revaluation. And as imports into Japan suddenly relatively cheaper and export prices from Japan higher, Japanese companies in many industries were forced to seek alternative locations to obtain cost improvements that could not be achieved at home.

What had undoubtedly been intended as an impediment to Japanese economic growth was turned to Japan's advantage. As trade surpluses continued, the money thus accumulated was recycled in considerable part by direct investment. Three-quarters of all Japanese investment abroad since the signing of the peace treaty in 1951 was made in the late 1980s, after the revaluation. Two-thirds of all investments by Japanese companies in East Asia was made in that same brief period from 1985 to 1990.

In the late 1980s, Japan's *kaisha* began to move abroad in earnest—to globalize. Initially, heavy investments were made in the United States. A good deal of this investment (like most in western Europe) was in corporate infrastructure sectors—distribution arms of Japan's general trading companies, banks that set out to win U.S. market share on the strength of their revalued currency, and brokerage firms moving to position themselves in Wall Street–centered world finance.

Japanese investment in manufacturing in the United States has generally been in those sectors around which the United States has built trade barriers—steel, automobiles, consumer electronics, and machine tools—with the total amount temporarily swollen by a few spectacular

•

acquisitions, notably the Sony and Matsushita Electric forays in Holly-
wood and entertainment software.

The direct investment patterns of Japanese companies in East Asia
have been quite different from those in the developed West. First, acquisitions are rarely an entry method in developing countries, where acquisition candidates are few and the climate for acquisition largely unfavor-
able. Second, the amounts of individual investments are relatively smaller
than those in the economies of the developed West, but the numbers of
investments are comparatively quite large. Finally, the main thrust of investment in East Asia has been in manufacturing.

INVESTMENT PATTERNS IN EAST ASIA

East Asia accounts for only 15 percent of Japanese foreign direct investment, while nearly half has gone to the United States and Canada, as
shown in Table 9–1. This small proportion of total investment in East
Asia might suggest a failure of Japanese companies to pursue Asian opportunities aggressively rather than a government-led effort to dominate
the area.[3]

Table 9–1   Japanese Direct Investment Abroad (percent)

	1951–91 (cumulative)	1991
United States	42	43
Canada	2	2
Asia	15	14
Middle East	1	0
Europe	19	23
Africa	2	2
Oceania	6	8
Latin America	13	8
Total	100	100
	($352 billion)	($42 billion)

Source: Data from *Sekai to Nihon no Kaigai Chokusetsu Toshi* (Tokyo: Nihon Boeki Shinkokai,
1993), pp. 521–22.

•

Seen in terms of numbers of investments rather than amounts, however, the full scope of the push of the *kaisha* into East Asia becomes clearer. The number of East Asian investments considerably exceeds those in North America, with about 5,000 Japan-related companies in East Asia compared with only 3,800 in North America. The East Asian investments clearly are much smaller in capitalization, in part because of the smaller scale of investment and in part because of a greater use of local partners and local borrowings in the financing of these Japan-related companies. (In accordance with OECD definitions, a company is termed "Japan-related" when a Japanese company holds 10 percent or more equity in the firm.)

Japanese direct investment in Asia has been, to an unusual degree, in manufacturing. Within East Asia, Japan-related companies in Hong Kong and Singapore are nonmanufacturing, reflecting the position of these two great city-states as centers for finance and communications. Leaving them aside, two-thirds of all Japan-related investments in East Asia are in the manufacturing sector, a quite extraordinary concentration compared with Japanese investment in the rest of the world. Less than 20 percent of Japanese direct investment in the United States has been in manufacturing, and only one-quarter of Japanese total world investment.

Moreover, these East Asian investments by Japanese companies are large-scale employers of labor. Of the roughly 2.5 million persons employed by Japanese companies outside Japan, 1 million are employed in East Asia, twice the number in the United States, and as might be expected, disproportionately in manufacturing. Looked at politically, local governments might not be fond of the Japanese investor, but that investor is handy for labor-surplus economies such as those of Southeast Asia.

It is noteworthy that there is essentially no Japanese direct investment in South Asia, that is, less than 1 percent of all Japanese overseas investment has been in India, Pakistan, Bangladesh, and Sri Lanka. For Japanese companies, it appears, Asia stops at Thailand, and South Asia is seen as a distinct area. The changing policies of South Asian governments, notably India, toward deregulation are beginning to attract Japanese attention, but skepticism about the climate for investment in these countries remains the rule.

Within East Asia, Japanese investment has been distributed across all the economies in the region. This contrasts with Japanese investment in western Europe, where there has been a high concentration in the

•

United Kingdom and the Netherlands. These countries are seen as more hospitable owing to their more open economic policies favoring foreign investment and more familiar language and legal climates, than economies such as France or Germany. African investment is limited in amount and dominated by Liberia by reason of shipping laws and registrations, with a similar situation in Panama for Latin America.

The Textile and Clothing Industry

Historically speaking, industrial development usually begins with the textile industry: entry costs into much of the industry are not high, so a shortage of capital is not a major barrier; the technology is usually available; and most important, in much of the processing of textile materials, unskilled labor can be used. There are of course exceptions within this broad industry grouping, but in general textile manufacturing has been the starting point for industrialization, first in Britain, then in Japan, then in Asia's NICs, and, on all evidence, next in Indonesia and China.

For Japanese industry, textiles accounted for one-third of total exports from 1910 until the mid-1950s. The consistently high relative importance of textiles in terms of both total manufactured product and exports continued over substantive changes, from silk and silk products to nylon and polyester, and from no-fashion "dollar blouses" to high-fashion styles. As wages rose and comparative advantage was lost, the place of textiles and clothing in Japan's industrial structure and in export sales dropped precipitously and is now only 3 percent of exports, with a world share in textiles exports about the same as that of Britain, France, and the United States.[4]

There is a nice irony in the fact that the intensity of U.S. pressures on Japan to restrain textile imports peaked in the mid- and late-1960s, just at the time that the decline of the Japanese industry was taking place. Now embodied in the grotesque form of the Multi-Fiber Agreements, these protests marked the beginnings of the long trend of American protectionist policies, subsequently applied to steel, autos, electronics, and machine tools.

East Asia's share in world exports of textiles and clothing has grown dramatically. Notwithstanding Japan's reduced output, East and Southeast Asia now account for 40 percent of that trade, double the rate of three decades ago and approximately equal to the combined share of

●

western Europe and North America. Southeast Asia's share may continue to grow, but it is now much less significant than China's share of world trade in these products. Just as rapid economic growth in first Japan and then the more recently industrialized economies of East Asia led to a gradual relocation of world textile and clothing activity away from Europe, so China's growth is beginning—and is likely to continue—to add to that trend of relocation in East Asia. Thus suppliers of textiles and clothing in higher-income countries can expect increased competition from East Asia as China's industrialization proceeds.[5]

These successive relocations of the textile industry are both inevitable, given industry economics, and from a broader perspective, desirable in allowing less developed economies to build an industrial base on the experience they gain in this industry. The general response to the shift, noticeable in the United States particularly, has been pressure for protection of the home market. In the Japanese case, however, there has been no recourse to higher tariffs, import quotas, and the like. Instead, leading firms in the textile and clothing industry have themselves gone abroad in pursuit of lower factor costs.

Toray

Toray, a major Japanese synthetic fiber producer, illustrates the forces at work as a large company struggles to deal with changing economics and shifting trade restrictions. With total sales nearing $5 billion, Toray's international investments go back to the early 1960s, when several overseas ventures were established to combat trade barriers; these were small operations widely scattered in Africa and Latin America, as well as in Hong Kong and Thailand. The real shift toward globalization took place in the early 1970s, however, in response to the protectionism of the Multi-Fiber Agreement, when major investments were made in Indonesia, Malaysia, and Thailand.

The immediate result was near disaster. All these investments showed losses for 10 to 15 years, with little growth and depressed prices. Toray's concept was right, but its timing was very wrong. By contrast, Toray's Japanese rival in synthetic fibers, Teijin, disinvested, a move Toray felt unable to make because of continuing commitments. Until 1985 it was Teijin that was seen as both smart and lucky, while Toray bled red ink.

With the 1985 exchange rate revaluation, all that changed. Today

●

Toray's overseas export sales are nearing the $1 billion level, 80 percent of which is from subsidiaries in Thailand, Indonesia, Malaysia, and Hong Kong. Profit margins are good, at the 20 percent level, and two firms in Thailand and one in Indonesia have been taken public on the local stock exchanges. Toray is expanding capacity in both Indonesia and Thailand, with a three-year, ¥20 billion expansion underway in Indonesia.

Currently 60 percent of Toray's output in Indonesia and nearly all its Malaysian output is exported, as these Southeast Asian subsidiaries replace Japanese plants as Toray's export base. Already the next stages of investment are appearing, as Toray begins to invest in plastics for the electronic industry in Malaysia and Thailand and sees Vietnam and China as interesting for the company "ten years from now."

Toray expects annual growth in Asia in its industry to be about 7 percent. The company finds what it calls the "new three" of Indonesia, Thailand, and Malaysia far more interesting than the "old four" of Hong Kong, Singapore, Taiwan, and Korea, and expects a free-trading Asian bloc within the next 10 years or so.

The experience of another major Japanese textile company, Unitika, parallels that of Toray on a somewhat smaller scale. Unitika, with annual sales of about $3 billion, has plants in Hong Kong, Thailand, and Indonesia. The Indonesian operation is the largest, with 1,400 employees. Sales there have doubled in the past four years, while profits have increased by over five times. Again, the company's performance has flourished since the yen rate changed in the 1985–86 period, making exports from Indonesia highly competitive.

Unitika's Indonesian subsidiary, P.T. Unitex, was taken public in 1982, with Unitika retaining 28 percent of the shares, Marubeni (the general trading company) holding 16 percent, and local partners and the public holding the balance. Marubeni became Unitika's partner in establishing the venture, one of the first examples of a general trading company facilitating Japanese manufacturing investment abroad.

Asahi Chemical Industry Co.

A variation on this textile investment pattern is offered by Asahi Chemical Industry Co. Asahi Chemical, a $10 billion sales company, is highly diversified but has still about 20 percent of its sales in textiles and apparel. Asahi Chemical's forays abroad began with an acrylic production plant in Korea in the 1960s that was extended to produce polyester and continues

•

to operate. Although both Toray and Teijin pulled out of Korea, Asahi Chemical finds it a very difficult country in which to operate, but maintains its operations there.

However, Asahi Chemical has also moved into Indonesia, where it has a majority holding in an acrylic and nylon operation, with 1,150 employees. A somewhat similar operation in Taiwan is about half the size. Perhaps because of a lesser commitment to Southeast Asia, Asahi Chemical seems particularly conscious of the emerging position of China.

These three major textile companies each have major East Asian investments, and since the yen revaluation, have been doing very well in their offshore Asian operations. These operations are substantial in scale, in many cases made more local by selling shares to the public in the host country. The result is a model of economic restructuring—a mature and declining Japanese industry moving capital and technology abroad to the mutual advantage of the Japanese economy and the developing economies of the area. Where are the U.S. and European textile companies as their economies mature and Asia grows?

The Auto Industry

Investments in the East Asian economies by Japan's auto companies have been driven less by the economics of production than by local restrictions on marketing. Throughout the area, with the exceptions of Hong Kong and Singapore, local governments have aspired to establish indigenous auto production operations. As a result, Japan's auto companies have quietly proceeded to capture those markets that have been open to them.

Korea, as always, is a special case where a substantial and still rapidly growing domestic industry has been established. Japanese autos are barred from the Korean market, and in turn Korean autos are not sold in Japan (rather like the Italian/Japan standoff, where both sides have stayed out of the other's turf). Japanese parts and designs, however, have been critical to the success of Hyundai, for example, in which Mitsubishi Motors and Mitsubishi Corporation are both substantial shareholders. Similarly, Kia Motors has drawn on Mazda and Ford technology, and both those companies are Kia shareholders.

Taiwan is also a special case where Japanese firms hold significant but

●

minority share positions in local companies, in a market that is closed to
exports from Japan—and to majority share positions as well. Interestingly, Taiwan is becoming an export market for Japanese autos produced
in the United States—a means by which the Japanese firms can circum-
vent Taiwan restrictions that have not been applied to U.S. products.

The rest of the East Asia auto industry is largely a Japanese game. As
Table 9–2 indicates, in all of Southeast Asia Japanese automakers have
overwhelmingly large shares of the market, with the apparent exception
of Malaysia, owing to that country's joint venture with Mitsubishi Motors to produce a local car, a program that, after some years of problems,
seems finally to be achieving success.

Honda

As one of the most international of all Japanese companies, the views and
position of Honda regarding East Asia are of special interest. Sales in East
Asia are still under 6 percent of Honda's worldwide sales. They are
growing much faster, however, than the corporate average, and this high
growth is expected to continue. Honda estimates its current share of the
Asian market to be about 8 percent and has set a target market share of
14 percent by the year 2000. They expect the Asian market to double in
total size over the same period, so one may conclude that Honda intends
to quadruple the volume of its Asian sales within the next few years.

Honda executives note that motorcycle sales gain ground when a

Table 9–2   Auto Market Shares, 1991 (by Country)

	Japanese Makers	U.S. Makers	All Others	Total
Thailand	95.2	—	4.8	100.0
Indonesia	95.1	1.4	3.5	100.0
Philippines	99.7	—	0.3	100.0
Malaysia	47.9	6.3	45.8★	100.0
Singapore	69.5	2.8	27.7	100.0
Hong Kong	83.2	2.4	14.4	100.0

★42.2% share is Proton, a national auto with equity, technology, and management
links to Mitsubishi Motor Corporation.

Source: Data from "Asia-Oceania Car Market," booklet, International Public Affairs Division,
Toyota Motor Corporation, Tokyo, August 1992.

●

bike can be purchased with three to four months of salary, and that auto sales sprint ahead when an average annual salary will buy a car. To hasten this process, Honda's plans include a new style of car for first-time buyers in the expanding markets of Indonesia and China.

No doubt Honda will do well in the area, but the position of Toyota is formidable as well, with major shares in all the markets of the area and firm leadership in Indonesia and Thailand. Toyota's marketing organizations in East Asia employ more than 15,000 people in nearly 450 sales outlets, with total sales of some 265,000 vehicles.[6]

The future of autos in Southeast Asia from the perspective of the Japanese auto industry seems to have two main components. One scenario focuses on the building of an integrated auto manufacturing system in Southeast Asia, as illustrated by the Toyota and Honda investment patterns for the area, summarized Figure 9–1. These moves result from "the formation of a regional parts complementation agreement signed in 1988 by ASEAN members. The Accord, known as the Brand to Brand Complementation (BBC), provides for a halving of tariffs on intra-regional trade in components between units of the same manufacturer. This has paved the way for the creation of regional car parts complementation schemes which had been impossible due to member nations' strict protectionist auto trade policy."[7] It is quite likely that Southeast Asia will have a fully integrated automobile industry in place in a few years— owned by the Japanese with local partners in all key locations.

The second component to the policies of Japanese automakers in Southeast Asia is the establishment of a position in China. Here Honda may have an advantage in its leadership in the motorcycle industry. As the Chinese move from their now ubiquitous leg-powered bicycles, the next stage—as was the case in the 1950s in Japan—is to a gasoline-powered motorcycle, and thence as incomes rise, to four-wheeled vehicles.

Chinese policy has leaned away from the Japanese makers toward the Europeans and Americans, with Peugeot and Volkswagen in lead positions. All of the Japanese auto companies are establishing themselves in China, however, without major investments as yet. Given its geographic proximity and product suitability, a strong Japanese auto position in a liberalizing Chinese market seems inevitable. Honda especially has the advantage of being able to build production and market position from motorcycles and then apply that experience to small cars. The Japanese product line fits China's developing needs.

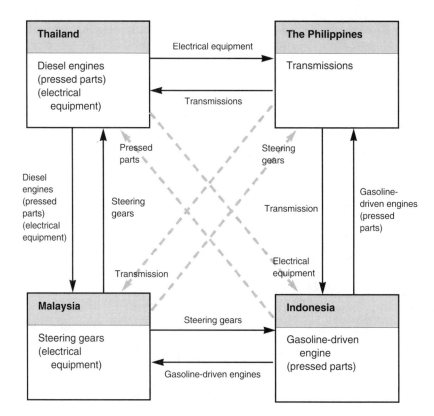

**Figure 9–1   Auto Parts Production System in ASEAN: The Case
of Toyota Motor Corp.**

Source: Reprinted from "Asia-Oceania Car Market," booklet,
International Public Affairs Division, Toyota Motor Corporation, Tokyo,
October 1990, p. 15.

The Electronics Industry

The shift of textile manufacturing operations from Japan to Southeast
Asia was driven by cost factors, while the development of the Japanese
auto industry in the area was driven by attractive but protected markets.
The impetus for the shift of electronics manufacture has elements of both
cost pressures and market interest.

Japanese investments in the electronics industry in Asia are of special
significance to the development of the area. "Those NIEs which have

●

enjoyed the most rapid economic growth in recent years also have highly dynamic electronics industries. This applies in particular to the four leading East Asian NIEs, i.e., South Korea, Taiwan, Singapore and Hong Kong, where electronics goods and services account for a sizeable and increasing share of value-added and exports, and of industrial employment. There is nothing fortuitous about this correlation, since electronics has dominated world trade growth and most of those countries have pursued export-led industrialization strategies, in which electronics has been a leading export item."[8]

The OECD study of electronics in the developing economies provides a measure of the importance of the industry to East and Southeast Asia. "Singapore relies most heavily on electronics, with one-fourth of its industrial labour force employed there. In Hong Kong and Taiwan, roughly one in ten industrial workers is an electronics worker. In Korea and Malaysia, the proportion is only slightly lower. In Thailand, roughly one in twenty industrial workers is an electronics worker. In Brazil, the figure is one in fifty and in India and in Indonesia, just over one in two hundred."[9]

U.S. companies were pioneers in electronics manufacturing investment in East Asia, back in the era when the assembly of semiconductors was highly labor-intensive, and chips were shipped to Asian assembly centers for wiring and reshipment to world markets. As this early—and substantial—U.S. approach suggests, there was little if any interest in East Asia as an end market, or even as an integrated production site. The basic impetus to invest was to obtain low-cost, relatively efficient labor to improve competitive positions in home markets.

Japan's *kaisha* too followed this route initially but were less than satisfied with the quality of output, and turned instead to automation in simple assembly operations to solve their labor supply problems. As a result, the *kaisha* have moved toward establishing integrated operations with local partners in East Asia, with a considerable portion of output aimed at local markets.

Matsushita Electric Industries

The company most deeply involved in East Asian electronics, and most representative of the Japanese approach, is Matsushita Electric Industries (MEI), which, in Asia as elsewhere, markets both its National and Panasonic brands. MEI actively invested outside Japan in East Asia very early, and since the 1960s has built a major position in the area, which accounts for half of the company's offshore production. MEI has a total of 47 companies in the area, employing nearly 50,000 people.

Matsushita's first venture in Asia was in Taiwan, with a local partner, to manufacture radios and record players. The Taiwanese operation has been a real success, exporting more than US$200 million annually, with total sales over US$580 million. The president is Ms. Y. M. Hong, with operating management in the hands of MEI executives.

In contrast to the Taiwanese success, Matsushita withdrew from Korea, where it produced TVs for the US market in the 1970s after several years of operations. One reason given for the move was escalating Korean wages and another the fact that the Korean venture became re-dundant after Matsushita's acquisition of Motorola's Qasar operation in Chicago. However, in discussing the Korean experience, MEI manage-ment also refers to Korean government interference in the operation. In any case, like many other Japanese efforts in Korea, this one did not succeed.

Its Korean experience was not typical of MEI's record in East Asia, however. Currently MEI operates a major facility in mainland China, as a 50–50 joint venture with the government of Beijing. The venture's chairman is the former vice mayor of Beijing, and another former city official acts as director as well. The plant produces television tubes, with current volume at 1 million per year. MEI management notes the good supply of engineers in China as part of the reason for its success, and believes it is necessary to look to Asia in terms of its own markets, not in terms of supplying product to Japan or the West.

Matsushita even has substantial operations in Indonesia, where elec-tronics investments by most companies are only now taking place. MEI entered Indonesia in 1970, in a majority MEI-owned joint venture with Gobel, a non-Chinese Indonesian business group. The National Gobel venture has 3,000 employees and has grown on average 20 percent per year. Dividend payout rates are 20 to 30 percent, with aggressive rein-vestment of earnings.

Overall, the Matsushita's 37 manufacturing companies in East Asia sell 70 percent of their output in the area, with about 10 percent going to Japan and approximately 20 percent exported to the United States and Europe. Managing Director Tahara, in charge of Asia and the Middle East for the corporation, credits this high level of Asian sales to the fact that Matsushita supplies not only finished products to the area but a high

•

percentage of parts that are sold to other producers. He claims that MEI's Singapore and Malaysian factories hold a 20 percent share of the world market for small compressors for air-conditioning and refrigeration units.

Organizationally, Matsushita has taken advantage of Singapore laws to set up its regional headquarters there, an increasingly common phenomenon among Japanese companies. Asia Matsushita Electric (S), Pte Ltd, currently with a staff of about 500, provides financial, accounting, logistical, and sales support for the 38 Matsushita companies located in ASEAN, with special emphasis on training. In 1992, AMS, the Singapore regional unit, provided 52 different training courses for 2,000 employees from throughout the region. This massive program is aimed at what the company sees as its biggest problem area—shortages of engineers, and managers throughout East Asia and the need for higher levels of education and training.

MEI is highly optimistic about the potential of the Philippines—largely owing to the high levels of education there and the wide use of English—but as yet has invested little owing to the continuing political uncertainties in the Philippines (a common Japanese company view of that country). Vietnam is seen as for the future, but "not yet in our business."

Matsushita's massive presence in East Asia is due in part to the interests of the company's legendary founder, Kohnosuke Matsushita, who, for example, negotiated personally with the company's Indonesian partners in setting up that venture. Other features that have contributed to MEI's success include the company's willingness to involve local partners and maintain their relationships on a long-term basis; its exceptional emphasis on staffing and training at all levels of area operations and a willingness to invest in training local personnel; its focus on the local fast-growing consumer markets as key; and its emphasis on parts production, building the potential for the Japanese producers in the area to establish an integrated consumer electronics industry in Southeast Asia.

NEC

The *kaisha* on the industrial side of the electronics industry have smaller positions in East Asia and have been rather slower in building them. NEC, from its traditional base in telecommunications, has diversified into computers with great success, dominating the Japanese personal computer market, and into semiconductors, where it is now the world's

•

largest producer. Perhaps owing to this product mix, however, just under one-quarter of NEC's sales are overseas, about US$6 billion, and one-fifth of that is in Asia. Asia, for NEC, is a rather smaller market than is western Europe.

Having said this, NEC management now declares that "from now on, Asia is the consuming continent and we will push harder." NEC has a total of 12 manufacturing operations in East Asia, and like Matsushita has nothing in Korea but a considerable presence in mainland China, as well as Taiwan. Having a total 6,500 employees in the area, NEC, with its relatively high-technology product line, needs to work more closely with the headquarters units than is the case with Matsushita's operations, centering on consumer electronics. An illustration of NEC's East Asian activities was its supplying fiber-optic telephone system with digital switching installed in Hanoi in late 1992—the kind of product and project that would require a Japanese supply base and Japanese government aid support.

Hitachi

Hitachi, like NEC, has a less extensive position in Asia than Matsushita. Like NEC, Hitachi's focus, although very widely diversified, is on balance in the heavier equipment sectors. The company's origins are in the power generating business, and its culture is still shaped in good part by this. Management speaks of "low-end products" produced in Southeast Asia by low-cost labor, with big projects still managed from Tokyo. Like Matsushita, Hitachi's center of Asian operations is in Singapore, but Korea and Taiwan are controlled from Tokyo, as is activity in mainland China. Hitachi management feels the company was slow to get into Singapore and Malaysia but pursues power generation projects from that base. Not surprisingly, Vietnam is seen as a market with high potential for renovation projects as well as new equipment, to be managed out of Bangkok.

The general impression one receives of Hitachi's activities in Asia is one of slow moves on a limited basis. This impression was reinforced by discussions in Indonesia, where Hitachi has only a representative office but a very active sales effort for heavy equipment through the Japanese trading companies that are well established in Djakarta. Hitachi's product line has been a factor in its development pattern. Another factor may well be its organization, which treats each factory as a profit center and

•

thus finds it quite difficult to focus corporatewide resources on a region or project. Thus, for example, Hitachi Taiwan is focused almost entirely on air-conditioning equipment and has only about 1,000 employees.

Overall, however, the position of Japan's electronics industry in East Asia is considerable: "Of cumulative Japanese electronics/electrical equipment (E/E) investment (until 1988 totalling in the world economy $10.2 billion), 29 percent went to developing regions, most to developing Asia. Moreover, E/E investment represented one-fifth of all Japanese manufactuing investment in developing Asia, the single largest sectoral share. From 1983 to 1988, Japanese E/E investment in developing countries more than tripled, while that going to East Asian NIEs grew even more rapidly, i.e. 3.75 times."[10]

"The strategic importance of these Japanese investments in East Asia is determined by the fact that the major growth in markets will be in this area. Even in the traditional sector of power generating equipment, 'according to all the big suppliers, the Asia/Pacific region will be a key growth market over the next five years, accounting for 29 percent of the world's capacity additions, says GE. Siemens, the big German supplier, expects the Asian market to account for 37 percent of expected world demand over the next decade."[11]

Textiles, autos, and electronics are major sectors of strength for Japan's economy, and it is therefore not surprising to find each of these industries, in its own fashion, heavily engaged in the markets and economies of East Asia. What of Japan's less distinguished sectors? Where Japanese industry is weak, how do Japanese companies fare in East Asian competition?

Consumables

On the whole, in the purely consumable product sectors, Japanese companies are less active in East Asia and seem to fare less well. The food and beverage sector is an example. Japan's food companies are for the most part rather small by the standards of this highly concentrated industry. One of Japan's few major firms in packaged foodstuffs that has a presence in East Asia is Ajinomoto, a pioneer in the seasoning monosodium glutamate (MSG) and now widely diversified into processed foods, chemicals, and pharmaceuticals.

The Asian division of the company accounts for approximately 40

•

percent of Ajinomoto's overseas sales of about $1.2 billion. MSG is its main product in the Asian area, with factories throughout ASEAN and local partners in most locations. Competition is local; in Indonesia the main competitor is a Korean company selling a close copy of the Ajinomoto brand and product. In addition to the basic, long-established flavoring businesses, several years ago Ajinomoto acquired a 50 percent interest in the Asian operations of the Knorr subsidiary of America's CPC (Ajinomoto now owns Knorr's Japan operations). A recent Thai investment is aimed at exporting frozen foods back to Japan.

Ajinomoto certainly holds a major position in Asia, with a well-accepted and widely used product, sold in small packets at very low prices, that allows for local flavoring variations (for example, a chicken-flavored seasoning developed especially for Indonesia is sold in packets at 2 or 3 cents U.S. each). Indeed, in the processed food field, only Uni-lever or Nestlé might be as widely represented in East Asia as Ajinomoto.

Beverages are quite another story. The domestic beer and beverage business in Japan has many international competitors, not least of all Coca-Cola. However, the giant in the domestic beverage market, bol-stered by its more than 50 percent position in beer, is Kirin, with sales of well over US$10 billion. Yet Kirin has virtually no position in Asia, only a license to San Miguel of the Philippines to sell Kirin in Hong Kong and some minor activities in Taiwan and Hong Kong. Because local compet-itors in East Asia dominate their markets, and Japan is a very high-cost site for beer production, exports are uncompetitive. In addition, foreign competitors like Europe's Heineken have stolen the march on Kirin in East Asia.

One of Kirin's two major competitors in Japan, Sapporo Breweries, does report some minor export sales but declares that it intends to reduce its dependency on beer over time, and is investing heavily in urban de-velopment projects in Tokyo and Sapporo. Indeed, the company's one major effort abroad is a minority position in a large hotel and restaurant complex in Beijing.

Some of the disadvantages faced by Japan's consumer products com-panies as they seek to exploit the markets of East Asia are illustrated by the case of Kao Corporation, Japan's leading toiletries and personal prod-ucts company. With sales of nearly $5 billion, Kao is one of Japan's most interesting and best-managed companies, with major market share posi-tions and an outstanding record of automation of company operations.

•

Innovations such as the concentrated detergent Attack have enabled Kao to hold Procter and Gamble, Unilever, and Colgate Palmolive, along with its local competitor Lion Corp., at bay in the giant Japanese market.

Yet Kao is still badly outgunned throughout East Asia, despite major efforts at investment. "Unilever reckons that in East Asia as a whole its detergent and personal product sales are ten times as big as Kao's and four times as big as P&G's. Unilever is an old hand in Asia. Its parents set up shop in India and Indonesia in the 1890s. Unilever's Thai operations began in 1932. Europe and America are still far more important to the company, but Asian sales are growing more than twice as fast as sales in either region and are expected to double in the next five years."[12]

The Big Three—Unilever, P&G, and Kao—are in fact competing for world position and confront one another in each of the markets of East Asia. The stakes are not small. The markets in developed countries are mature, and share changes are costly and hard to come by. By contrast, the markets in East Asia are growing rapidly: Kao estimates the shampoo market in East Asia outside Japan and Korea at $1.3 billion, and toothpaste at about $800 million.[13]

Success in the competition for Asia is critical to Kao's long-term position. A regional headquarters has been set up in Singapore, with an executive vice president in residence to manage the area. Kao has not entered the Korean or Chinese markets as yet, feeling somewhat disadvantaged in each, and yet it must see those markets as critical. The company is prepared, however, to take the long view. The Indonesian operation, up against Unilever in a country in which that company is one of the two or three largest listed companies and has a century-long history, has grown by a factor of four in the last six years and is now at break-even. Kao staff manage the local joint venture with an Indonesian partner, and the local manager says they are on target to achieve profitability within ten years: "We are a global organization because our competitors are global."

Services

In manufacturing, Japanese corporate efforts in East Asia cover a broad range—from market leaders to struggles for any share to general indifference. The service sector presents quite a different pattern, with varying degrees of involvement in East Asia, depending on the specific type of service industry.

Financial Services

It will come as no surprise that Japan's banks are very active throughout East Asia; indeed, the number of Japanese bank branches, subsidiaries, and representative offices is even greater in Asia than in North America and western Europe. Banking is of course always regulated, but within the constraints of regulation, Japanese banks are very active throughout the region, even in Korea, where most types of Japanese businesses are only modestly represented, if at all. The one market in which Japanese banks appear to be outnumbered is Taiwan, where the advantages of an American affiliation remain strong.

The insurance sector is much less penetrated by Japanese firms, and then, only by casualty insurance companies. Japan's giant Tokyo Fire and Marine Insurance Company states as its modest mission the following of Japanese clients abroad, profitably. A decade or more ago, Tokyo Marine was more ambitious, to its subsequent regret for various reasons: the scale of the East Asian casualty insurance markets is small; insurance is not used as widely as in more developed markets; and Japanese firms have only limited experience of the market as a base for underwriting risks. In addition, government policies normally restrict the role of foreign insurance companies to a minority interest in a local firm.

Yasuda Fire and Marine similarly aims at insuring Japanese firms as they need coverage in East Asia. Yasuda has wholly owned operations in Singapore and Hong Kong, and minority interests in Indonesia, Malaysia, Thailand, and the Philippines. Yasuda reports rather good profits from the area, with quite firm prices in the markets. Yasuda is tying up with a Vietnam firm, but there, as in much of the rest of the region, it is concerned with future political uncertainty. East Asia for Yasuda is still far from a single market, requiring a cautious, country-by-country approach.

In other service sectors as hotels, the Japanese position is limited, with regional companies based in Hong Kong and Singapore seeming to be making the running. Media—television, print, and radio—are not in Japanese hands, despite a brief effort by Japan's national television operation to play a regional role in TV newscasting. Even restaurant franchises, a sector that is well developed in Japan, are not a Japan-led sector in the rest of East Asia.

Retailing

The one extraordinary exception to this pattern of limited investment is retailing, and the situation is really quite remarkable for two reasons. First, retailing is not usually cited as one of Japan's strengths. Indeed, one hears of overstaffing, excessive service, high prices, and restrictive practices that limit the size and number of outlets. Second, retailing is considered to be deeply rooted in local customs, practices, and tastes, and the field is littered with failed efforts to transplant retail management from one society to another.

Yet Japanese department stores and supermarket operations are moving aggressively and successfully across East Asia, despite legal restrictions in many markets. In contrast to Western practice, their entry method is not by acquisition of existing operations (e.g., Marks and Spencer buying Brooks Brothers). Instead, the Japanese enter new markets by building new stores in major urban centers under Japanese management.

A total of 78 Japanese retail stores had been opened in Asia by early 1992, with many more announced and planned.[14]

Where limits on retail investment remain—in Korea and Indonesia, for example—Japanese retailers have entered into partnerships and licensing arrangements. The earliest of these stores, established in the early 1970s, were small, averaging only 6,000 or 8,000 square meters of floor space, but the sizes are now in the 120,000 to 170,000 square meter range.

It is estimated that 40 percent of Hong Kong department store sales and 50 percent of Singapore department store sales are through Japanese branches. The first wave of investment in retailing in Asia was initiated by the department stores—Mitsukoshi, Sogo, Isetan, and Daimaru. The second wave has been led by supermarket and discount store operators. Their pace of development and scale of operations are greater than those of the department stores and are accelerating. These include such chains as Jusco, Uny, Seiyu, and notably Yaohan.

Yaohan is a Hong Kong–based supermarket chain that originated in Shizuoka, a provincial city some 200 kilometers from Tokyo. The

•

founder and still controlling owner of Yaohan is Kazuo Wada, who declares that much of his strength derives from his firm adherence to a religious sect known as *Seicho no Ie*. Frustrated by the limits on his operations at home, Wada first expanded to Brazil, but failed there. He opened his first Asian operation in Singapore in 1974 and now has 17 retail outlets in six Asian countries outside Japan. In 1990, Wada moved his company headquarters to Hong Kong, where he now has fashion boutiques, a chain of restaurants, and even the mansion on Hong Kong's Peak that was the former residence of the head of the Hong Kong and Shanghai Banking Corporation.

Yaohan is positioned at the lower end of the market and price range, and Wada sees a major opportunity for his company in China. He operates a store in Shenzen and has announced further investment in two shopping centers in Shanghai, one in Beijing, and one in Guangzhou. In relocating his company, Yaohan Department Store Co. of Japan will become one of the Hong Kong parent company's many retailing units.

Yaohan is the most spectacular of the Japanese retailing moves into Asia. It is not alone, however. In Taiwan, a difficult terrain for Japanese retailers because of government restrictions, the leading convenience store chain is the 7–11 stores. They are owned directly by Southland of the United States, but Southland in turn is now owned by Ito-Yokado, the second-largest and arguably best-managed of all Japan's supermarket operations. Many years ago, Ito-Yokado licensed the 7–11 technology from Southland. Five thousand franchise outlets later, Ito-Yokado rescued Southland from bankruptcy and the licensee became the owner. The chain will be a real asset in expanding retail in high-rent, land-poor Asian cities where effective franchises are especially attractive.

There is no indication of any slowing of Japanese retailer interest in East Asia. The next market of interest appears to be China, with announcements of plans to expand into China already made by Seibu, Yaohan, and Daiei. The Chinese government has indicated to several of the major Japanese department stores, including Takashimaya, that they would be welcome to open stores, but concerns about infrastructure shortcomings and supply problems are delaying decisions.

It might be noted that the success of Japanese retailing in East Asia has an implicit message regarding Asian attitudes toward Japan. Surely if resentment of Japan were so acute as is sometimes suggested, retailing would be the last sector in which to expect Japanese success. These Japanese retail stores make no secret of their identity, and their nationality is hardly unknown to the crowds of local housewives who patronize them. When next assessing attitudes in Asia toward Japan, the retailing phenomenon must be kept in mind.

From a business point of view, an urgent issue has to be the procurement policies of these successful retailers. Are these retail operations a conduit for Japanese goods? Might they be a channel by which U.S. and European companies can reach East Asia's consumers?

In interviews with the management of these retail operations in Tokyo, all stated that there is no special procurement guidance from Tokyo. Goods offered for sale are not necessarily "Japanese," but where local supplies are not available offshore purchasing occurs. For example, Isetan's head of international operations states, "Each branch does its own purchasing. For instance, if the Singapore store wants to buy Italian shoes, they go to Italy and attend the shows with other store managers and make their own decisions about what to buy. We have purchasing offices in most European countries to expedite the process."

He continues, "If the country has very open trade laws, we import most of the goods. Malaysia and Thailand are relatively closed, so only about 20 percent of the goods we sell there are imported. Importing from Japan is not easy nor necessarily profitable. Sometimes we sell things from Japan. Clothes made in Japan are especially popular in Asia. We don't sell much electronics because Japanese makers have already established their distribution routes. They don't need us."

These reports of autonomy in purchasing are borne out by survey data suggesting that only 10 percent of food suppliers, 20 percent of clothing suppliers, and 25 percent of consumer electronics suppliers to Japanese retailers abroad are Japanese companies, the great majority of suppliers in each case local.[15]

Nonetheless, Japanese retailers are becoming a major force in East Asian retailing, with their share rising in all locations. Central access from Tokyo to Japanese retail networks in Asia may be possible, and certainly merchandising and promotion programs on an Asia-wide scale can be worked out through the retailing headquarters in Japan to the advantage of the Japanese—or Western—supplier.

Trading Companies

A discussion of Japan's international service sector would be incomplete without attention to the enormous general trading companies, the *sogo*

●

shosha. The largest of these—C. Itoh, Mitsubishi Corporation, Mitsui and Co., Marubeni, and Sumitomo Trading—have sales of ¥20 million million and more, and their worldwide presence and multiplicity of activities are legendary.

Certainly the *sogo shosha* are critical factors in Japanese overseas investment. The nine general trading companies are credited with a total of 2,475 separate investments abroad.[16] Because the worldwide total of Japanese overseas investments is given as 13,522, it appears that nearly 20 percent of all Japanese investments abroad have been made by the *sogo shosha.*

Mitsui and Co. has the largest single number of foreign investments, a total of 568. The range of activities covered is extraordinary, from coal mining to graphics, from Chinese printing equipment to Arizona real estate. As might be expected, the largest proportion is commodity-related—petroleum, ore, foodstuffs, and the like—the handling of which has long been the core business of the general trading companies.

Mitsui and Co., like the other *sogo shosha,* has increasingly taken equity positions in new ventures. Indeed, the organization of consortia of investors in large and risky projects has become a major activity of the trading companies as they adopt some of the functions handled by merchant banks in other economies. These also include supporting the activities of manufacturing firms, especially in economies where the manufacturer may have limited experience and where the general trading company has been operating for some time.

Thus Mitsui and Co. is a minority investor in two of the companies that Toray Industries operates in Thailand, Toray being a key member of the Mitsui group with a long history of links to the company dating from pre–World War II days. (Indeed, the individual who put Toray together in the postwar period, a key business leader in Japan's reconstruction, Mr. T. Tashiro, was a manager in Mitsui and Co.'s London office before the war.)

However, Mitsui and Co.'s support for manufacturing investors is not limited to Mitsui group firms. NEC, a Sumitomo group company, has Mitsui as investor in its Thai venture. Bridgestone Tire, also not a group firm, has Mitsui capital in its large operation in Indonesia.

The trading company role is especially valuable in frontier investment areas. In Indonesia, Marubeni in particular has joined with local interests, including the Salim group, in developing industrial parks to which Japanese corporate investors are invited and in which investments

•

the trading company will often take a position. Marubeni is a 16 percent equity holder in the Unitika venture in Indonesia, mentioned earlier. Again, in Indonesia, C. Itoh holds a 5 percent equity position in the large Gobel National venture of Matsushita. Obviously, Itoh's capital was not required, but presumably its experience and position in Indonesia was seen as necessary, even by as powerful a company as Matsushita.

The forthcoming moves into Vietnam by Japanese companies will certainly be facilitated by the fact that the major trading companies have for some time been maintaining staff in that country, even when economic relations between Japan and Vietnam have been at low ebb. Trading companies have reduced utility in sophisticated markets or in dealings involving high value-added products. However, in the frontier areas and in the commodity sectors, the staff and financial resources of the *sogo shosha* are a powerful support to Japan's corporate investors.

Performance and Prospects

East Asia is now the site for 5,000 Japanese-invested companies and more than 1 million employees. It has not, however, been the most favored site for Japanese investment; nearly one-half of total Japanese foreign direct investment has gone into the United States and Canada. Indeed, it can be argued that relative to the size of the economies of East Asia, much less their importance to Japan politically, Japanese companies have underinvested in East Asia.

However, Japanese investment in East Asia has been more successful than investment in the West. The most recent survey by the Ministry of International Trade and Industry of profitability of Japanese investment abroad shows a consistently higher level of profits from Japan's Asian investments than from investments in Europe, with investments in North America reporting the poorest performances, showing losses in 1990. In contrast, investments in Asia show consistent profits, rising rather steadily over the period from 1985 to 1991 (see Appendix Table 13).

Arguably, many of the North American investments are of a large scale, particularly those in steel and auto and electronics plants, and are relatively recent. Losses in the first years of these sizable new operations would not be a surprise. No doubt the poor overall performance in recent years of the Canadian and American economies is also a factor.

•

Nonetheless, the poor profitability of investment in North America has continued now over a six-year period, with no indication whatsoever of any improvement.

It can hardly come as a surprise then that, given this profit performance and the increased hostility toward Japan displayed in the West, especially in the United States, the management of Japan's largest companies report plans to reduce investments in North America sharply to a level equal to about one-fifth of total Japanese investment (as opposed to one-half, as reported previously), with European investments levels constant at one-quarter of the total and with East Asia becoming the site of 40 percent of total direct investments, up drastically from historic levels of approximately 15 percent.[17]

The survey results are given additional credence by the report in mid-1992 that in the first half of the year, Japanese investments in China was three times greater than the same quarter a year earlier, this at a time when the Japanese economy is in a period of slow growth during which foreign investment could be expected to decline sharply.

The forces driving Japanese investment in East Asia have not abated. The fact is that East Asia is where the growth is, where the profits are, and where the labor power and material resources needed by Japan's *kaisha* are in greatest abundance. Add the fact that the Japanese economy is now experiencing its greatest trade surpluses in history—thus generating massive cash flows that must be recycled abroad—and it becomes safe to assume that high levels of direct investment will continue, but they will now focus to an unprecedented degree on East Asia, causing all the growth and area-integration forces that will continue the transformation of the region.

The role of Japanese investment in East Asia in the integration of the area can be seen as well in the pattern of the flow of goods, as shown in Table 9–3. As would be expected, nearly all the products from Japanese subsidiaries in Europe and North America are sold in their respective domestic markets (even though Honda America Manufacturing is the largest exporter of U.S. cars to Japan's market). These investments in the West were aimed at market penetration and at overcoming trade barriers against exports from Japan.

There has been a view that Japan's Asian investments were aimed at reexport to Japan, taking advantage of lower factor costs to improve competitiveness at home. In fact, however, as testimony to the growing size of these markets, 60 percent of the output of these Japanese subsidi-

•

Table 9–3   **Sales Destination of Japan's Overseas Manufactures, 1991**

	Sales in Country of Manufacture as Per-cent of Total	Exports as Percent of Total Sales	Exports to Japan as Percent of Total Sales
All Locations	76.2	23.8	8.4
North America	89.4	10.6	4.1
Europe	93.9	6.1	1.9
Asia	54.5	45.5★	15.5

★To Other Asia, 15.6%.
  To Japan, 15.5%.
  To North America, 8.5%.
  To Europe, 4.3%.
  To other, 1.6%.

Source: Reprinted from "Dai 22-kai Waga Kuni Kigyo no Kaigai Jigyo Katsudo Doko Chosa no Gaiyo," Ministry of International Trade and Industry (MITI), Tokyo, March 1993, p. 16.

aries in the area is sold in the country of manufacture. In any case, nearly 85 percent of East Asian–produced Japanese goods is sold in East Asia, including Japan. These investments in Asia are not primarily for low-cost sourcing of products for the Japan home market. By producing for the area, they further its economic integration.

At the level of management organization and operations, the Japanese approach to the area seems similar to that of firms of other nationalities. They face the usual problems, familiar to all multinational companies, of seeking to resolve issues of geographic and product line control, with Japanese firms taking the same matrix approach as Western multinationals.

If there is a difference in this regard, it may be in the degree of decentralization of decision making regarding Asian investments on the part of Japanese companies. Especially in the highly diversified electronics companies, a great deal of authority is vested in the product divisions—or in the case of Hitachi, in its factory organizations—with less corporate planning and top-down decision making. One result is the ability of Japanese companies to make relatively small investments in the area.

These are, after all, for the most part still small economies. The initial scale of investment in any given business is likely to be correspondingly limited in size. It is not easy for a large multinational, headquartered in

•

New York, London, or Frankfurt, to identify and pursue a one- or two-million-dollar project in Kuala Lumpur, Changmai, or Surabaja. Perhaps because of geographic proximity, perhaps because of greater experience, perhaps because of less centralization in decision making, Japanese firms seem better able to seize upon these limited opportunities—which, when repeated and augmented over time, add up to significant investment positions in these countries.

A further and related difference in management practices was highlighted in a discussion in Jakarta with the country manager there for one of America's largest and most successful companies. This manager, himself an Asian and resident in Jakarta on behalf of his company for more than a decade, explained the problems he encounters when a large Indonesian project is under consideration. He reports that invariably the closing stages of negotiations involve a delegation from headquarters accompanied by legal representatives. The delegation sees as its responsibility the identification and resolution of every possible contingency in the matter under negotiation.

He also observes that a Japanese company, in a similar situation, is willing to settle for an overall general agreement, with the understanding that details will be worked out if and as the project proceeds and succeeds. He notes that there is a willingness on the part of Japanese senior management to accept some ambiguity and uncertainty, a willingness that appeals especially to the Japanese who share the view that matters can be worked out if both parties are interested in working together—and if not, why enter the deal initially? This is a real difference in approach, and to the advantage of the Japanese.

That the *kaisha* do have difficulties in managing their businesses in East Asia is clear enough, even with relatively good profit performances and generally ambitious growth plans. The Japan External Trade Organization (JETRO), a MITI-related agency, recently surveyed Japanese companies in Korea, Hong Kong, Singapore, Thailand, Indonesia, Malaysia, and the Philippines, asking about major problems in local operations.[18] In the developing economies of ASEAN—Thailand, Indonesia, and the Philippines—the major issue noted is the lack of infrastructure. In each of these economies, electric power, water supply, and transport are real bottlenecks for Japanese (and other) operations. Problems with customs and tariff administration were also seen as particular to these economies.

In contrast, in the more developed economies of Korea, Hong

Kong, Singapore, and Malaysia, personnel management was cited as the most difficult area, with specific reference to problems of recruiting and retaining staff where job-hopping is customary. Interestingly, it was in these economies that competition was cited as a problem, not an issue in the less developed economies. Curiously, partner relations and political issues were not cited as problems.

A recurring issue in discussion of Japanese investment, not only in East Asia but in the West as well, is whether the *kaisha* operating abroad have a disproportionate number of Japanese expatriates in the management of their foreign subsidiaries. Similar complaints have been made of all foreign companies operating abroad. It seems likely in fact that all foreign investors are seen, no doubt accurately, as reserving top management positions for nationals of the investing country, and the newest investors, the Japanese, are the current targets for this recurrent complaint.

Proportionately and in absolute terms, the indications are that there is only slim justification for this complaint regarding Japanese companies in East Asia. Leaving to one side Singapore and Hong Kong, we find that staff dispatched from Japan make up less than 1 percent of the total labor force. The proportion is higher for Hong Kong and Singapore, as indeed it is for the United States, because in these locations a high proportion of investment is in nonmanufacturing—banking and the like—where expatriates are used in greater proportion.

In any case, the number of Japanese dispatched abroad is surely not large, especially when it is remembered that most of these investments are recent, and Japanese firms have had only a short time to recruit and train local managers—in economies where qualified management personnel are likely to be few.

Toray perhaps provides a representative example of the situation. All Toray's Asian operations are headed by a Japanese sent from home. Toray management justify this on the grounds that local staff do not have the requisite technical and management expertise, and that communication in Japanese with the home office is critical. However, there are about 10,000 Asians in Toray's operations, with a total of only 90 Japanese. Toray reports that the number of Japanese expatriates is likely to stay at this level for some time, as no locals are yet ready to take over operations.

Toray, like Matsushita, NEC, and other major Japanese companies, has a program bringing Asian staff to Japan for training for periods of 3 to

●

12 months, in addition to training programs in the field and at area head-quarters. Ajinomoto, with 57 Japanese in Asian operations out of total staff of over 6,000 sends groups for training to Japan from each of its Asian factories each year so that by the time employees are promoted to division manager (*bucho*), they have been to Japan several times and are well integrated into the company. If Japanese firms are unusual in Asia, it may be in the extent to which they offer formal training for local staff—and risk job-hopping by the personnel they train.

The forces that have been driving Japanese manufacturing and marketing investment in East Asia have lost none of their power. The yen continues to strengthen with the double effect of making exports from Japan less competitive, thus encouraging sourcing of products from abroad, while making foreign assets and foreign factors of production less expensive for the *kaisha*. So long as the dollar remains the major currency for trade exchange and so long as many Asian economies peg their exchange rates to the dollar rather than the yen, this force will continue as a major factor favoring increased Asian investment. Lower land and labor costs in East Asia are additional factors, also reinforced by an appreciating yen.

The rapid growth of East Asia's economies and markets is a new factor pulling the *kaisha* into investing in the area, the more so as growth in the early 1990s in Japan itself and in the other developed economies has been even slower than usual relative to the growth in East Asia. With this has come a new and equally powerful influence—Japanese investment in East Asia is profitable, far more profitable than investments made in the United States and a good deal more profitable than investments in western Europe.

So the positive factors are many and powerful. The negatives are less significant. Most of the area now quite actively seeks foreign investment and there has been steady relaxation of restrictions; controls over investment seem not to be a major issue in most of the region. Nor does there appear to be any special problem or hazard associated with a Japanese identity, as Japanese firms gain management experience abroad and the advantages of Japanese investment becomes more evident than before.

The result in an increasingly impressive presence, not only in manufacturing and marketing but also in retailing, banking, and other services. Japanese investments are not crowding out other investments. Rather, companies from the other developed economies of the world are not making the investments that the growth and potential of the area call for,

●

whereas the Japanese are. Moreover, in industries like autos and consumer electronics, Japanese companies are putting in place integrated industries in Southeast Asia that will over time make it very difficult for competitors from Europe and the United States to penetrate these markets.

There is no inherent Japanese competitive advantage in the area. Indeed, most of the region's governments would, quite naturally, like to balance the Japanese presence with investments by companies from other countries. The *kaisha* are capturing East Asia's growth not only owing to their own efforts but also to the competitive failures of their American and European counterparts, most of whom will realize too late the critical strategic importance of East Asia's economic successes.

10

•

AFTER THE SEA CHANGE

There is nothing temporary or fragile about the enormous economic changes taking place across East Asia, called here a sea change. Moreover, the successes in country after country reinforce the continuing process, as policies continue to focus on economic issues and as market forces are steadily driving growth. Countries with improving living standards are apt to continue current policies rather than looking for new solutions.

For these reasons, and owing to the momentum of savings and investment that is now in the system, it seems reasonable to expect continued rapid economic growth for the area. Consider some of the factors at work. Recent investment, both domestic and from abroad, has been heavy. Many of these investments will become productive over the next two to three years, helping ensure continued growth as they come on stream.

Moreover, the high savings rates in virtually the entire area go far to ensure a continuation of high investment, and these savings rates are unlikely to diminish rapidly. In terms of foreign investment, the two main suppliers of new capital to the world, Japan and Taiwan, continue to run very great surpluses on their current accounts that will be recycled, with an increasing proportion of investment moving to East Asia rather than

•

to the West. With the capital and technology involved in these investments, along with the superb labor supplies throughout the area and increased depth in experienced corporate management, the resources necessary for continued rapid growth seem in ample supply.

The great trends that have set all this sea change in motion continue. Northeast Asia—Japan, Korea, and Taiwan—will in sequence move toward higher technologies with greater research investments and with movement offshore to Asia of the less advanced of their industries, those most raw material– and labor-based, that fit best the current needs of developing Southeast Asia. And the great, added impetus from the entrepreneurial-driven Overseas Chinese population throughout East Asia continues as key to the continuation of the growth process as coastal China becomes an increasingly integral part of the economy of the area as a whole.

It is of course critical to the continuation of this extraordinary progress toward prosperity for the peoples of East Asia that the process of area integration continue. The integration of East Asia has been a market-driven process, not one initiated or even planned by governments. The area groupings like ASEAN and APEC have had little impact as yet on the rapid integration of the area, unlike the government intervention and bureaucracy building associated with European integration. The process in Asia, admittedly less advanced, has been a generic one and is arguably the more solid for not being governmentally imposed.

In any case, it is a region where governments are putting economics first, and the economics being applied, even in the socialist states of China and Vietnam, is market economics, encouraging private investment, capital markets, foreign investors, and open trade. Progress toward greater integration of the region has not been limited to economics, however. In the early 1990s, rapid and quite startling readjustments of nation-state relations have taken place as well.

Notably, Korea entered into diplomatic relations with Russia, China, and Vietnam, restating its view of its future as belonging to the mainland of Asia. China for its part renewed relations with Russia and Vietnam, while taking the initiative in the Korean rapprochement. Vietnam broke through its terrible isolation by gaining observer status in the ASEAN grouping, establishing relations with Korea and the reinstitution of aid supplies from Japan. ASEAN set in motion the first meaningful tariff reduction program for the area, a necessary first step to market integration. Japan moved military personnel abroad for the first time in postwar history as part of a Japan-led effort to resolve Cambodian's problems.

All these shifts to economic and political integration of the area, with major efforts to resolve remaining issues, are owed in some degree to the end of the cold war and the retreat of the superpowers from the area. The cold war is not ended in all aspects in Asia—no treaty yet exists between Japan and Russia, the Koreas remain divided, and there are continuing problems in former Indo-China. Nonetheless, the confrontations the cold war reinforced are much eased, and the diminution of the roles of the former Soviet Union and the United States in the area has encouraged further integration.

Russia is not a major factor in East Asia now, if only because its energies are being directed inward to deal with a collapsing economy and relations with eastern Europe and the fragmented elements of the former Soviet Union. There is little time, energy, or funding left for East Asia, nor is there likely to be any for some time. Any Russian mass migration would be to Europe. A nuclear capacity remains but occasion for its utilization toward East Asia is not easy to imagine. The Russian-trained Vietnamese officials are learning Japanese and English.

The United States remains the world's only superpower and a major player in the Pacific area. Its position in East Asia is rapidly changing, however, and its policies are failing to keep pace with the change in the realities of its role in the region. The great change is the rapid diminution of the U.S. economic position in East Asia. Still a massive absorber of imports, the United States is no longer Japan's largest market, has not been for most of Southeast Asia, and has quickly diminishing importance for what have been its dependencies—Korea and Taiwan.

The change in market involvement in the United States by East Asia's economies is accompanied by the marked reduction in U.S. corporate investment in the area. The private money investing in Asia is now Asian. U.S. companies are playing a small and shrinking role. Like the marketplace change, these investment changes are by private companies, not by governments. U.S. companies are failing to maintain position in the economies of East Asia, and the United States economy as a whole will pay for that failure.

Nor do government funds from the United States in any way help

the imbalance between East Asian importance and U.S. efforts. Even in
the Philippines, where surely the U.S. obligation is great, Japan is by a
multiple a more important supplier of aid. In the area as a whole, the
United States is out of the aid business. Indeed, in the case of Vietnam,
where an argument of obligation also might be made, the United States
leads an effort to block assistance to that country. Both private and public
investment from the United States is at a low level compared with the
total flows into the region.

A less dramatic diminution of military role has taken place. After the
retreat from Vietnam, the U.S. position in Southeast Asia was limited
largely to the long-held, large bases in the Philippines. These have now
been closed. At the same time, the numbers of U.S. forces in Korea and
Japan are being reduced, and that will continue. As U.S. economic leverage has diminished, so has the U.S. military/strategic position in the region.

There have as yet been few signs of an appreciation by the government of the United States of its loss of leverage. Demands on Japan in
trade and other economic matters, demands on China with respect to its
internal affairs, objections to regional trade group proposals excluding the
United States, demands for support of the U.S. position in international
relations all continue as before, in apparent assumption of unchanged
U.S. status and power. Increasing disagreements and real conflicts can be
expected as a result, if there is no U.S. review and redirection of its attitudes and policies toward East Asia. (And continuing condescending references to the important economies of East Asia as "dragons" or "tigers,"
like cartoons in a Disney-produced film, say a good deal about current
U.S. attitudes.)

None of the above is meant to be a prediction. Continued economic
success in the region for some years is virtually assured. Continued integration of the region in general is a near certainty. The virtual disappear-
ance of Russia from the East Asian scene, despite Boris Yeltsin's bluster,
is a fact. And the loss of leverage of the United States in the affairs of the
area is also a fact. Predicting the future is another problem.

Some of the influences on the future can be identified, however, and
some of their effects foreseen. Against the background of high probabil-
ity of continued growth and integration, there are forces that can work
to the advantage of these basic trends and other forces that can work to
frustrate them.

●

A WORLD OF REGIONAL
TRADING BLOCS

First, let us examine issues on the economic front that can present major problems. Chief among these is the division of the developed world into trading areas that might become protectionist blocs. Although the full integration of the EC will be a longer process than the drafters of the Maastricht Treaty proposed, the moves to harmonization within the market are going forward. Despite protestations, the use of dumping rules has been protectionist, as have been the decisions on the import of Japanese autos into Europe. Europe talks an open market but acts rather differently, to the considerable concern of Japan and the rest of East Asia.

Similarly with the North American Free Trade Area. Billed simply as a reduction of tariffs, with the potential for wider application of the reductions, the concept was unexceptionable. In fact, with the local content embellishments in particular, NAFTA too appears to East Asians to be protectionist. The local content rules raise the further concern that investments in lower-cost sourcing that might otherwise be made in East Asia will be made in Mexico to access NAFTA.

With these concerns goes the fact that the United States has over the past two decades moved increasingly to protectionist trade policies, beginning with the Multi-Fiber Agreement and now extending even to machine tools. The domestic focus of the 1992 election rhetoric, with what many in Asia saw as "American First" themes in prominent display, increased concerns over closing markets.

In fact, closing markets are likely. With the Congressional Budget Office and others forecasting long-term U.S. economic growth of 2 percent, while East Asia grows at 7 percent, trade pressures on an undersaving, underinvesting U.S. economy will create a substantial political reaction. Even without improved performance, assuming constant market shares of U.S. goods in East Asia and East Asian goods in the U.S. market, "the constant-market-share calculations indicate that exports to the Pacific Basin developing countries will account for 1,021,200 U.S. jobs in 2000, while imports from the Pacific Basin developing countries will cost the United States 2,198,400 potential jobs."[1] In an underperforming and retreating U.S. scene, that means more protection from imports. The United States does not blame itself for its trade problems.

•

The United States needs goods from Asia to run its economy—witness the fiasco over punitive dumping duties on computer displays that forced U.S. production offshore, or the effort to embargo Toshiba goods that proved vital to many U.S. producers. This fact does not prevent protectionism but merely makes it more costly. East Asian growth could be slowed by European and especially U.S. moves to protectionist trading blocs.

Should that happen, the initial East Asian response, and especially that from Japan, will be an effort to negotiate, while beginning to put together an Asian group to improve negotiating leverage. This is the rationale for Mahahtir's East Asia Economic Caucus—"hang together or we hang separately." These kinds of confrontations have a way of getting out of hand. Asia will be reactive, not proactive, because Asia is served by open trade and damaged by closed trading blocs. But if there are to be blocs, we can assume Asia will have its own. Multinational companies with an eye on insurance need begin—as Honda and Matsushita are now—to put fully integrated operations in each of the great trading areas.

POLITICAL RISKS FOR EAST ASIA

It is suggested on occasion that East Asia is too diverse, in terms of language, economic status, form of government, ethnic composition, and religion, to be able to coalesce into an effective regional group. But that surely was also a widely held view of Europe when the Treaty of Rome was signed in the mid-1950s. The diversity of Asia is not all that much greater than the divisions in Europe, whose nations devoted much of their resources for centuries to trying to eliminate one another. An external threat of a closing world could go far to cancel out the effects of diversity.

Indeed, it is argued by some that the groups and nations of Pacific Asia are not prone to trying to force values and ideologies on others. "A spirit of tolerance . . . may already have contributed to the way in which Pacific Asia was able, more or less, to contain its myriads of racial, religious and linguistic differences in these past troubled decades. Considering the extremely complex ethnic and cultural mosaic of the region, this has been a remarkable accomplishment . . . and may offer a model for the

•

rest of the world."[2] East Asia's diversity may not, after all, be a real barrier to regional organization.

If Western protectionism and trading blocs are a major economic hazard, what are some of the political problems?

An immediate issue is the question of a reasonably smooth reversion of Hong Kong to Chinese sovereignty in 1997 as scheduled. The curious effort of the British to introduce some modest measure of democracy into Hong Kong after 150 years of total neglect of the matter and only 5 years before reversion might well be seen as an effort to discredit the current Chinese leadership and to slow China's progress by interfering with the development of the South China economic zone. The British would not be alone in worrying over increased Chinese economic power, and the Hong Kong episode is for Britain an inexpensive ploy— it has nothing to lose in the game and might damage China.

Should the reversion go reasonably well, it will set a pattern of sorts for Taiwan. There is an independence movement of substance in Taiwan, and that movement, especially if it advances with perceived Chinese mismanagement of Hong Kong, could put off political integration for a long time. But that lack of political integration need not matter much if economic integration is allowed to continue on its recent course. The marketplace is voting strongly for close economic relations, whatever the political structure. It is to be hoped that the Hong Kong reversion will go smoothly enough that the current development of coastal China will continue uninterrupted.

China figures largely in speculation about East Asia's future in another way, the issue of succession, which is a more general issue in much of East Asia. These are young countries for the most part, whose governments do not have very long histories and who have had generally strong leaders. Thus succession is a delicate matter. Deng Xiaopeng's successor is not by any means clear and Deng's reformist policies are by no means unanimously accepted. What of the succession in China? And could a turbulent China fragment again in something of the manner of the Soviet Union, as China itself has in the not distant past?

The coastal provinces of China are doing well, generating tax revenues and foreign exchange that could serve them well as separate provinces. As income differences widen between the coastal provinces and the hinterland, surely the issue of decentralization, or federation, arises—even in a Communist—dominated country. There must be tensions now. A sustained struggle over succession, or a long period of uncertainty, could

•

make the fragmentation of the nation more possible. What would this mean for the rest of Asia? Not a great deal, provided the coastal provinces could continue in close economic interaction with the rest of East Asia.

The leading observer of the coastal development of China argues, "China's present reforms and market opening policies are irreversible. Also definite are the further integration of the South China Sea coastal provinces with the rest of the Western Pacific economies. This trend further underscores the movement of the Western Pacific region toward a self-sustaining economy.[3]

Questions about succession are by no means limited to China. Indonesia has known only two presidents, and the successor to Suharto is already a major topic of discussion. The issue of succession to Kim II Sung in North Korea may well have more risk—and opportunity—for Asia even than these other questions of succession, none of which have answers at this time. It should be noted though that the process of succession to strong leaders has on the whole gone fairly well—from Chiang Kai-shek to Chingguo to Taiwan-born Lee; from Park to Chung to Roh to Kim; from Lee to Goh. There is plenty to go wrong in all these cases, and some that has, but thanks in part to Confucius, the process has been managed fairly well more often than not.

MILITARY BUILDING AS A HAZARD

In addition to the Hong Kong/Taiwan issue and the chronic concern over succession, there has been increasing discussion of military armaments and military tension as an issue in East Asia. Continuing arms sales competition (in Taiwan between the United States and France) and cut-rate sales of armaments by Russia and China have been factors in this speculation. The matter seems overblown. The combined military budgets of Japan, the NIEs, ASEAN, and China are about 6 percent of world military expenditures, with Germany alone at 5 percent and the United States at 30 percent. Although there may be some argument about the exact numbers, Asia's do seem small. Japan accounts for half of the military budget of the area and does not seem bent on combat.

The Asian Development Bank has provided a recent analysis that reports military budget reductions for three of eight countries in the area, with Singapore arguably the most warlike from these numbers (see Appendix Table 14). There are areas of dispute. The Vietnam–China border

•

is one. The Spratly Islands in the South China Sea are almost always cited as a potential problem area. Japan has disagreements with Taiwan and Korea over continental shelf areas that may bear oil. And so with other territories, mainly questions of title to islands in an island-strewn area.

Assuming a reasonably prosperous East Asia and no really disastrous problems of succession in any of its governments, we find it very hard to see major military actions between these countries over the coming years. A different pattern would obtain with a major failure of the economies, with nationalistic issues being used by military leaders to vent frustrations. But this is not an area of ideologues but of pragmatists. And the pragmatists are now in control.

A less discussed area of potential political problems but one of increased concern is that of population movements, of mass migrations: "As seen in the cases of Eastern Europe, political upheaval and internal conflicts might trigger massive population movements regardless of social and political barriers . . . For example, some 1.3 million people moved from ex-Comecon countries to the West in 1990. An estimated 2 million people a year could quit the former Soviet Union itself when its new emigration law takes effect. Likewise, internal conflicts in China and the collapse of the authoritarian regime in North Korea will instigate outflows of population and therefore could be a trigger destabilizing regional stability in the North Pacific. This possibility demonstrates the need for potential impact countries to assist in peaceful transition in China and North Korea."[4] One Japanese estimate is that there is a total of 160 million unemployed in China. Japan's total population is 125 million. We may assume that for this reason among others Japan places the highest possible importance on stability in China, and cannot cooperate with U.S. or other Western moves to destabilize that country.

POTENTIAL FOR EVEN GREATER GROWTH

These seem to be main issues for the East Asian region, problems that could adversely affect the progress of the area. There are important potential pluses for the area as well.

1. Integration of Vietnam into the region as a fully participating member. This process is now well underway, with Japanese aid

●

resumed, ASEAN involvement in process, and Chinese relations reestablished. U.S. policy remains a barrier.

2. Cambodian stability. Cambodia is of importance in its potential to create major problems, especially among China, Vietnam, and Thailand. Japan's efforts to help solve the problems are important for the area in many ways, not least as an earnest of the good intentions of postwar Japan.

3. Continuation of the Korean unification process. This is perhaps the highest-risk situation in East Asia, not likely to be solved quickly—indeed, the German case argues against quick solution. The combined economies over time could be formidable, but certainly a successful reunification is not likely until the twenty-first century.

4. Russian-Japanese peace treaty and economic integration of the Russian Far East into a Sea of Japan zone. The impact of a peace treaty would be negligible in economic terms. It might, however, accelerate Japanese and Korean investment in Sakhalin and Russian Far East resource development, and with the Tumen River project, start bringing together the Koreas, northeast of China, and Japan's Asian prefectures into an economic zone of sorts.

5. Competent, stable Philippine government, with land and tax reform to begin to move the Philippines into the East Asian economic tide.

Each of these potential events and developments could have a most positive impact on the development of the East Asian region as a whole. And each is, to varying degree, within the realm of possibility in the decade of the 1990s. The balance is not a bad one for East Asia. There are real issues that can present major problems, but positive factors within reach will provide further impetus to existing growth patterns.

JAPAN AS A REGIONAL PLAYER

There remains the question of Japan and its future role in the region. Of Japan's economic role and its magnitude, there can be no doubt. The remaining piece to the economic role is increased share of the Japan mar-

●

ket for Asian imports. Given the rate of increase of manufactured goods imported into Japan from Asia since the mid-1980s, this is not likely to remain a problem for long.

In political terms, Japan's objectives in the area are stability, prosperity, and peace. It does not seek to change any governments, nor even to try to improve them. It has no plans, nor even a faint political mandate, to rearm. There is no urgent threat to the nation, nor indeed is there a visible threat to the region. There is time therefore for the scars of the past to heal, for economic aid and investment programs to bring the area more closely together, and for Japan to develop the skills and the receptivity in the region for a larger role that may yet prove needed.

Still, the shape of East Asia over the next few years will not be driven only by events and relations within the region. The policies of the major powers toward the region and with one another will be major influences as well. It seem unlikely that the European Community, or its key members, will be significant players in the region, even though some European companies will be very important. The EC will be fully preoccupied in industrial and financial terms with its own internal issues and those of eastern Europe, it would appear. And Europe's powers have in any case treated the strategic issues of East Asia as largely the province of the United States. That is unlikely to change in the near future.

The issues for East Asia in the intermediate term of the next five to ten years with respect to major power relations are focused on the two great powers of East Asia itself, Japan and China, and the United States. The key relationship will be that of the United States with Japan. These represent the world's largest economies, with complex relations with each other and in the region. And the relations of China with the United States and Japan will do much to determine that nation's role in the region over the next few years.

For its part, China will remain a poor country, an economy one-eighth the size of Japan's, by no means insignificant but not yet a major industrial or financial power. Moreover, issues of succession to current leadership and the problems of holding together regions of greatly different economic success are likely to keep domestic issues the main concerns of China for some years. Internationally, China has now established reasonably good relations on its flanks with Korea, Russia, and Vietnam. Major items of unfinished business center on Hong Kong and Taiwan; to reach settlement of these matters, China will need to be seen as a reasonably and relatively open economy, a constructive member of the region.

•

IMPLICATIONS FOR THE
UNITED STATES

The position of the United States in the region is currently a fast-diminishing one. As one measure, total fund flows into East Asia from the United States are little more than one-third of the flows from Japan, even though the U.S. economy is one-third larger than Japan's. The strategic commitment of the United States to East Asia is diminishing as well, beginning with the retreat from Vietnam, the closing of the Philippine bases, and gradual troop withdrawals from bases in Korea and Japan.

This is despite the considerable and even increasing importance of the region to the United States. The East Asian region is the largest and fastest-growing market in the world for U.S. goods, and U.S. trade across the Pacific has exceeded that across the Atlantic for more than a decade. East Asia is also a critical supply source that the U.S. economy has come to depend increasingly upon for the flow of consumer products and key industrial components.

What may well prove most important to the United States is the flow of funds from East Asia to make up the shortfall in U.S. capital formation. The East Asian economies are saving economies, as demonstrated by the favorable trade balances of Japan, Taiwan, Hong Kong, and China. The pools of Asian funds are very large indeed, with $70 billion in Japanese foreign exchange reserves, $80–$90 billion in Taiwan, and $40–$50 billion in China, a significant fraction of total world reserves. Japan as a source of funding of the U.S. deficit has already been critical for some years. As with trade, East Asia is essential in U.S. financing, and there will be no alternative funding source in the 1990s as Europe tends to its own problems.

Finally, the security dimension of East Asia for the United States cannot be overlooked. Not only is an economically stable and prosperous East Asia now critical to the U.S. economy, but a politically stable East Asia is critical to U.S. security, the more so as overall U.S. strategic capacity is reduced in the world. A measure of the region's importance to U.S. security is the fact that three of America's last four wars started in East Asia. The region's increasing economic weight only makes the security aspects more important still.

In spite of these factors, the U.S. position in East Asia is tapering off. Moreover, the trend is likely to continue. Certainly U.S. budgetary pressures will result in further reductions in military forces in the area, if only to bring U.S. commitments in line with U.S. capacity. In the area of

•

trade relations, there has been a general worsening of U.S. trade balances with the area, along with continued U.S. overconsumption and underinvestment. To the large deficits in trade with Japan and Taiwan can now be added a rapidly growing deficit with China. And thus trade frictions, now focused on Japan, will sour relations more broadly in East Asia.

The fact is that U.S. trade policy is not international policy but instead is driven by domestic political concerns. Trade imbalances therefore become the problems of the trading partner, not of the United States, in the U.S. view. This mind-set seems unlikely to change and will most certainly result in the continuation of the U.S. trend toward protectionism that began with the textile negotiations of the late 1960s and has since spread across a wide range of product areas. The growth of East Asia and the competitive success implied by that growth, along with a perpetual failure of the United States to deal with its own economic problems, certainly means increased trade tensions with East Asia and increased trade barriers in the United States.

While the reality of budget pressures and trade imbalances shapes policies, so do attitudes. Asia is remote and of marginal concern to a U.S. public increasingly hostile toward Japan and that appears to be turning inward as the cold war ends and domestic problems grow more serious. It is not surprising then that in the 1992 election campaign Japan and Asia were hardly mentioned, and a coherent national policy toward the East Asian region seems not to exist. Even the issue of relations with Vietnam remains unsettled.

Does all this really matter very much? Events in East Asia are moving forward without U.S. involvement. ASEAN takes shape, the China coast opens to trade and investment, China and Korea get together as do Korea and Russia, Hong Kong reversion proceeds in its fashion—all without U.S. help or hindrance. Yet is surely is in the U.S. interest to be able to shape these events and ensure that U.S. objectives are served as East Asia moves forward.

U.S.-JAPAN COOPERATION IN THE REGION

In this issue of U.S. involvement in East Asia, Japan is key. Both the United States and East Asia are vital to the long-term stability and success of Japan economically and politically. It is clear that the balance of Japan-

•

ese interest is shifting toward Asia, and that shortsighted U.S. policies are reinforcing that shift. But it is also clear that Japan will go a very long way to avoid having to make a choice between the United States and East Asia, a choice that in a well-ordered world would not be required.

Japan can help ensure a U.S. position in East Asia commensurate with U.S. resources. Japan will support a continued U.S. military presence in the area, as it does now with its underwriting of the cost of U.S. troops in Japan. The United States and Japan together can bring into effect an Asian equivalent of Europe's Conference on Security and Cooperation in Europe (CSCE), which can provide the postcold war regional security arrangements now required in East Asia. Japan has already gone to some lengths to put off the proposal for an East Asian economic group that would exclude the United States by insisting on U.S. membership in the Asia Pacific Economic Cooperation group. Japan's interest in the region is first of all stability. It is an objective that the U.S. can join in seeking.

All of this would be part of the "partnership" that both the United States and Japan often speak of and very seldom practice. Certainly the interests of the East Asian region would be well served by such a partnership and badly served by a confrontation between Japan and the United States, or the region and the United States. Japan has an interest in an expanded international role, including a permanent seat on the Security Council, and a larger role in the Asian Development Bank and World Bank that could be—but are not—supported by the United States. The United States has an interest in an ongoing position in the East Asian region that has been—but may not always be—supported by Japan.

This kind of cooperation is one option but not the most likely. The more likely option is drift, with continued trade frictions, an absence of positive programs that would engage the resources of the two countries in common efforts, and a lack of vision on both sides as to how the two countries might together shape their futures and the future of the region. This slow drift apart, in policies, actions, and attitudes, seems likely to bring Japan and the United States to confrontation over time, not merely the seemingly endless bickering over the mechanics of trade, but real differences.

Perhaps the most serious near-term outcome of this drift would be a move to trading blocs, with U.S. trade conflicts with Japan and then with China fostering U.S. protectionism and East Asian regionalism. The North American Free Trade Agreement provides an institutional struc-

●

ture from the U.S. side; the proposed East Asia Economic Group could provide the structure from the Asian side. A constant diminution of the U.S. position in East Asia, with a gradual shift of Japan's interests toward Asia in the context of trade conflicts, could—even without a point of crisis—lead to the formation of trading blocs. The hope must be that both self-interest and common sense on the part of the Americans and the Japanese—and East Asians more generally—will prevent this from happening. The prosperity and security of both the United States and Japan depend greatly on a stable and open East Asian region in which they share a leadership role.

APPENDIX

Appendix Table 1   Japan's Export Markets for Electronics, 1992 ($ billion)

	Asia	Europe	North America	Other
Consumer Electronics: of which	$50	$59	$57	$12
Color TVs	15	0.9	0.4	0.7
VCRs	17	11	15	3
Industrial Electronics	55	91	130	15
Electronic Components	182	88	136	17
TOTAL	$287	$238	$323	$44

Exchange rate in 1992: US$ = ¥126.7

Source: Newsletter of the Electronic Industries Association of Japan 6:4 (April 1993), p. 8.

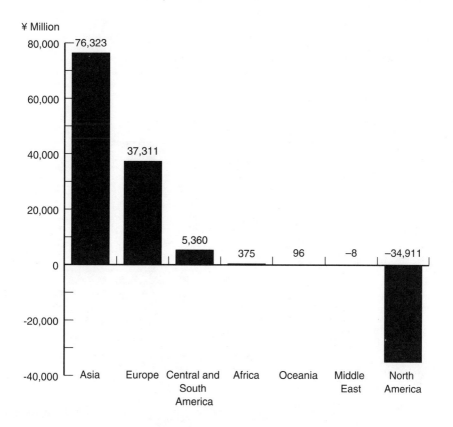

Appendix Figure 1   **Japanese Electrical Machinery Industry's Income Before Tax and Extraordinary Items by Region, 1991**

Source: Data from a summary by Gemini Consulting of "Dai 21-kai Waga Kuni no Kaigai Jigyo Katsudo," ed. by Industrial Policy Bureau (Tokyo: MITI, May 1992).

●

Appendix Table 2   Official Development Aid (ODA) to East Asia, 1990

	Total ODA ($ million)	Donor Countries (percent)					
China	1,416	Japan	51	Germany	16	Other	33
Indonesia	1,518	Japan	57	Netherlands	12	Other	31
Malaysia	459	Japan	81	—		Other	19
Philipppines	1,100	Japan	59	United States	22	Other	19
Thailand	732	Japan	57	France	16	Other	27

Source:Data from "Waga Kuni no Seifu Kaihatsu Enjo 1992" (Tokyo: International Assistance Association, 1992), p. 29.

Appendix Table 3   ASEAN Attitudes Toward Japan, 1983 and 1992 (percent, 1983 in parens.)

Which country do you know best?

Respondents	Japan		United States		China		Great Britain	
Indonesia	65	(76)	22	(12)	3	(2)	3	(3)
Malaysia	47	(32)	19	(13)	8	(19)	3	(8)
Philippines	34	(28)	56	(53)	2	(5)	0	(1)
Singapore	8	(24)	16	(17)	10	(23)	2	(9)
Thailand	30	(22)	38	(30)	9	(13)	3	(6)

How do you feel now about Japan in World War II?

	Indo-nesia		Malay-sia		Philip-pines		Singa-pore		Thai-land	
Cannot forget bad aspects.	29	(27)	40	(27)	37	(20)	31	(29)	18	(23)
There were bad aspects, but they do not matter now.	52	(28)	33	(42)	37	(41)	44	(39)	36	(32)
No problem whatsoever.	18	(36)	19	(25)	11	(36)	19	(29)	27	(27)
Don't know.	2	(9)	8	(6)	16	(3)	4	(8)	19	(18)

Source: Data from "ASEAN Shokoku ni okeru Seron Chosa, heisei 4-nen 8-gatsu," (Tokyo: Japanese Ministry of Foreign Affairs, August 1992), pp. 1 and 6.

Appendix Table 4   Coastal China, 1991

Province	Population (million)	Share of GNP (%)	Growth of Real GNP 1980–91 (annual, %)	Per Capita Income (RMB)	Ranking by Economic Strength Among All Provinces*	Number of Japanese Companies
GUANGDONG	64	9.0	13.9	2,143	2	67
FUJIAN	30	2.8	12.7	1,493	—	19
SHANGHAI	13	4.3	4.3	5,201	4	54
JIANGSU	68	7.3	9.2	1,826	5	25
SHANDONG	86	7.9	10.8	1,575	3	18
LIAONING	40	5.4	7.4	2,180	1	46
TOTAL	303	36.8	9.6	—	—	229
Nation	1,158	100.0	9.0	1,392	—	363
Percent of Nation	26	36.8	—	—	—	63

*Rating of economic strength of province from 1 to 10 on resources, industry level, agricultural base, capital infrastructure, relations with foreigners, standard of living, by the Japan External Trade Organization (JETRO).

Source: Data from *China Statistics Yearbook 1992* (Beijing: China Statistics Publishing Company, 1992), and from *Kaigai Shinshutsu Kigyo Soran* (Tokyo: Toyo Keizai Shinposha, April 1992).

•

Appendix Table 5   The South China Regional Economy Compared with the ASEAN Economies, 1991

	Area (thousand sq. km)	Population (million)	GNP 1989 (US$ billion)	GNP per Capita, 1989 (US$)	Exports (US$ billion)	Imports (US$ billion)
Guangdong and Hong Kong	178	70	116	1,658	112.2	108.8
Thailand	514	57	91	1,600	28.4	37.6
Malaysia	330	18	45	2,458	34.4	36.8
Indonesia	1,919	188	111	591	29.3	25.9
Philippines	300	63	46	725	8.8	12.9

Source: Reprinted from Kyoko Yasukuni, article in *Pacific Business and Industries* (Tokyo: Mitsui Taiyo Kobe Research Institute) Vol. III, No, 13 (Sept. 1991), p. 46

Appendix Table 6   China's Trade Partners, 1980, 1985, 1991 (percent)

	Exports from China			Imports to China		
	1980	1985	1991	1980	1985	1991
Total Amount ($ billion)	$18	$27	$72	$20	$42	$64
Asia	63%	69%	74%	38%	53%	59%
Hong Kong	24	26	45	4	11	27
Taiwan	—	—	1	—	—	6
Japan	21	22	14	24	36	16
ASEAN	6	10	6	4	3	7
Europe	22	19	13	23	23	20
EC	13	8	9	13	15	13
Former USSR	1	4	3	1	2	3
United States	6	9	9	23	12	13
Rest of World	9	3	4	16	12	8
TOTAL	100	100	100	100	100	100

Source: Ma Chengsan, *Hattensuru Chugoku no Taigai Kaiho—Genjo to Kadai* (Tokyo: Ajia Keizai Kenkyusho, 1992), pp. 52–53.

●

Appendix Table 7   Foreign Investment in Taiwan, 1980–90

| | Value ($ million) | Share (percent) | | |
Year	Total	Japan	United States	Overseas Chinese
1980	466	19	24	48
1985	702	21	47	6
1990	2,302	36	24	10
Cumulative 1952–90	13,252	28	25	15

Source: Japan Economic Institute Monthly Report No. 27A, 19 July 1991, p. 10.

Appendix Table 8   Direct Investment in Malaysia, Indonesia, and Thailand 1986–91 ($ million)

	Japan	Taiwan	United States
Malaysia	1,800	2,010	476
Indonesia	5,032	2,771	1,675
Thailand	12,532	3,426	3,780
TOTAL	19,364	8,207	5,931

Note: Statistics are drawn from each recipient country.

Source: Tsai-Yi Wo, "Taiwan Economic and Industrial Structure Change and Relationships Among Asia-Pacific Region" (Tokyo: Institute of Developing Economies (21 Jan. 1993): 33.

Appendix Table 9   East Asian Real Economic Growth Rates, 1960–2010 (annual average, percent)

	1960–70	1970–80	1980–90	1990–2000	2000–10
Japan	10.7	4.6	4.4	4.5	3.7
NIEs	9.3	8.9	8.3	6.8	6.0
ASEAN	5.4	7.3	5.1	6.7	6.5
China	4.0	5.8	8.5	6.5	5.1
United States	3.8	2.7	2.8	2.3	2.7
Germany	4.4	2.7	1.9	2.2	2.3
World	5.1	3.4	2.7	2.8	3.2

Source: Data from "Takyokuka Jidai no Sekai Chizu," ed. by Hisao Kanamori (Tokyo: Nihon Keizai Kenkyu Senta, May 1992), p. 255.

●

Appendix Table 10 **FDI in ASEAN, 1986–90: Share of Investing Countries in Total (percent)**

Investing Country	Indonesia	Thailand	Malaysia	Philippines
Korea	7.1	1.8	2.1	1.7
Taiwan	8.5	9.1	30.3	17.2
Hong Kong	8.8	6.2	3.4	16.4
Singapore	3.9	4.4	7.8	1.7
NIEs Total	28.3	21.5	43.7	36.8
Japan	20.4	32.7	29.0	25.6
United States	6.9	8.2	5.1	16.3
Other	44.4★	37.6	22.2	21.3

★"Multicountry," which includes Japanese and other investors, makes up most of this category, peculiar to Indonesian statistics.

Source: Reprinted from Junko Sekiguchi, "Transformation of ASEAN Manufacturing Industry and Its Outlook," *Pacific Business and Industries* (Tokyo: Mitsui Taiyo Kobe Research Institute), Vol. IV, No. 14 (1991), p. 5.

Appendix Table 11   **Savings and Investment, 1965 and 1992**

	Gross Saving as Percent of GDP		Gross Investment as Percent of GDP	
	1965	1992	1965	1992
Indonesia	8	36	8	35
Malaysia	24	30	20	36
Philippines	21	15	21	22
Thailand	19	34	20	36
Singapore	10	46	22	40
United States	21	15★	20	16★
Germany	29	28★	28	22★
Japan	33	34★	32	33★

★1991.

Source: Data from Asian Development Bank, *Asian Development Outlook 1992* (Hong Kong: Oxford University Press, 1992), pp. 294–95; The World Bank, *World Development Report 1992* (New York: Oxford University Press, 1992), p. 235.

●

Appendix Table 12   **Japanese Manufacturing Investment Abroad: Operating Profit Margins, 1985–91 (percent)**

	All Regions	North America	Asia	Europe
1985	1.3	-0.5	2.9	1.7
1986	1.4	0.7	2.3	1.2
1987	2.2	0.4	4.0	2.0
1988	2.9	0.7	4.4	2.3
1989	1.8	0.2	3.8	2.3
1990	1.8	-0.9	5.0	3.2
1991	0.9	-1.9	4.8	-0.6

Source: Data from "Dai 22-kai Waga Kuni no Kaigai Jigyo Katsudo Doko Chosa no Gaiyo. (Tokyo: MITI, March 1993) p. 24.

Appendix 13   **Military Expenditure and Economic Growth**

Country	Military Expenditure			Average Growth (percent) 1981–90	GDP Growth (percent) 1981–90
	Average ($ million) 1988–90	Average per Capita ($) 1988–90	Percent of GDP, 1990		
Korea	7,916	187	3.9	4.9	9.9
Taiwan	6,397	320	4.8	4.6	8.5
Singapore	1,378	512	4.8	6.9	6.3
Thailand	2,233	40	3.2	3.3	7.8
Malaysia	1,732	100	4.6	0.5	5.2
Indonesia	1,820	10	1.5	-4.5	5.5
Philippines	633	10	1.6	-0.1	1.0
China	6,400	6	1.6	-1.7	10.1

Source: Asian Development Bank, *Asian Development Outlook 1992* (Hong Kong: Oxford University Press, 1992), p. 25.

NOTES

Chapter 1. Sea Change

1. Estimates from Deutsche Bank Capital Markets, Tokyo. Professor Kenneth S. Courtis, President, provided these data.

2. Population and GDP data unless otherwise noted are from *World Development Report 1992* (New York: Oxford University Press, 1992), and from *Asian Development Outlook 1992* (Manila: Oxford University Press, 1992).

3. Andre de Jong and Gerrit Zalm, "Scanning the Future: A Long-term Scenario Study of the World Economy 1990–2015," in *Long-Term Prospects for the World Economy* (Paris: Organization for Economic Co-operation and Development, 1992).

4. Samuel Brittain, "Eastward, Look, the Land is Bright," *Financial Times* 10 (Dec. 1992).

5. Derek Healey. *Japanese Capital Exports and Asian Economic Development* (Paris: Development Center, Organization for Economic Cooperation and Development, 1991), 21.

6. Yuichiro Yamagata, "The Role of Japan's Aid in Asia's Development," *Economic Eye,* (Summer 1992): 26.

7. These data are from "Capturing the Asian Potential: Insights for Western

•

Multinationals, A Report from A. T. Kearney." Mr. William Best of that firm's Hong Kong office generously made the report available.

8. Akira Iriye, *Across the Pacific: An Inner History of American East Asian Relations,* rev. ed. (Chicago: Imprint Publications, 1992), 380, 381.

9. Quoted in Anthony Rowley, "Asia Above the Gloom," *Far Eastern Economic Review,* (Dec. 1992): 52–53.

10. Noda Yosuke and Sato Yurie, eds., *Ajia Shokoku no Chuki Keizai Kozo* (Tokyo: Ajia Keizai Kenkyjo, 1992), 7.

11. Jane Jacobs, *Cities and the Wealth of Nations: Principles of Economic Life* (New York: Vintage Books, 1985), 31

12. Ibid., 42.

13. "The Asiaweek 1000," *Asiaweek,* 18 Dec. 1992, 52ff.

14. Keidanren Review, no. 134, April. 1992, 4.

15. Flemings Research, "Trade Watch," 18 Nov. 1992, 5.

16. T. Hashida, "The Greater China Economic Zone," *Nomura Asia Focus* (June 1992): 16.

17. Ibid., 17.

Chapter 2. Ensuring Competitive Success

1. Mark Clifford, "Spring in Their Step," *Far Eastern Economic Review* 5 (Nov. 1992): 56.

2. Ibid., 57.

3. Ibid.

4. James Capel Japanese Service, 7 Dec. 1992.

5. Tokyo Keizai Data Bank 1992, 42–43.

6. So much for Japanese stereotypes. Mabuchi Motors has no *keiretsu* ties, is exceptionally profitable by any standard, has virtually no debt with interest income exceeding interest expense regularly, and competes very successfully with such giants as Matsushita Electric.

7. "Uniden Corp.," James Capel Pacific Limited, 13 Oct. 1992.

8. Seiki Satomura, General Manager, Asia Division, International Tire Operating Division, Bridgestone Corp., Tokyo.

9. These share data come mainly from Toyota Motors, and we are obliged to Takeharu Inuzuka, Assistant Manager, International Public Affairs, for providing the most recent data from their files. Malaysia's Proton is included here in the Japan share totals.

10. "Matsushita Group: Conclusive Management in Malaysia," *Tradescope* (October 1992): 7–8.

11. Shojiro Tokunaga, "Japan's FDI-Promoting systems and Intra-Asia Networks: New Investment and Trade Systems Created by the Borderless

●

Economy," in Shojiro Tokunaga, ed., *Japan's Foreign Investment and Asian Economic Interdependence* (Tokyo: University of Tokyo Press, 1992), 37 ff.

12. Mark Clifford, "A New Frontier: US Electronics Firm Expands in Asia," *Far Eastern Economic Review* 17 (Sept. 1992): 62.

13. "First Shots in a Photo War," *Asian Business* (Oct. 1992): 56.

14. Kenneth S. Courtis, "The Challenge of Leadership Across the Pacific: Japan and America's New Administration," *Deutsche Capital Markets (Asia)* 17 (Dec. 1992): 5.

15. Be careful of predictions, too, including those in this book. A well-known American economist wrote a volume of high praise of Europe, concluding that "Future historians will record that the twenty-first century belonged to the House of Europe." Lester Thurow, *Head to Head,* (New York: William Morrow, 1992), 258. Shortly thereafter, with splendid rhetoric, a British commentator wrote, "Europe is now a high-cost, high exchange rate, high-tax, high-welfare, technologically obsolescent, partly corrupt, undynamic, low-investment, low-growth, over-regulated, high-unemployment, non-competitive economy based on a rapidly ageing population." William Rees-Mogg, "Edinburgh fiddles while Europe burns," *The Independent* 7 (Dec. 1992).

16. A recent estimate has it that while about half of manufacturing investment in the developed economies is for new plant and equipment, the proportion is higher than 80 percent in East and Southeast Asia. "Capturing the Asian Potential: Insights for Western Multinationals, A Report from A. T. Kearney," 4.

17. Nihon Keizai Shimbun Feb. 1991.

Chapter 3. Japan in Asia

1. Y. Ojimi, "The Basic Philosophy of Japanese Industrial Policy," published by The Boston Consulting Group, Inc., no date.

2. See, for example, the useful summary of opinion poll results on Japan by William Watts, "Japan Focus of America's Worst Fears," *Japan Times,* 15 July 1992.

3. Japan Economic Institute, *Japan's Expanding U.S. Manufacturing Presence, 1990 Update* (Washington, D.C., Japan Economic Institute, June 1992), 1–2.

4. John W. Sewell and W. Patrick Murphy, "The United States and Japan in Southeast Asia: Is a Shared Development Agenda Possible?" in Kaoru Okuizumi et al., *The U.S.-Japan Economic Relationship in East and Southeast Asia* (Boulder: Westview Press, 1992), 124–25.

5. Anthony Rowley, "In Their Own Backyard," *Far Eastern Economic Review* (19 March 1992): 40.

•

6. Quoted in Saito Seiichiro, "The Pitfalls of the New Asianism," *Japan Echo,* 19, Special Issue (1992): 17.

7. Masahide Shibusawa et al., *Pacific Asia in the 1990s* (London: Routledge, 1992), 137.

8. Asian Development Bank, *Asian Development Outlook 1992* (Hong Kong: Oxford University Press, 1992): 25.

9. Kent E. Calder, *Japan's Changing Role in Asia: Emerging Co-Prosperity?* (New York: Japan Society, 1991), 11.

10. Richard P. Cronin, *Japan's Expanding Role and Influence in the Asia-Pacific Region: Implications for U.S. Interests and Policy.* Congressional Research Service, The Library of Congress, Washington, D.C., September 7, 1990.

11. Ibid., 49.

Chapter 4. Asia's New Economies

1. Toshio Watanabe is professor of economics at Tokyo Industrial University, Tokyo, Japan. He is the author of several books dealing with regional economies, including *Nishi Taiheiyo no Jidai* (Tokyo: Bungei Shunju, 1989), *Ajia Shin-Choryu* (Tokyo: Chuko Shinsho, 1990), and *Ajia: Shin-Keizai Chizu no Yomikata* (Tokyo: PHP Research Center Publication, 1991).

2. Lee Tsao Yuan, "Sub-regional Economic Zones in the Asia-Pacific: An Overview." Unpublished paper prepared for the International Symposium on Regional Cooperation and Growth Triangles in ASEAN, Singapore, 23–24 Apr. 1992.

3. State investment in Guangdong reached a high of about 70 percent of total investment in 1979 as the SEZ program began. However, by 1990, state investment accounted for less than 2 percent of the total, with foreign capital accounting for more than 20 percent. See T. Watanabe, ed., *Hokuto Ajia no Shindotai,* JETRO, p 136.

4. Andrew Tanzer, "The Mountains Are High, The Emperor Is Far Away," *Forbes,* 5 Aug. 1991, 70.

5. Main sources for these estimates include *Kanan Keizaiken,* Noburo, Maruyama, Ajia Keizai Kenkyujo, Mar. 1992, p. 395; *Ajia: Shin Keizai Chizu no Yomikata,* T. Watanabe and Takeshi Aoki (co-author), PHP, p. 34: *Hokuto Ajia no Shindotai,* T. Watanabe, 67.

6. Tokyo: Nihon Kokusai Boeki Sokushin Kyokai; *China Provincial Statistics 1992,* p. 68.

7. *International Herald Tribune,* 17 Mar. 1992, 9.

8. *Asian Wall Street Journal,* 4 June 1992, 5.

9. *Asahi Shimbun,* 29 Sept. 1992, 6.

●

10. Toyo Keizai Tokei Geppo, "Taigai Kaiho Susumu Chugoku Keizai," Sept. 1992, 24.

11. See the discussions in *Growth Triangle,* ed. Lee Tsao Yuan (Singapore: Institute of Southeast Asian Studies, 1991).

12. See for comment the *Financial Times,* 8 July 1992, 7, and *Far Eastern Economic Review,* 14 May 1992, 32.

13. Keizai Kikaku Cho Sogo Keikaku Kyoku, ed. (Tokyo: Okurasho Insatsukyoku, 1992), 1.

14. Jim Rohwer, "When China Wakes," *The Economist,* 28 Nov. 1992 5.

15. Takyokuka Jidai no Sekai Chizu: 2010-nen no Sekai to Nihon (Tokyo: Nihon Keizai Kenkyu Senta, 1992), 4.

16. Ma Chengsan, *Hattensuru Chugoku no Taigai Kaiho: Genjo to Wadai* (Tokyo: Ajia Keizai Kenkyusho, 1992), 86–87.

17. Masahide Shibusawa et al., *Pacific Asia in the 1990s* (London Routledge, 1992) 112.

Chapter 5. Taiwan and Korea

1. Marcus Noland, *Pacific Basin Developing Countries: Prospects for the Future* (Washington, D.C.: Institute for International Economics, 1990), 32ff.

2. Tony Michell, *From a Developing to a Newly Industrialized Country: The Republic of Korea, 1961–1982* (Geneva: International Labour Office, 1988, 14.

3. The issue of the role of government, drawing heavily on these Northeast Asian experiences and examples, has given rise to a considerable literature and controversy. In theologicallike argument, a "free market" view explaining growth in market terms with minimum government role is set in opposition to a "governed market" view suggesting that the role of government needs be pervasive and interventionist—in the manner attributed to Japan's Ministry of International Trade and Industry. For a detailed and thorough review and assessment of the issues, perhaps the best source is Robert Wade, *Governing the Market* (Princeton: Princeton University Press, 1990).

4. Attila Karaosmanoglu, Vice President, World Bank, "Asia and the New Balance in Development Strategies." Address to the World Institute for Development Economics Research, Helsinki, 16 Sept. 1991.

5. Wade, *Governing the Market,* 346.

6. Not all are small. Wang Yung Ching's Nan Ya Plastics, Formosa Chemicals and Fibers, and Formosa Plastics have total unconsolidated sales of some $5 billion, the largest PVC producer and second-largest synthetic fiber producer in the world. He started by taking over a government-built PVC plant in 1957. See ibid., 80, for background. Again, China Steel, mostly government owned, is a $2.4 billion business. There are large Taiwan operations.

•

7. Masahide Shibusawa et al., *Pacific Asia in the 1990s* (London: Royal Institute of International Affairs, 1992), 74.

8. Noland, *Pacific Basin,* 35.

9. *Far Eastern Economic Review,* 9 Apr. 1992, 59.

10. Carl Goldstein, "The Bottom Line," *Far Eastern Economic Review,* 17 Sept. 1992, 24.

11. "Lee Lai To, "Taiwan and the Reunification Question," in David S. G. Goodman and Gerald Segal, eds., *China in the Nineties.* (Oxford: Clarendon Press, 1991).

12. Michell, *From a Developing,* 11.

13. *Asian Development Outlook 1992* (Hong Kong: Oxford University Press, 1992), 84.

14. Damon Darlin, "Asia's Consumer Class Continues to Grow," *The Asian Wall Street Journal's Asian Economic Survey* (Hong Kong: Dow Jones (Asia), 26.

15. Michell, *From a Developing,* 15.

16. Louis Kraar, "Korea's Tigers Keep Roaring," *Fortune,* 4 May 1992, 25.

17. "Big Business in Asia," *Nomura Asia Focus* (June 1991): 12.

18. Wade, *Governing the Market,* 323–34.

19. For an effort to explain the difference away, see ibid., 320.

20. Steve Glain, "Foreign Firms React to Korean Red Tape by Pulling Out Funds," *The Asian Wall Street Journal,* 5 May 1993, 1.

Chapter 6. The Challenge of Southeast Asia

1. This discussion takes no account of Brunei Darussalam, the sixth member of ASEAN. It is similar to Kuwait, called by a cynic an oil plantation. Brunei has a population of about 260,000 and an area of about 6,000 square kilometers, entirely under the control of Sultan Hassanal Bolkiah, with what may be the highest per capita GDP in the world from its oil wealth. It is tempting to speculate about the possible long-term independence of the sultanate. Access to Brunei's oil power and wealth could greatly change many nearby nations. For a highly readable review of the sultanate, see James Bartholomew, *The Richest Man in the World,* (London: Penguin Books, 1990). See also Mary Ann Weaver, "In the Sultan's Palace," *The New Yorker,* 7 Oct. 1991, 56–93.

2. Eric Stone, "Trading on ASEAN's Future," *Asian Business* (July 1992): 21.

3. Mancur Olson, *The Rise and Decline of Nations* (New Haven: Yale University Press, 1982), 75, 77.

4. It is remarked that the Asian Pacific is a Japanese lake. It clearly is not. It is an Asian lake in which Japan is a large fish but not the only one. If direct investment is a measure of corporate interest and strategic intent—and it surely is to a degree—U.S. and European companies are failing to respond to the Southeast Asian opportunity.

5. Phillippe Regnier, *Singapore: City-State in South-East Asia* (Honolulu: University of Hawaii Press, 1991), 39.

6. "The Sixth Malaysian Plan (1991–95)," *Nomura Asia Focus.*, 5 (Oct. 1991): 11

7. Kenzo Horii, "Disintegration of the Colonial Economic Legacies and Social Restructuring in Malaysia," *The Developing Economies* 29, no. 4 (Dec. 1991): 303.

8. Mohamed Ariff, *The Malaysian Economy: Pacific Connections* (Singapore: Oxford University Press, 1991), 52–53.

9. S. Gordon Redding, *The Spirit of Chinese Capitalism* (New York: de Gruyter, 1990), 31.

10. Clark D. Neher, *Southeast Asia in the New International Era* (Boulder, Colo.: Westview Press), 44.

11. Asian Development Bank, *Asian Development Outlook 1992* (Hong Kong: Oxford University Press, 1992), 146.

12. Nigel Holloway et al., "An Insurance Policy," *Far Eastern Economic Review* (25 July 1991): 53.

13. Edward Balls, "Building Trade Blocs in East Asia and the Pacific," *Financial Times,* 3 Feb. 1992, 2.

14. Peter Drysdale, "Open Regionalism: A Key to East Asia's Economic Future," *Pacific Economic Papers* 197 (July 1991).

Chapter 7. Indonesia and Vietnam

1. Anne Booth, ed., *The Oil Boom and After* (Singapore: Oxford University Press, 1992), 421.

2. Ibid., 355.

3. *Economist* (10 Aug. 1991): 20.

4. David Joel Steinberg, ed., In Search of Southeast Asia, rev. ed. (Sydney: Allen & Unwin, 1987), 307.

5. *Far Eastern Economic Review* (30 Apr. 1992): 54.

6. S. Gordon Redding, *The Spirit of Chinese Capitalism* (New York: de Gruyter, 1990), 22.

7. The *konglomerat* are listed and described in "Pertanda Zaman di wah Konglomerat," *Warta Ekonomi* 37, (11 Feb. 1991): 20–65.

8. Booth, *The Oil Boom,* 33.

9. Nigel Holloway, ed., *Japan in Asia* (Hong Kong: Far Eastern Economic Review, 1991), 96.

10. Interview by Brian Riordan, 3 Sept. 1991.

11. Robert Shaplen, *A Turning Wheel,* (New York: Random House, 1980), 236.

●

12. Booth, *The Oil Boom*, 238–39.

13. Masao Araki, "Japan's Tet Offensive," *The International Economy* (Jan./Feb. 1992): 20.

14. Asian Development Bank, *Asian Development Outlook 1992*, (Hong Kong: Oxford University Press, 1992), 150.

15. See, for example, "Special Report: Indochina," *Nomura Asia Focus* (Aug. 1992): 1–2.

16. "Vietnam," *Financial Times Survey* (14 Nov. 1991): 1.

17. Steinberg, *In Search of Southeast Asia*, 130.

18. Melanie Beresford, "The Impact of Economic Reforms on the South," in *Doi Moi: Vietnam's Economic Renovation, Policy and Performance*, Dean K. Forbes et al., eds. (Canberra: Australian National University, 1991, 120.

19. Hisao Kanamori, "Vietnam Revs Up for Economic Takeoff," *Economic Eye*, (Summer 1992): 22.

20. Graham Allibrand, "Whither Vietnam," in *Doi Moi*, 246–47.

Chapter 8. Networks, Groups, and Growth

1. Lucian W. Pye, *Asian Power and Politics: The Cultural Dimensions of Authority* (Cambridge, Mass.: Harvard University Press, 1985), 325–26.

2. Edward Chen and Gary G. Hamilton, "Introduction: Business Networks and Economic Development," in Gary Hamilton, ed., *Business Networks and Economic Development in East and Southeast Asia* (Hong Kong: University of Hong Kong, 1991, 8–9.

3. S. Gordon Redding, *The Spirit of Chinese Capitalism* (New York: de Gruyter, 1990), 3.

4. *Economist* (18 July 1992): 21.

5. Akira Suehiro, "Capitalist Development in Postwar Thailand," in *Southeast Asian Capitalists*, ed. Ruth McEvoy (Ithaca, N.Y.: Cornell Southeast Asia Program, 1992), 39.

6. Hara Fujio, "Mare-Ka Seisakuka de Katsuro o Saguru—Mareshia," in Yu Chung-Hsun, *Sekai no Chainizu* (Tokyo: Saimaru Shuppankai, 1991), 58.

7. Heng Pek Koon, "The Chinese Business Elite of Malaysia," in *Southeast Asian Capitalists*, 127.

8. Kunio Yoshihara, *The Rise of Ersatz Capitalism in South-East Asia* (Singapore: Oxford University Press, 1988), 48–50.

9. Ruth McVey, "Materialization of the Southeast Asian Entrepreneur," in *Southeast Asian Capitalists*, 15.

10. *Yozo Tanaka et al.*, "Overseas Chinese Business Community in Asia: Present Conditions and Future Prospects," in RIM, *Pacific Business and Industries* 2 no 16, (1992), 13.

●

11. Wellington K. K. Chan, "Chinese Business Networking and the Pacific Rim: The Family Firm's Roles Past and Present," *Journal of American-East Asian Relations* 1 (Summer 1992): 174–75.

12. McVey, "Materialization of the Southeast Asian Entrepreneur," in *Southeast Asian Capitalists,* 9.

13. Yoshihara, *The Rise of Ersatz Capitalism,* 58.

14. Jamie Mackie, "Changing Patterns of Chinese Big Business," in *Southeast Asian Capitalists,* 183.

15. James McGregor, "Fujian Gets Boost from Overseas Chinese," *Asian Wall Street Journal,* 4 June 1992, 1.

16. Lynn Pan, *Sons of the Yellow Emperor.* (London: Mandarin, 1991), 228–29.

17. Ibid.

18. For these Japanese views see especially the article "A Comparison of Overseas Chinese Enterprises and Japanese Enterprises," in the daily JETRO publication *Tsusho Koho.* Inoue Ryuichi, "Kajin Kigyo to Nihon Kigyo no Hikaku," *Tsusho Koho,* 10 June 1992, 16.

19. Yozo Tanaka et al., "Overseas Chinese Business Communities in Asia: Present Conditions and Future Prospects," *RIM* 2 no. 16 (1992);18–19.

20. Hidemasa Morikawa, *Zaibatsu* (Tokyo: University of Tokyo Press, 1992), 3–4.

21. "Japanese corporate networks have evolved from *zaibatsu* to business groups and further to the recent network industrial organization. This evolution is seen as a gradual loosening of the intercorporate linkage and blurring of corporate boundaries." Kenichi Imai, "Japan's Corporate Networks," in *The Political Economy of Japan,* vol. 3: *Cultural and Social Dynamics,* Shumpei Kumon and Henry Rosovsky, eds. (Stanford: Stanford University Press, 1992), 228.

22. For a general discussion of the *chaebol,* see Richard M. Steers et al., *The Chaebol* New York: Ballinger, 1989). More detailed analysis is in Kim Dong-Ki and Kim Linsu, eds., *Management Behind Industrialization: Readings in Korean Business,* (Seoul: Korea University Press, 1989).

23. Yozo Tanaka et al., in RIM, 19–20.

Chapter 9. Japan's *Kaisha* in East Asia

1. From the *Korea Times,* 23 June 1992. Also reported in the *Herald Tribune,* 24 June 1992.

2. Unpublished paper by Urban C. Lehner, Editor, *Asian Wall Street Journal,* prepared for the seminar, Japan and East Asia, Sophia University, 4 Feb. 1992.

3. Neither the numbers in Table 9–1 nor any others dealing with foreign investment are entirely accurate. Some sources tabulate planned but not yet

•

executed investments. Others include retained earnings and local borrowings in the investment totals, while the Ministry of Finance data do not, nor is allowance made for revaluation of older investments. The proportions of investment flows shown in these data seem likely to be reasonably accurate, even if absolute levels are in question.

4. These data are drawn from Kym Anderson, eds., *New Silk Roads: East Asia and World Textile Markets* (Cambridge: Cambridge University Press, 1992).

5. Ibid., 38–40.

6. A detailed review and analysis of the situation in Southeast Asia, and the changing fortunes of foreign companies in the area, is provided in Richard F. Doner, *Driving a Bargain: Automobile Industrialization and Japanese Firms in Southeast Asia* (Berkeley: University of California Press, 1991).

7. "Japanese Trade and Direct Investment in East Asia," an industry-by-industry analysis of characteristics. Paper by F. Uryu et al. Research Institute of International Trade and Industry, Tokyo, 1992, 7–8.

8. Dieter Ernst and David O'Connor, *Competing in the Electronics Industry: The Experience of Newly Industrializing Economies* (Paris: Organization for Economic Cooperation and Development, 1992), 95.

9. Ibid., 96.

10. Ibid., 146.

11. *Financial Times,* 31 July 1992, section 3, I.

12. *Economist,* 1992, 15 Aug. 58.

13. H. Kawanaka and T. Sasaki, "Recent Trends in the Southeast Asian Toiletry Industry," *Pacific Business and Industries* 2 (1991): 38.

14. *Ryutsugyo no Kokusaika.* Ed. K. Uemura (Nihon Keizai Kenkyu Senta). Series Kenkyu Hokoku No. 79, 1992, 24.

15. Ibid., 33.

16. *Kaigai Shinshutsu Kigyo Soran '92* (Toyo Keizai), 88ff.

17. The Export-Import Bank of Japan, "Results of a Survey on Overseas Direct Investment for FY 1991," Background Paper, Tokyo, Dec. 12, 1991, 2–4.

18. *NIES, ASEAN de no Nikkei Kigyo (Seizogyo) no Katsudo Jokyo* (Tokyo: Nihon Boeki Shinkokai, 1992), 24–26.

Chapter 10. After the Sea Change

1. Marcus Noland, *Pacific Basin Developing Countries: Prospects for the Future* (Washington, D.C. Institute for Developing Economies, 1990), 169.

2. Masahide Shibusawa, "Pacific Asia in the Post-Cold-War World," *IHJ Bulletin* (Spring 1992): 2.

●

3. Toshio Watanabe, "The Western Pacific will be dynamic," *Nikkei Weekly, 15 Feb. 1992, 6.*

4. Won Bae Kim, "Population Movements in the North Pacific," Working Paper Number 8, Feb. 1992, East-West Center, Honolulu.

INDEX

●

●

●

●

●

●

●

•

●

●

•

•